Bruce's Timeline of Our World

Bruce Tapping

Clink Street

Published by Clink Street Publishing 2024
Copyright © 2024
First edition.
ISBNs:
978-1-914498-65-7 – paperback
978-1-915785-00-8 – ebook

For my daughters, Ana and Petra, and also for their amazing, wonderful bunch of friends.

When I write this you are all young, but history turns quickly and soon you will be young adults.

As you grow, I hope this book helps you learn that there is a much "Bigger Picture" out there.

Slow down, take your time, and remember what is important.

To Ana and Petra
&
all their friends.

"If you don't know history, then you don't know anything. You are a leaf that doesn't know it is part of a tree."

— Michael Crichton

This is not a heavy historical book.

It's an easy to ready, simple, and fascinating timeline of all the major people and events that have made up our world from the beginning of time until today.

It's the ultimate coffee table, or interesting bathroom browsing, read!

Contents

Introduction

I have written this timeline as I've always wanted a perspective as to how we all fit into this world.

I grew up hearing of, and reading about, dinosaurs, Julius Caesar, Jesus, Richard the Lionheart and the Crusades, the Renaissance, the Tsars, the Great Wall of China and many more great events, people and places, but I had no real idea as to how they had shaped the world, or in which order they had occurred.

Humans tend to think we are the only important thing on the planet and this thinking makes us trample on own environment. I hope this book helps to add some perspective as to who we are and how we fit onto this planet, which has been around far longer than we have.

It is a simple timeline from the formation of the universe through to the emergence of humans, our empires, the present day, and covers all the major events along the way including how our countries were formed and when.

It is meant to be an enjoyable, user friendly "guide" to our history – from the beginning of time until now, and our place in it.

In many cases, especially in BCE times, it is not possible for dates to be pinpoint accurate. For example, where scientists may argue exactly how many billions of years ago rocks first formed (4.5–3.7 billion), I have provided a rough guide date of 4.4 billion years ago as probably the earliest date they would have likely started forming.

CE and BCE date usage

I have decided to use the CE and BCE date usage purely for practical reasons, in that its name is not tied to any group, or religion, but the dates are aligned with AD and BC which is the more traditional western timeline.

CE stands for Common Era
BCE stands for Before the Common Era.
The CE is the same as AD
The BCE is the same as BC

AD means Anno Domini which is Latin for the "Year of Our Lord", therefore signifying, for Christians, the supposed year that Jesus was born.

BC means Before Christ.

The BC/AD system has been in place since 525 when a 6th century monk by the name of Dionysius Exiguus introduced it as a means of keeping track of how many Easters there had been. As Easter signifies Christ's death, and as he was a Christian monk, Dionysius wanted to record the number of years since Christ's death.

It is assumed that Dionysius used the Bible's detail on Jesus being in his thirties when he died to establish the year of his birth. There is no exact science to establish the exact year Jesus was born, meaning the 1st year of AD (CE) itself is an approximate assumption. Historians now consider Christ's actual birthday to be probably 7 BCE.

There is also no Year "CE Zero", meaning the day after 1 BCE December 31, is 01 January CE 1.

If you enjoyed this book and are interested in further books I have written, and am writing, or if you want an updated version of Bruce's Timeline of Our World, please go to www. brucetapping.com for more information.

Bruce.

Chapter 1.   Universe Creation–Dinosaur Extinction

**14 billion years ago –
65 million years ago**

14 billion years ago
The Big Bang

The theory is that at the beginning of time, everything was one huge singular mass.

When Edwin Hubble invented the Hubble Telescope in 1929 it was observed that the galaxies were drifting apart. Backward reasoning therefore meant they were once together. A singular mass at the beginning of time, calculated at approximately 13.8–14 billion years ago.

This singular mass is known as "singularity" and why it suddenly started expanding outwards... is a mystery, but the point at which it did is called the Big Bang.

Whilst there is general agreement that the universe has been expanding since that point in time billions of years ago, there is still discussion as to whether there was a Big Bang from singularity before expansion started. In other words, interestingly, it is only the very first second that there is disagreement on. Was it an instant Big Bang, or was it something else? (Creationists could use this unexplained "first second" to bring in their theory of creationism)

If it was the "instant Big Bang" then there must have been the exact amount of matter needed to create our universe at the rate it has been created. Also, our temperatures (in the greater scheme of things) were too perfectly uniform. It seems suspiciously perfect to some, who therefore propose cosmic inflation as another theory. This theory states that if you wanted the universe to have those exact temperatures and amount of matter that it did, you would first need to have set it up that way. In this theory, before the actual

Big Bang, there was a constant flat universe with uniform properties everywhere. This then rapidly expanded to the point it is at today.

However, as with all hypotheses, the theory as to how it all started is constantly evolving, especially with the introduction of new technologies. In 2022 the James Webb Space Telescope was launched, more advanced than the Hubble Telescope, and can view objects further than previously viewed (and therefore from a time earlier than viewed before) which means new theories are now evolving which may add to, or adapt, our present theories.

13 billion years ago
Galaxies formed

After the Big Bang, gravity caused giant clouds of dust and gas to gather together, which they did in groups, and these groups are what we call galaxies, which are countless.

Stars were formed under further immense gravitational pressure, which caused clouds of gas and dust to shrink together until their matter was so dense, and temperatures so high, that an enormous amount of energy was given off in a nuclear reaction. This reaction created stars, emitting light and heat in a continual reaction thereafter.

This process of galaxy formation took billions of years.

4.6 billion years ago
Our sun and galaxy formed

Our galaxy is called the solar system and is called that because we gravitate around our sun, which itself is just a normal star among over 1000 million others in our galaxy alone. The only thing that makes our sun special in comparison to any other star, is that it happens to be our closest.

As galaxies are often spiral, including our own, (which is like a flattened spiral plate), when we look out to space at night, we look out across the "plate" and see a tail of grouped together stars. This is our view of the stars within our galaxy – which we have aptly named the Milky Way.

4.5 billion years ago
Earth, planets and our moon formed

In a similar manner to how clouds of gas and dust formed to create our sun and other stars, clouds of gas and dust also created other rocky worlds. These were Earth and the other planets in our solar system.

There are two main theories as to how our moon formed. One theory is that a space collision, from something crashing into Earth, caused fragments to split off into space, with gravity then forcing these fragments to bind together. Earth's own gravity then caused this newly formed mass to remain circling our Earth, creating our moon.

An alternate theory is that Earth and Moon formed together when two huge objects crashed together and then collided again. As the fragments settled under gravitational forces, they clumped together into two separate objects, Earth and our moon, with the moon bound to us by Earth's gravity.

4.4 billion years ago
Rocks formed, Oceans formed

Initially Earth was so hot it was just a mass of molten magma, but as it gradually cooled, the first rocks were formed.

These are referred to as igneous rocks which are rocks formed from the cooling of molten magma.

After the Earth formed, and over a period of millions of years, and around the time the moon-forming collision occurred, hydrogen and oxygen atoms were escaping from Earth into our atmosphere.

Initially Earth was extremely hot and any water on it would have boiled. Over millions of years however, Earth cooled and the water vapour in our atmosphere started to rain down. This rain occurred for centuries and settled onto the cooler Earth, creating our oceans.

3.7–3.5 billion years ago
First life on earth

It's not known exactly how life was first formed but it is agreed that some form of chemical change must have occurred.

Initial forms of life have been found in small rock like objects called Stromatolites – fossils of which from Greenland have been found to contain a type of single celled (prokaryote) bacteria called cyanobacteria within them.[1]

Further fossils of rocks discovered in Australia found other bacterial forms dating from a similar timeframe.

3.5 billion–600 million years ago
First Ice Ages

Between 2.4 and 2.1 billion years ago the first Ice Age occurred.

Ice Ages are an occurrence of a global temperature drop that creates an expansion of glacial ice sheets.

The second Ice Age occurred 850 million to 635 million years ago.

600–500 million years ago
Multi-celled organisms evolved, fish appeared on Earth

Almost 3 billion years after simple single celled (prokaryote) organisms appeared, the more complex multi-celled (Eukaryote) organisms evolved.

Jellyfish and the first shelled animals occurred after that, at the beginning of what is known as the Cambrian explosion – a period of time, about 550 million years ago, where, within 10 million years, there was an explosion of life forms, during which the first chordates appeared (life forms with a notochord, or spinal rod, to support them).

The first fish evolved at the end of this period, about 500 million years ago.

The oceans' corals also started forming 500 million years ago.

500–300 million years ago
Pangea, first plants, insects and reptiles appeared, first fire

At this time there were no individual continents. There was one Earth mass surrounded by the oceans, and this supercontinent was called Pangea.

Just under 500 million years ago, the first plants appeared on land. It was sometime just after this that the first fire occurred on Earth (we know this from evidence of charcoal, originating 420 million years ago), presumably from a lightning strike, as there was now plant material to burn. [2]

The third Ice Age occurred 460–430 million years ago.

This was also the period around 400 million years ago when the first completely terrestrial (land) animals appeared. Sharks evolved around 400 million years ago and over the next 100 million years other fish and corals continued to evolve in the sea and, eventually, closer to 350 million years ago, the first amphibious animals evolved.

Between 350 and 300 million years ago the first carboniferous plants evolved on land and the first insects and reptiles appeared.

300–65 million years ago
Dinosaurs, mammals and the first birds appeared

Between 360 and 260 million years ago the Earth entered its fourth Ice Age.

300 million years ago new types of reptiles evolved, with dinosaurs and the first mammals then making their appearance 250–200 million years ago.

Between 250 million and 100 million years ago the first crocodiles went through various evolutions. By 80 million years ago it had evolved into a ten-metre, ten-ton version.

About 200 million years ago the Earth's single continent, Pangea, split into two major continents. Laurasia in the north and Gondwanaland in the south.

150 million years ago saw the evolution of our first birds, followed soon after by our first flowering plants. Around 145 million years ago the continents had further split, due to plate movement, into the early formation of our current seven continents, but they were still closely grouped together.

65 million years ago
The Alvarez event, dinosaur extinction, mammals developed quickly

65 million years ago a huge meteorite crashed into Earth.

This caused a huge change in the Earth's climate creating a massive tidal wave and sending clouds of dust and other particles into the atmosphere, blocking out sunlight and dramatically dropping temperatures.

This event is known as the Alvarez event after its proponent Luis Alvarez.[3]

This catastrophic event is thought to have caused the extinction of 75% of all species, including the dinosaurs. This mass extinction is known as the K–T extinction as it marks the end of the Cretaceous (K) period, and the beginning of the Tertiary (T) period.

Evidence of this giant meteorite strike includes the huge crater showing where it impacted, in Mexico.

Chapter 2. Early Primates, Humans – through until the Stone Age

65 million years ago– 5000 years ago

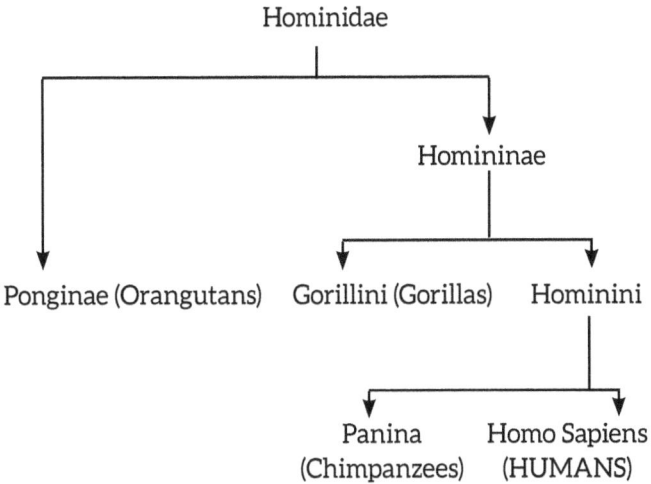

```
                        Hominidae
                            |
    ┌───────────────────────┴───────────────────┐
    |                                            ↓
    |                                        Homininae
    |                                            |
    |                              ┌─────────────┴─────────────┐
    ↓                              ↓                           ↓
Ponginae (Orangutans)    Gorillini (Gorillas)            Hominini
                                                              |
                                                  ┌───────────┴───────────┐
                                                  ↓                       ↓
                                               Panina              Homo Sapiens
                                            (Chimpanzees)           (HUMANS)
```

65–35 million years ago
The first primates appeared on Earth, current continents formed

It is estimated that it took 4 million years for Earth to recover its biodiversity after the meteorite impact that led to the K–T extinction. (In the first chapter this was explained as "This mass extinction is known as the K–T extinction as it marks the end of the Cretaceous (K) period, and the beginning of the Tertiary (T) period.")

With predatory dinosaurs removed from Earth, some birds evolved into large flightless carnivores. Mammals began to flourish and around 60 million years ago the first primates appeared. These primates were more squirrel-like in appearance than ape-like.[4]

Around this time, 50 million years ago, megalodon, the largest shark to ever exist evolved, and later, approximately 45 million years ago, the ancestor of the great white shark evolved.

Also at this time, 55 million years ago, the ancestor of the modern crocodile evolved from earlier crocodilian forms.

The largest mammal that ever inhabited Earth (Paraceratherium) lived about 40–39 million years ago, a 16 ton, five metre tall, long-necked rhinoceros-type creature.

At this time, our current seven continents formed and slowly drifted apart from each other towards their present day positions. About 40 million years ago, India slowly crashed into Asia, creating the Himalayan mountain range. Africa split from Asia and the Red Sea was formed.

35–7 million years ago
First monkeys, cattle and hominins appeared

About 33 million years ago world geology changed dramatically. North America and Europe separated and moved closer to their current positions.

During this period there were also great changes in climate as winters in the northern hemisphere became colder. Much of the similar animal life we see today evolved, including large cats and dogs.

Monkeys first appeared about 35 million years ago, and apes about 25 million years ago. 21 million years ago apes were living in Africa and by 14 million years ago had spread up to Southern Europe. Cattle also appeared approximately 14 million years ago.

By 9 million years ago the apes in Africa evolved into two separate lines – one that led to gorillas and the other to humans and chimpanzees.

7–2.6 million years ago
Early man and the Stone Age

Hominidae is the name for the larger family of Primates that includes Hominini which are the specific sub-family that humans belong to.

Generally it is believed that the first Hominids evolved in Africa and from there they spread north, however there is no consensus among experts as to the exact location the

Hominins first evolved from other primates, with suggestions including Africa and Central Europe, Greece, and Turkey.

However, around 7 million years ago the Hominini line split, one line leading to chimpanzees and the other to early humans.

By about 3.5 million years ago these "early humans" started using stones as tools. This therefore was the beginning of the Stone Age.

Approximately 2.5 million years ago, the early human line evolved into the Homo group, including Homo Erectus and these early humans started to walk upright on two feet.

2.6 million–300,000 years ago
Current ice age. Human development. Human use of fire and clothing

The fifth, last and current Ice Age started 2.6 million years ago and we are still in it. An Ice Age is defined as a period of time when the poles remain frozen year-round. This Ice Age is the one we refer to as "The" Ice Age and it peaked 18,000 years ago

Just over 2 million years ago the early humans' brain had grown larger, and greater use of tools developed. Early humans then started to walk fully upright and and started spreading northwards into Europe. They also started using fire. By 700,000 years ago these early humans had started cooking.

The earliest evidence of clothing is from 500,000 years ago, around about the same time as Neanderthal Man evolved – a separate species from modern-day humans. Neanderthal man died out around 40,000 years ago.

Evidence out of Israel shows early humans were regularly using fire 400,000 years ago. Possibly they were using flints to start fires but there is no hard evidence that this is the time when man learned to start fires. It could have been as much as 1 million years ago, or even at a more recent stage.

By 300,000 years ago the early human had evolved into modern-day Home Sapiens, physically the same as modern-day humans, and speech then evolved.

300,000–100,000 years ago
Spread of humans, first structures built

Between 250,000 and 200,000 years ago humans started to inhabit Southeast Europe and West Asia. Approximately 180,000 years ago it appears man started wearing clothes more permanently.

Around 120,000 years ago the woolly mammoth first appeared on earth.

By 100,000 years ago the earliest use of man-built structures occurred in Egypt.[5]

100,000–16,000 years ago
Modern human development, human art and music, peak of The Ice Age

Some of the earliest evidence of human settlements come from Australia approximately 40,000–30,000 years ago and the movement of people into China and Japan occurred around a similar time.[6]

Around the same time, music appeared, with the first flutes originating from Germany.

Evidence of the earliest human art occurred around 35,000 years ago–a mammoth ivory carving found in Germany–and dogs became domesticated in Europe and Siberia 20,000 – 30,000 years ago, and the first use of pottery was in China approximately 20,000 years ago.

The most recent glaciation period, often known simply as "The Ice Age," reached peak conditions some 18,000 years ago, as this was a period when glaciers spread out across large parts of the Earth, not just the poles. The ice grew to more than 12,000 feet thick, as ice sheets reached as far south as Northern America, Northern Europe and Northern Britain.

16,000–5000 years ago
Agriculture started, wheel invented

The first humans in North America are believed to have moved there around 16,000 years ago.

Evidence found from the Middle East shows early human agriculture originated there 10,000 years ago.

There is evidence of possible early warfare in Kenya approximately 6000 years ago.

Around 5000 to 4000 years ago the woolly mammoth became extinct.

Roughly 3500 years ago, the wheel was invented in Mesopotamia. Initially it was not invented for transport, but as a potter's wheel in pottery.

Chapter 3. The Bronze and Iron Ages, the Egyptian and Roman Empires

3000 BCE–CE1

5000–3000 years ago
Egyptian Empire and the Pyramids, the Bronze Age, first writing

5000 years ago (approximately 3000 BCE), the Egyptian Empire began. Egyptians had started farming around the Nile as far back as 7000 years ago (5000 BCE) and over the next 2000 years started to form kingdoms, ruled by pharaohs. [7]

One of the first civilisations to start writing, the Egyptians used papyrus as early paper and they studied maths and science.

The pyramids began to be built 4650 years ago (2650 BCE) with the largest pyramid, the Great Pyramid at Giza built around 2589 BCE (4589 years ago). The pyramids were finished being built by about 4150 years ago (2150 BCE).

Of the many pharaohs, some famous ones were Tutankhamun who ruled from 1336–1327 BCE, Ramesses I (1295–1294 BCE), and Rameses II (1279–1213 BCE).

Around about the same time, approximately 5000 years ago (3000 BCE), the Bronze Age devoloped as Man started using and trading bronze, an alloy of copper and tin. Bronze had more uses than previous stone age tools, especially for cutting.

During this time, as man became more organised and skilful in using bronze tools, agriculture became more prolific as man kept animals and started storing the food he had grown.

The earliest written records of Chinese civilisation date back to over 3000 years ago, from the Shang Dynasty, which ruled in the Yellow River valley.

3000 years ago–814 BCE
Iron Age, the Phoenicians, Carthage

The Iron Age took over from the Bronze Age, approximately 3200 years ago (1200 BCE) and lasted until approximately 500 BCE, although in some areas of Europe and Asia it lasted into the early CE years.

> The Iron Age was the period when man started to use iron or steel (an alloy of iron and carbon) instead of bronze as it was a stronger alternative.

> The Iron age was the last of the three prehistoric Ages – Stone, Bronze and Iron. Although iron continued to be used after the end of the Iron Age, these ages ended at the time when man started to record his own history, and therefore these newer ages are no longer classified as "PRE-historic".

The Phoenician Empire was established and existed from approximately 1500 BCE to 300 BCE and centred around what is modern-day Lebanon and Syria.

> The Phoenicians founded Carthage in 814 BCE[8] as a city-state in what would be modern-day Tunisia. The Phoenicians founded many cities along the Mediterranean coastline and the Iberian Peninsula to conduct trade and moor their fleets.

753 BCE–60 BCE
Rome was founded, Homer, Hannibal, Roman Republic,
the Mayans, Carthage independence, Persian Empire,
Confucianism, Taoism, Buddhism, Classical Greece,
Pythagoras, Socrates, Aristotle, Alexander the Great,
Archimedes, Qin Dynasty, the Silk Road

In 753 BCE Rome was founded. Mythology states it was founded by two brothers, Romulus and Remus, with Romulus killing his brother in an argument over deciding the exact location of the city. Various Kings ruled Rome for 200 years until senators took over and Rome became a republic in 509 BCE. [9]

The word Republic means "public affair" and this Roman Republic is from where we now use the term in its modern sense to denote a country that is run as a public affair by represented officials of the public, rather than a kingdom.

It was around this time, 750 BCE, that Homer supposedly wrote both the *Iliad*, detailing much of Greek mythology and the Trojan War, and the *Odyssey*, bringing to life many stories of the Greek gods. These stories and their being attributed to Homer, have not been factually proven, remaining therefore myths. [10]

Also around this time, Hesiod wrote *Theogony* which depicted the origin of the world and its creation by the great deities of Greek mythology–first the Titans and then the Olympic gods. As these are myths rather than facts, we don't cover the supposed dates of these creations in this book, but as a matter of purely interest we can list the gods and events briefly here:

Gods and Goddesses[11]

Zeus – King of the Gods and God of the Sky

Hera – Zeus' wife and Goddess of Marriage

Athena – Zeus's daughter and Goddess of War and Wisdom

Apollo – God of Music and Arts

Poseidon – God of the Sea and Rivers

Ares – God of War

Artemis – Goddess of Hunting and Chastity

Demeter – Goddess of Earth's Fertility and of Farming

Aphrodite – Goddess of Love

Dionysus – Greek God of Wine (known as Bacchus to the Romans)

Hermes – God of Trade and Wealth

Hephaistos – God of Fire and Metallurgy

Hades – God of the Underworld and of the Dead (Hades has been included here as a 13th God, but is not considered to be one of the original Olympian Gods)

Events[12]

1800 BCE – beginning of the World which is then ruled by the Titans

684–1674 BCE – Zeus fights the Titans and wins

1344 BCE– Pegasus the winged horse is born

1246 BCE – Jason and the Argonauts' voyage occurs

1203 BCE – Helen is abducted by Prince Paris of Troy

1193–1183 BCE – The Siege of Troy, which is eventually conquered by Agamemnon using the Trojan Horse to break the siege and enter the city.

Although the Mayans had been around since pre 2000 BCE it was between 750 BCE and 500 BCE the first Mayan cities were developed, housing large temples with impressive architecture. The Mayan people were not one specific group but rather the term Mayan is a modern-day term to describe the various peoples of parts of south and central America, from Mexico to Guatemala and Belize.

Carthage gained independence from the Phoenicians in 650 BCE and became a major hub for trade for the western Mediterranean over the next 300 years.

During this period a number of Mediterranean wars ensued, including the Sicilian Wars (Carthage against the Greeks) and the Punic Wars (Carthage against the Roman Republic).

It was during the Second Punic War, in 219 BCE, that Hannibal,[13] a revered general in the Carthage Army, invaded Italy. To do so he marched an enormous army which included infantry, cavalry and African elephants across the Alps mountain range. In Italy Hannibal won a number of battles but was never able to conquer Rome itself. His army withdrew from Italy in 203 BCE.

In 550 BCE the Persian Empire was formed under Cyrus the Great[14], who defeated various kingdoms including Media, Lydia and Babylon. His empire also became known as the Achaemenid Empire. This huge Empire eventually spanned from Europe to North Africa and through to India's Indus Valley.

In China, Confucius was born in 551 BCE.[15] He began a teaching career when in his thirties and later played an important role in promoting the values of teachers. He believed strongly in learning as a means towards self-realisation, but also believed in the concept of serving others and became active in politics to promote these ideas. Frustrated at other politician's lack of interest in his ideas, he went into self-imposed exile at age 56 for 12 years. He returned at age 67 and concentrated on writing for the remainder of his life. His thoughts and works created followers of Confucianism which spread throughout China. Confucianism centred around ethics as a means to maintain order among people.

Around the same time, approximately 500-400 BCE, with no real known exact origins, Taoism began forming into a religious system. Lao Tzu is often credited with being the person who started teaching Taoism but this is unproven, as is his actual existence.

In India or Nepal around 500 BCE, Siddhartha Gautama, born into a wealthy family initially, left his material life behind and engaged in wondering as a holy man seeking truth and meditation, during which he experienced enlightenment and spent the remainder of his life teaching his practices which became known as Buddhism.

In Greece this period (500–323 BCE) was known as the Classical period of Ancient Greece. Between 495 and 429 BCE, Pericles, who was an important Greek statesman, over-saw the development of the Acropolis (the highest point in Athens) and the development of its most important buildings including the Parthenon and the Temple of Athena Nike.

It was in 490 BCE that the Greeks won an important vic-tory against the Persians, and a runner was dispatched to Athens from the site of the battle, a place called Marathon, 26 miles away. This legend gave way to the modern mar-athon race although the actual modern marathon dis-tance was only formalised for the 1908 Olympic Games in London, supposedly to appease a member of the royal family who wished for the event to start in the grounds of Windsor Castle, and finish at the Royal Box at the Olympic Stadium, which extended the event to 26.2 miles.[16]

Pythagoras was born and lived in Greece from about 570 BCE through to 490 BCE. One of the most famous philos-ophers and mathematicians in history, Pythagoras is best known for his mathematical theory stating the opposite side of a right-angle triangle is equal to the other two sides.

Socrates was born in 470 BCE in Athens and became known as one of the founders of Western philosophy. Socrates went on to tutor Plato who in turn, in the 380s

BCE, founded the Academy in Athens, a research institute for maths, science and philosophy. Plato published, among many publications, *The Republic* in which he writes about Socrates' talks and thoughts on justice.

At age 18, Aristotle joined the Academy where he remained for 20 years. Aristotle went on to write across a vast number of subjects but was famed most for his writings on ethics.

356 BCE saw the birth of Alexander the Great who succeeded his father as King of the Greek Kingdom of Macedon at age 20 in 336 BCE. Over the next ten years he created one of the largest empires of its time stretching from Greece down to North Africa and he was undefeated in battle, cementing his place in history as one of its greatest military commanders. Alexander was tutored by Aristotle in his younger years.

In this third Century, Archimedes had his "Eureka" moment when he realised (supposedly whilst bathing) that the weight of water displaced by an object was equal to the buoyant force then created underneath that object. Archimedes was a famed mathematician in Greece at the time who also calculated the value of PI. Eureka means "I have found it" in Greek and Archimedes is said to have shouted it out when he realised his theory of buoyancy.

In 221 BCE the first unified Dynasty in China – the Qin Dynasty – was established by Emperor Qin[17]. Although work on different walls had begun earlier by various smaller kingdoms who were protecting their territories, it was under the new first unified territory that Emperor Qin ordered that these individual walls be joined together into one great wall, the Great Wall of China.[18]

Also constructed around this time, was the Terracotta Army. Qin, whilst in power, started the construction of his own Mausoleum. The Terracotta Army was constructed as an afterlife guard for this Emperor's tomb. It was believed to be completed by 206 BCE.[19]

This Qin Dynasty lasted until 207 BCE when it was replaced by the Han Dynasty. Under the Han Dynasty trade increased and the Silk Road trade routes were born.

60 BCE–CE
Julius Caesar, Paris, Antony and Cleopatra, Octavian, Octavia, the Roman Empire

The Roman Republic lasted 500 years until 60 BCE when Julius Caesar, along with Crassus and Pompey, formed a triumvirate of power. Julius Caesar's powers increased due to his success in the Gallic Wars, during which he twice invaded Britain, in 55 BCE and 54 BCE.

It was also at this point, in 52 BCE that the Romans began their settlement at Paris' left bank, developing a rich city of baths and theatres. Paris was established although not then named Paris.

Meanwhile, the Roman Senate, threatened by Caesar's military strength, ordered him to return to Rome, probably to be charged with waging war without their permission. Instead, Caesar crossed the Rubicon River with his armed legion in 49 BCE. At the time it was illegal to enter Rome with an army, with all arms to be laid down and left north of the Rubicon. This brought about the expression, to "cross the Rubicon" meaning to cross a line and accept what consequences then occur.

A four-year civil war ensued with Caesar victorious. He took over Rome in 45 BCE and became Rome's first dictator.

Also in 45 BCE Caesar introduced the 12-month calendar – known as the Julian Calendar. This replaced the previous Roman calendar which was a lunar based calendar, based on phases of the moon.

Further fighting occurred in order to bring back the Republic, and Julius Caesar was assassinated in 44 BCE (by Marcus Brutus on the Ides of March).

After Caesar was assassinated, Rome was ruled by three of his supporters, who joined forces to create a 2nd Triumvurate. Mark Antony, a general, Marcus Lepidus, another one of Caesar's generals, and Octavian, Caesar's great nephew and adopted son. These three rulers then defeated Caesar's murderers and then ruled separate parts of the Republic.

Mark Antony, as one of the three Roman leaders (along with Octavian and Marcus Lepidus), took control of Egypt which was ruled by Cleopatra.

In 40 BCE, to divert war between Antony and Octavian, Antony married Octavian's sister Octavia, but he was also involved in a relationship with Cleopatra at the time.

In 36 BCE Marcus Lepidus was thrown out of the triumvirate of rulers, and in 33 BCE Antony and Octavian had disagreements, creating a split between the two.

Civil war broke out between 32-30 BCE when Octavian declared war on Cleopatra. Antony was defeated in battle and fled to Egypt with Cleopatra where they both committed suicide.

In 27 BCE Octavius declared himself Caesar – meaning Emperor – and changed his name to Augustus meaning "Venerable". Thus he became Augustus Caesar–first Emperor of the Roman Empire.

The Roman Empire began.

Chapter 4.   Jesus – the end of the
             Roman Empire

             CE 1–CE 499

CE 1-39
Jesus, Pontius Pilate, the Roman Empire, Xin Dynasty

Both the Roman historian Tacitus and the Jewish historian Flavius Josephus published historical volumes that objectively recount stories of a person known as Jesus that corroborate the New Testament. Both Josephus in CE 93 and Tacitus in CE 116 wrote that Jesus was sentenced to death by Pontius Pilate. Without therefore verifying the other New Testament stories of the resurrection and other miracles, it is at least historically proven that Jesus did exist, was crucified, and had followers.

> The estimated date of Jesus' crucifixion is between 30–37 CE, with his birth being estimated as being between 2 BCE–7 BCE. The period after his crucifixion therefore saw the beginning of Christianity being established.

In China there was a brief rebellion against the Han Dynasty and from CE 8–CE 23 China was ruled by the Xin Dynasty.

CE 40-99
Roman Empire expanded to Britain, London established, Queen Boudicca, The Eastern Han Dynasty, Emperor Nero, Rome burns, Colosseum built, Gladiators, Early Christian teachings by Matthew, Mark, Luke, John and Paul, Mount Vesuvius, Buddhism entered China.

Around this same period, the Roman Empire was expanding across Western Europe, Africa and Eastern Europe. Under orders from Emperor Claudius, Britain was invaded in CE 43. Two major battles occurred before Rome managed to conquer Britain, the Battle of Medway and the Battle of the Thames.

Between CE 47 and 50 Rome established as its capital the city of Londinium on the Thames at the site of the present-day City of London. London was created.

Over the next 15 years Rome expanded its territory through Britain as far west as Exeter.

In CE 60 or 61 the Roman expansion was briefly halted by the uprising and rebellion of the Welsh Queen Boudicca, before she was defeated.

In China, when the Han overthrew the Xin rebellion and resumed ruling again, the new Han Dynasty became known as the Eastern Han Dynasty.

In CE 64 two-thirds of Rome was burned in a fire.[20] The emperor at the time, Nero, was extremely unpopular, and perceived as "decadent". The myth that followed the fire was that Nero played his fiddle as it burned, but whilst this is not literally true, it is meant to mean he was an ineffective leader.

After the fire, Nero blamed the Christians for the fire, and also went onto build himself a palace on land the fire had cleared, further increasing his unpopularity. Nero's reign ended in CE 69.

Between CE 70 and CE 75 the Colosseum was built. It held up to 80,000 spectators to watch gladiatorial contests as well as battle re-enactments and theatrical dramas.

After Jesus' death the initial teachings of Christianity were delivered by his followers, Mathew, Mark, Luke and John, who wrote the first four books of what became the New Testament sometime between 70 CE and 110 CE. Further books of the New Testament were written by other Christian leaders some of whom, like Paul, only converted to Christianity after Jesus' death.

In CE 79 Mount Vesuvius erupted and within the space of 25 hours the volcanic ash and lava completely enveloped and destroyed Pompeii, a city to the south of the volcano.[21]

> Accurate records of the destruction of the city are available because Pliny the Younger, a Rome magistrate and a writer, interviewed survivors and wrote letters to the historian Tacitus who recorded them. The volcanic ash also preserved Pompeii, meaning modern-day archaeologists were able to uncover the city and view life in those times.

In China under the Eastern Han, trade increased, and Silk Road trade grew with it. It was probably through this trade that Buddhism entered China during the 1st century CE.[22]

CE 100–199
Emperor Trajan, Roman Empire's peak size, Hadrian's Wall, Chinese Yellow Scarves Rebellion

The earliest archaeological remains of paper originate from this century in China, invented most likely by Cai Lun, a eunuch in the emperor's court at the time.

Under Emperor Trajan, the Roman Empire reached its peak size by the time of his death in CE 117. Trajan was a soldier in the Roman Empire rising through its ranks to power. Under his leadership the Roman Empire encompassed most of England, Western and Eastern Europe, the Middle East and North Africa.

In Britain, by CE 100 the Roman Empire had extended northwards as far as Tyne. In the areas not controlled by the Romans there were various warring tribes. In CE 122 Emperor Hadrian visited Britain and ordered a wall to be built in order to separate his empire from these warring tribes in the north (Scotland). Hadrian's Wall was then built and took approximately six years to build. It is 115km/73 miles long.[23]

From CE 161 to CE 180 Marcus Aurelius ruled as Roman Emperor. In a time when emperors had absolute power and were often therefore corrupted, Aurelius stood out as a Stoic and a philosopher. As a Stoic he stood for a set of individual ethics that could not be corrupted by temptation. As a philosopher Aurelius published various writings, one of the most famous being *Meditations*, a series of 12 books on self-improvement and his thoughts on Stoicism.

In China, rebellion broke out in 184 CE against the Eastern Han Dynasty. The rebels wore yellow and thus the rebellion is known as either the Yellow Turban or Yellow Scarves Rebellion. Largely suppressed within a year, the rebellion continued in pockets for another 21 years. The cause of the rebellion was the peasants' disquiet during these times of famine, poor wages in employment, and high taxes.

CE 200–299
Marcus Aurelius, Pax Romana, Gallic Empire, the Bantu People, the Chinese Jin Dynasty

Marcus Aurelius' reign was also considered the end of Pax Romana (meaning Roman Peace)[24]. For 200 years the Empire had seen relatively little strife within its borders. There had been external wars fought as it expanded, but mainly peace within its own borders. However after nearly 200 years, civil war and economic and political troubles were again seen within the Roman Empire in the 3rd century.

During this time from 260 CE to 274 CE, Britain, and most of what is present day France, split off to form the Gallic Empire as various Roman military leaders declared themselves emperors of this region without trying to take power away from the main Roman Empire headquarters of Rome. However the Gallic region was brought back under control of the Roman Empire after the Battle of Châlons in 274 CE.

> Further rebellion was seen in the east of the Roman Empire too, with the Palmyra region from Syria through to Egypt breaking away for three years, before also being brought back under control by Rome.

In Africa the spread of the Bantu people from West and Central Africa reached Southern Africa which previously had been inhabited by Khoisan peoples.

In China, after a period of rebellion, two different individuals proclaimed themselves Emperor in three different regions. The Han Dynasty ended and in its place three separate kingdoms were proclaimed in a period that became known as the Three Kingdoms Period. Further infighting occurred until power within one Kingdom was usurped by Sima Yan who conquered the other Kingdoms and established the Jin Dynasty in 265 CE.

CE 300–399
Roman Empire became Christian, Roman Empire split

In the 3rd century, the Roman Emperor Constantine converted to Christianity. It is not known whether this was for political or religious regions. Until 313 CE Christianity had been banned but Constantine lifted this ban.

By 380 the new Emperor Theodosius I declared Christianity as the official religion of the Roman Empire. This religion later came to become Catholicism but at this stage there were not specifically different branches of Christianity. Rather there were numerous Christian churches set up by Paul and other early religious teachers and these churches all taught varied versions and hymns of Christianity.

In Britain between 367 and 399, barbarian groups from Scotland, Ireland and even Germany ran a series of attacks against the Romans and created a state of lawlessness. Rome responded but the attacks grew stronger until 399 when peace was restored as the Romans brought in reinforcements.[25]

In 395 the Roman Empire split into two parts as it was too large to control from Rome alone. The Western Empire was ruled by Rome whilst the Eastern Empire was controlled by Constantinople.

CE 400–499
Romans departed Britain, Gaul, Vandals, Visigoths, Huns and Franks, the Byzantine Empire, split between Eastern Orthodox Church and the Roman Catholic Church

Between CE 407 and 409 the last remaining Roman troops were either withdrawn from Britain to help out in Italy, or were pushed out of Britain. By 409 Britain was no longer part of the Roman Empire.

During the early 5th century at least four nomadic groups were attacking the (Western) Roman Empire from outside of its borders. These were the Visigoths, the Vandals, the Huns, and the Franks, all Germanic.

The 'Goths', as the Visigoths came to be known, were thought to originate in Scandinavia or Poland and the latter's reputation had them described as a dark force – hence the Goth culture of black attire. In CE 410 the Visigoths managed to invade Rome, previously considered impenetrable.[26]

In CE 455 the Vandals also managed to invade Rome, led by their king, Geiseric. The Vandals originated in Scandinavia but chose to attack the Roman Empire's weaker southern borders in North Africa. They defeated the Romans there and took control of Carthage where they settled. The Vandals reputation for attacking the Roman Empire, and its properties, gave way to the modern word for destroying another's property.

From CE 434 to 453 the Huns, warriors in Northern Europe, were led by Attila who ran a series of assaults on the Roman Empire. These assaults were also instrumental in the gradual fall of the Western Roman Empire.

The Franks had settled in Gaul. Gaul was an area that included most of Western Europe including what we now call France, Belgium and Luxembourg as well as parts of Switzerland, Holland, Germany and Italy. Gaul had been under Roman control since the 2nd century BCE. In 486 however the Roman occupation of Gaul ended as the last Roman Emperor there was attacked and defeated by King Clovis I of the Franks. Clovis I went onto establish the Kingdom of the Franks and this area became known as France.

In CE 476 Odoacer, another German barbarian leader, took control of Rome from what was to be the last of the Roman emperors, Romulus Augustulus, and became King of Italy.

The Western Roman Empire had ended. The Eastern Roman Empire continued from Constantinople but as this became known as the Byzantine Empire, in reality, the Roman Empire had ended altogether.

The Byzantine Empire continued as a Christian empire with Greek as its language and lasted until 1453.

In CE 451 a Council was held in Chalcedon (part of modern-day Istanbul), and the head of the eastern branch of Christianity in Constantinople was declared of equal importance to the pope. The pope was the head of the Christian church in the west and was considered by Rome to be the overall head of the Christian religion. This was the beginning of the split between the Eastern Orthodox Church and the Roman Catholic Church.

Chapter 5. The Early Middle Ages (The Dark Ages)

CE 500–CE 999

After the fall of the Roman Empire, for the next 500 years Europe was run by barbarians, and these times became known as the Dark Ages.

Also called the Early Middle Ages or Early Medieval times, medieval from Latin "Medius" meaning middle and "Aevum" meaning age.

CE 500–599
Anglo Saxons, Gaul, Paris, AD/BC established, Prophet Muhammad born, Hagia Sofia, St Catherine's Monastery, Chinese Grand Canal completed

In Britain, no longer ruled by the Romans, various new Barbarian groups arrived. These included the Angles and the Saxons as well as Jutes and Frieslands, all from what we now call mainland Europe. The Saxons were a Germanic speaking tribe from today's Germany, Denmark and Holland. In Britain the Saxons established a number of kingdoms and fought battles against the Roman Britons who lived in Britain at the time. It was at this time that the legendary King Arthur supposedly lived and legend has it that he defeated the Saxons in a number of battles, slowing the Saxon's establishment of their kingdoms. The Saxons did settle though, and these new settlers became known as the Anglo Saxons, the people who settled in Britain after the Roman Empire.[27]

In Gaul, in CE 507 Clovis I, the first King of the Franks who had earlier defeated the Roman Emperor, defeated the Visigoths who then retreated to modern-day Spain and settled there. Clovis I then made Paris his capital. This was the beginning of Paris becoming the capital of the region to be called France, named after the Franks.

In approximately CE 525 Dionysius Exiguus introduced the AD, Anno Domini (in the Year of our Lord), time phrase.[28] He was doing this in order to introduce a new means for establishing at what point in the year Easter should fall. There was a dispute at the time between the Eastern Orthodox church and the Roman Church as to when Easter should occur and Dionysius wanted to have these two churches reach agreement. At the same time as trying to establish when Easter

45

should fall, Dionysius wanted to change the system of dating years from the Roman system in place at the time which dated years from when Emperor Diocletian was in power. As Diocletian persecuted Christians, Dionysius instead sought to date years from the date of Jesus' birth. As there was no means of knowing exactly when Jesus was born, Dionysius had to use the known history at the time. Today it is calculated that he was seven years out and that Jesus was probably born around 7 BCE.

In CE 537 the Hagia Sofia was re-built in Constantinople (modern-day Istanbul), having first been opened in CE 360.[29] At the time it was a Christian cathedral and an icon of Byzantine architecture in the Byzantium Empire. It remained a Christian cathedral until 1453 when it was converted to a mosque, before being turned into a Museum of Christian and Muslim artefacts in 1931, before being returned to a mosque in 2020.

Between CE 548 and 565, St Catherine's Monastery was completed at the base of Mount Sinai, the supposed place where Moses received the Ten Commandments. The monastery is the oldest Christian monastery in the world.

In China, the Grand Canal, the earliest parts of which dated as far back as the 5th century BCE, was first connected together as one "Grand Canal" during the Sui Dynasty between CE 581 and 618. The main reason for the canal was for trading, transporting valuable agricultural commodities from the far southern regions to Beijing, the capital in the north.

In the first half of the 6th century, a series of wars were continued between the Persian Empire under the Sassanids, and the Eastern Roman Empire as the two fought for territory.

In CE 570 the Prophet Muhammed was born in Mecca, mod-ern-day Saudi Arabia. Most of his first 40 years were spent as a trader. Although always religious, it was only at age 40 that he began to have revelations of appearances of the Angel Gabriel with messages from God. These occurred in CE 610 and are therefore discussed in the next chapter.

CE 600–699
Muhammad established Islam, Bulgarian Empire began

Muhammad, the prophet and founder of Islam, who was born in CE 570 in Mecca, was a trader until the age of age 40.[30] Mecca was a trading centre and a place where traders and travellers stopped to trade and worship various gods. Most of these gods were represented by idols that their fol-lowers worshipped, except the God Allah, who was not rep-resented by any idol. Married and religious, Muhammad meditated and worshipped, and in CE 610, when he was 40, the Angel Gabriel appeared to him whilst meditating. After this, Muhammad began to preach messages condemning the worshipping of idols. As his followers grew, he encountered more and more resistance from other prophets, as well as mer-chants who gained financially from the sale of the many idols of worship. Eventually in CE 622 Muhammad had to move from Mecca to Medina. The Muslim calendar's start date is marked from this year CE 622, and the migration is known as the "Hijrah".

Various battles occurred over the four years from CE 624–CE 628 as different groups within the Muslim communi-ties battled for control, but Muhammed and his followers eventually won. Muhammed's power base was now large

47

enough for him to return to Mecca which he did in CE 630 taking control of the city. Here he pardoned many of those who opposed him, and most of Mecca converted to Islam, and the idols that had been worshipped by the other religions were then destroyed.

Muhammed returned to Medina and died there in CE 632 at age 62.

One of the first people to have followed Muhammed was Abu Bakr, a close friend of his, and after his death many of Muhammed's followers believed Abu Bakr to be his successor. This group of people are Sunni Muslims. Abu Bakr became the first caliph – Agent of the Prophet.

However, one of Muhammed's children, a daughter named Fatima, had married Muhammed's cousin, Ali ibn Abu Talib, and another group of Muslims believed that he, Muhammed's cousin, should be Muhammed's successor and Caliph, not Abu Bakr. These people are Shi'ite Muslims.

In CE 627 the Battle of Nineveh occurred as the Persian Sassanid Empire continued to battle the Byzantium Empire. The Byzantines won. In CE 680 the Bulgarian Empire was established when the Bulgars defeated the Byzantines and established their own power base over their region. The Byzantium and Bulgarian empires existed in constant conflict thereafter.

CE 700-799
Islamic and Arabic culture spread, Charlemagne became King of the Franks, Viking era began

From 700 both Islamic and Arabic cultures spread westwards from Saudi Arabia (Mecca) and Syria (Damascus), throughout North Africa and to the Iberian Peninsula. Spain was invaded by Muslim forces in CE 711 and within seven years the whole Iberian Peninsula was under their control.[31] This rapid spread of Islamic culture was conducted by the Umayyad Dynasty. Prior to the Umayyads, Islamic rule was conducted through various governors in different states. There was a caliph who was the agent in charge, but there was no central state to govern. As Islam grew, the Umayyads formed a more central form of government and an Islamic Political State emerged. Arabic was established as the main political language, Islamic coins were introduced, and the Capital was moved from Mecca to Syria.

The Umayyad Mosque in Damascus was built In CE 715, with the dome completed in CE 789.

In France in CE 771, Charlemagne became King of the Franks. He had a goal to convert all his people to Christianity. He spent much of the next 20 years at war, and in 800 Pope Leo III made him Emperor of Europe.[32]

Around CE 791, the Vikings, who were Norse people of the Scandinavian region, started trading and conquering other parts of Europe. The first raids occurred on the British Isles. Of particular severity was their raid and destruction of Lindisfarne which was notable for two reasons. Firstly, it was an attack on Christian England, and secondly, because it was one of the earliest recorded Viking raids, it helps mark the beginning of the Viking era.[33]

CE 800–899

Charlemagne died, Vikings conquered new territories, the Kingdom of Scotland, Gunpowder, Cyrillic alphabet invented, Buddhism backlash in China, first king of England, Kiev became capital of Kievan Rus', Mayan civilisation collapsed

In CE 814 Charlemagne died having established a European cultural and intellectual identity known as the Carolingian Renaissance.

> The empire he had established covered most of Western Europe, and Charlemagne is considered the father of Europe.

Out of Scandinavia the Viking people continued to spread out to conquer territory. One of the best examples of Viking artefacts is the Oseberg ship which was buried in CE 830 and is on display today in Oslo. Across Britain the Vikings continued to conquer various kingdoms, installing their own rulers. This spread to Ireland where permanent settlements were set up, including Dublin in CE 841.[34] In CE 872 Harold I, having conquered Norway, became the first king of Norway.

From CE 840-843 under threat from Vikings, the Picts and the Scots created a union and the Kingdom of Alba was formed. This was part of the development of the Kingdom of Scotland.

Around CE 850 Chinese monks who had been using saltpetre for medicinal purposes for centuries and were looking for an Elixir for Life, discovered that when it was mixed with other chemicals including sulphur, it became extremely flammable. This was the discovery of gunpowder which was soon taken up by Mongols who used it for warfare.[35]

In approximately CE 860 St Cyril and St Methodius developed a new alphabet for the Slav people, based on the Greek alphabet, but with some additional sounds suited to the Slavic language. This alphabet is the Cyrillic alphabet now used across Russia, Belarus, Bulgaria, Serbia and numerous other countries.

In China in CE 841 Buddhism faced a backlash from the Royal Court due to its growing influence, with 250,000 monks and nuns forced back into civilian life and 50,000 monasteries were closed. This backlash lasted until CE 845.[36]

In England, Alfred the Great became King of Wessex from CE 871–899, having succeeded his brother Ethelred I[37]. Alfred defeated the Danish in a number of battles and in CE 886 he captured London and brought all England together under his control, becoming the first King of England.

It was also during this Century that Kiev, or Kyiv, previously already a loose settlement, was made the Capital of Kievan Rus', a new group of States in Eastern Europe.

It was during the 9th century that the south and central American civilisation of the Mayans collapsed. Although there is no proven singular reason for this collapse it is thought to be as a result of overpopulated cities, drought and warfare.

CE 900-999
Kingdom of England, Vikings raided Europe and Britain, Erik the Red, Song Dynasty established, Olav Tryggvason, Poland established, Kingdom of Ghana

In England, following the death of Alfred the Great, his son Edward the Elder became King of the West Saxons and his sister Aethelred became ruler of the Mercians. In CE 937 Edward's son Athelstan united both these areas and the Kingdom of England began.[38]

Vikings continued their raids through Europe and Britain. In Southern Europe they reached as far as Constantinople before being paid to leave.

In Britain, in CE 910 the Danes suffered a defeat at the Battle of Tettenhall which proved to be their last battle. In CE 981 Erik the Red left Norway and settled in Greenland and set up settlements there.[39]

In China the Song Dynasty was established in CE 960 by Emperor Taizu of Song and over the next 300 years the population of China doubled as rice cultivation expanded and there was greater food security.

In CE 955 Olav Tryggvason built the first Christian church in Norway. He had returned from battles in Britain where he had converted to Christianity and after taking the throne in Norway, he started converting Norway to Christianity.

CE 966 is seen by most historians as the date at which Poland was formed as state in its own right with the adoption of Christianity by its ruler at the time, Mieszko.[40] Mieszko had been born into the ruling family of a local dynasty. By adopting Christianity, he united his dynasty with that of another family dynasty and created a strong political union.

Throughout the 10th century, in Africa, the Kingdom of Ghana was at its peak, based on a strong trading empire of gold, iron and salt.

Chapter 6. The Middle Ages

CE 1000–CE 1499

Also known as Medieval Times, medieval from Latin "Medius" meaning middle and "Aevum" meaning age.

CE 1000–1099

Leif Eriksson set foot on North America, the Canon of Medicine, end of Viking era, Macbeth took the throne in Scotland, the Great Schism (1054), William the Conqueror crowned King of England, the Bayeux Tapestry, the Domesday Book, El Cid, The First Crusade

Around CE 1000 Leif Eriksson, a Norwegian raised in Greenland, probably became the first European to set foot on North American soil, almost 500 years before Christopher Columbus or John Cabot ever did. [41] Eriksson's father, Erik the Red, had formed the first settlement in Greenland after being banished from Iceland for killing his neighbour. According to Greenland legend, Eriksson heard of an Icelandic trader named Bjarni Herjolfsson who had sailed by the shores of America without disembarking. Eriksson followed Herjolfsson's route in reverse, crossed the Atlantic and set foot on what is modern-day Canadian soil, naming it Helluland, Icelandic for Stone Slab Land. They set up camp in what is now Newfoundland and spent winter there. It is believed that after about ten years' of trips to North America the Greenlanders stopped voyaging there due to the violent attacks they experienced from the indigenous North Americans. In 1960 Archaeologists excavated artifacts supporting the Norse or Viking settlement of Newfoundland dating them back to CE 1000.

In approx. 1020 to 1030 the *Canon of Medicine,* the world's first medical encyclopaedia, was authored by a Persian Muslim philosopher and physician called Avicenna. It set the standards for medicine for centuries to come.

In Norway, after the death of King Olav Tryggvason, another Olav became king, King Olav Haraldsson. In 1030 he was defeated in the Battle of Stiklestad. but by then he and the former Olav had managed to unify Norway as a Christian Kingdom, effectively bringing to an end the Viking era. Olav Haraldsson was canonised (declared a saint by the Roman Catholic Church) and became the Patron Saint of Norway.

In 1030 in Scotland, Macbeth succeeded his father as chief in the province of Moray and then killed his cousin Duncan I in battle (not in bed as was described in Shakespeare's play) and took the throne as King of Scotland in 1040. Macbeth died in battle in 1057.[42]

In 1054 the Christian church split in what became known as the Great Schism. Since the 3rd century under Constantine, Christianity had been the official religion of the Roman Empire. Various councils had been held over the century to solidify the Christian doctrine but differences emerged and by 1054 these could not be resolved. The Roman branch of Christianity believed in the supreme power of a pope and that he should have power over the patriarch (head) of the eastern branch. In 1054 the (Eastern) patriarch of Constantinople, Michael Cerularius was excommunicated by the (Western) Christian Church in Rome. It was the breaking point. The Christian Church separated into the Eastern Orthodox Church controlled in Constantinople, and the Western Catholic Church headed in Rome. The Orthodox Church did, and does not, acknowledge the Pope.

In England, in 1066 King Harold Godwinson defeated Norway's Harold Hardrada at the Battle of Stamford Bridge and then fought the Norman-French army under William Duke of Normandy at Hastings. Godwinson died in the fighting at the Battle of Hastings and William "the Conqueror" became King of England on Christmas Day

1066. Part of our knowledge of the Battle of Hastings and the Norman Conquest comes from the Bayeux Tapestry, a medieval embroidery 70 metres long.

> In order to fund his armies, William needed to know the wealth of his citizens so as to know who and how much to tax. To gain this knowledge, William commissioned the Domesday survey, which resulted in the publishing of the *Domesday Book* in 1086. It contained information on over 13,400 English settlements.[43]

In 1065 on the Iberian Peninsula (before the formation of Spain and Portugal), Sancho became King of Castile and appointed a 22-year-old as Commander of the Troops. This 22-year-old came to be known as El Cid. Over the next three decades he became a celebrated knight through various warring campaigns against the Moors and other kingdoms, and to this day remains a popular Spanish folk hero.

In 1095 at one of the Western Christian Councils, the pope, in answer to a plea for help from his Byzantine counterpart Alexius, requested Western European Christian kingdoms to help the Byzantine Christians fight off the Muslim threat and reclaim the Holy Lands. This marked the first of the Crusades. [44]

> The first Crusade occurred from 1096 through until 1099. The Crusading armies consisted of various separate entities and whilst some initial armies were defeated in battles, the main Crusaders won battles at Nicaea in Turkey, then Antioch in Syria, followed by Jerusalem in 1099. The crusade was bloody with huge casualties of men, women and children.

CE 1100–1199
Knights Templar, Portugal formed, Second and Third Crusades, Moscow established, Notre Dame, Genghis Khan, Thomas Becket, Peace Treaty between Rome and the Papacy

In 1118 the Knights Templar were formed by a French knight called Hugues de Payens. He did so with the support of the ruler of Jerusalem at the time, Baldwin II. The Knights were formed in order to protect Christian visitors to Jerusalem, many of whom were subject to attacks from Muslims, as they journeyed across Muslim lands to visit the now Christian controlled Jerusalem.[45]

Until 1139 the area of Portugal had been an autonomous region under the control of Henry of Burgundy. Fighting occurred frequently on its southern borders between Christians and the Islamic Moors. After Henry's death in 1112 his widow defended the country, but it was her son Alfonso I who had the most success in battles against the Moors in the south, before he then rebelled against his mother. In 1139 he won a decisive victory at the Battle of Ourique and was proclaimed King of Portugal by his army. The Kingdom of Portugal was formed. [46]

The Second Crusade began in 1147. After the success of the First Crusade, four Christian territories were established at Jerusalem, Edessa, Antioch and Tripoli. Muslim forces continued with their own holy war against these Christian states. In 1144 Edessa fell to the Muslims. The Christians in Western Europe called for a Second Crusade and the call was answered in 1147 by King Louis VII of France and King Conrad III of Germany. The Christians suffered two heavy defeats, the second of which was in Syria, effectively ending the Second Crusade.

In 1187 a Muslim leader, Saladin, began a campaign against the Christian Kingdom of Jerusalem, and won decisive victories and took back control of the city. Outrage in the West lead to the Third Crusade, lead primarily this time by King Phillip II of France and Richard I of England, known as Richard the Lionheart, as well as Emperor Frederick Barbarossa, the Roman Emperor. Barbarossa drowned in Syrian en-route, but Richard defeated Saladin at the Battle of Arsuf, captured the city of Jaffa, and regained Christian territories in the area. However, he did not lay siege to Jerusalem and instead Richard and Saladin signed a peace treaty which recognised Muslim control of Jerusalem but allowed Christians to visit the city. This treaty marked the end of the Third Crusade.

In the early 12th century the Kievan Rus' (see CE 800–900), a loose federation of states in Eastern Europe, began to disintegrate. However, Kiev, its capital, was well established by then and its over 400 churches signified its wealth and status as a city and the cultural heritage of the regions' people. By 1147 another settlement was established at a point on the Moskva River by Prince Yuri Dolgoruky. This was the establishment of Moscow.

In Paris in 1160 the Bishop of Paris, Maurice de Sully, suggested a single church be built on the site of two former Christian churches.[47] The first stones of this new church, Notre Dame de Paris, were laid in 1163 by Pope Alexander III.

In 1162 Genghis Khan was born and by age 20 began building an army to defeat and unite other smaller tribes and in doing so built the largest Empire in the world, the Mongol Empire.

In 1169 England's involvement in Ireland began with the Anglo-Norman invasion as Anglo-Normans gradually took over Irish land, and the English King Henry II landed there in 1171 to assert control.

Thomas Becket was murdered in 1170 in Canterbury Cathedral.[48] Becket was the former Chancellor of England, where he became extremely good friends with King Henry II. When the position of Archbishop of Canterbury became vacant, Henry appointed Becket to the post, whilst he still held his position as Chancellor. Henry wanted him to remain as Chancellor so he could link his government and the Church, but Becket resigned, creating a rift between him and the king, and by 1164 Becket had fled to France in exile. Under pressure from the pope, the king reassured Becket he could return safely to England. However, on his return, four knights, loyal to the King, assassinated Becket in the Cathedral.

> During the rift with Becket, and whilst Becket was exiled in France, in 1167 Henry II banned English students from studying in Paris. This resulted in a rapid rise in students studying at Oxford.[49] Teachings had occurred there since the 11th century, making it England's oldest university.

In 1177, after decades of fighting between the Roman Empire and the papacy, a peace treaty was signed between the Emperor Frederick I and Pope Alexander III. This was known as the Peace of Venice (1177).[50] Frederick acknowledged Alexander as the pope.

CE 1200–1299
*Fourth to Seventh Crusades, Cambridge University founded,
St. Francis of Assisi, Moors defeated in Spain, Magna Carta,
Great Zimbabwe, the Golden Horde, Kublai Khan, Marco
Polo, Switzerland established, William Wallace, the Ottoman
Empire formed*

In 1204 in Constantinople, when the Emperor Alexius IV
campaigned to have the Byzantine Church submit to the
Roman Church, other powers within his empire resisted and
Alexius was assassinated.[51] The Crusaders declared war on
Constantinople. This marked the beginning of the Fourth
Crusade which ended with the bloody conquest of, and fall,
of Constantinople.

> The Crusades continued for the remainder of the early
> twelfth century as the Crusaders fought against anyone
> who was opposed to Christianity, with battles fought in
> France and the Baltic. The Fifth Crusade occurred when
> the Crusaders unsuccessfully attacked Egypt in 1221.
>
> In 1229 Emperor Frederick II negotiated Jerusalem to
> again come under Christian control in what became
> known as the Sixth Crusade, however Jerusalem returned
> to Muslim control just ten years later.
>
> The final and Seventh Crusade occurred between 1248 and
> 1254 when Louis IX organised another Crusade against
> Egypt. This battle too was unsuccessful.

Cambridge University was founded 1209 and given a royal
charter by King Henry III in 1231, making it second to
Oxford as the oldest university in the England

Also in 1209, but in Italy, Francis Bernardone, later to become St. Francis of Assisi, decided to follow the teachings of Jesus and gave up all worldly material things, having previously been a wealthy merchant's son. In 1210 he walked to Rome to request permission to preach, which was granted, with this date marking the beginning of the Franciscan order.[52]

In 1212 the course of Spanish history was changed when the Battle of Tolosa Plains occurred, and the Moors were defeated by the Christian monarchs. The battle proved a turning point in the Moors' hold on the Iberian Peninsula, and the eventual Christian reconquest of the region.[53]

At Runnymede in England in 1215 King John, an unpopular king facing down rebellion, agreed to sign the Magna Carta, a Great Charter, laying out the rights of free men and holding the king and future kings to act within the rule of law. The document was reissued three times over the next decade and would go onto lay the foundation for the English system of Common Law. [54]

Although construction of the great walled Kingdom of Zimbabwe was believed to have started in the 11th century it is estimated that the actual kingdom was established around 1220. It flourished until 1500 as a centre for trading with travelling Arab, Portuguese and other merchants. [55]

In 1240 one of Genghis Khan's grandsons, Batu Khan, established the Golden Horde, a group of Mongols who conquered and ruled over most of Mongolia and Russia and as far east as part of Eastern Europe including Bulgaria and Ukraine. The Golden Horde ruled until 1502. [56]

In 1259 the Treaty of Paris was signed between Henry III and Louis IX in which Henry gave up his claims to land in Northern France but would retain the Channel Islands.

In China in 1260 another grandson of Genghis Khan, Kublai Khan, conquered the Song Dynasty, established the Yuan Dynasty and created the Chinese Empire of China, Mongolia, part of Siberia, and even extending into parts of the Middle East.[57]

Although currencies had been in use since 600 BC in Lydia (modern Western Turkey) when King Alyattes created the first coins, and the Chinese then introduced paper currency around 700BC, it was Kublai Khan who reintroduced paper money into his Empire and began managing the money supply, around 1270[58]

In 1275 the Italian Explorer and businessman Niccolò Polo and his son Marco arrived at the court of Kublai Khan in what is modern-day Beijing. They took on important roles for the emperor, and remained in the court for 16 years before returning to Italy as rich merchants. In Italy Marco financed a warship as Venice was at war with Genoa. Marco ended up captured and imprisoned, and whilst in prison he befriended a writer who wrote of his travels in China. This book became Europe's main source of information on China for centuries to come. Marco died in 1324 CE.[59]

In 1291 the three founding cantons of modern-day Switzerland decided to support each other militarily and economically. Although the date is disputed, this is considered the date of the beginning of Switzerland's democratic formation into a confederation.[60]

In 1297 the Scots, under William Wallace, secured victory over the English at the Battle of Stirling Bridge, cementing Wallace's place in Scottish history, and its fight for retaining its independence from the English.[61]

The Ottoman Empire, established between 1290 and 1300, lasted until 1922, reaching its peak by the mid 1550s and stretched from Hungary to Egypt, taking control of Constantinople and putting an end to the Byzantine Empire when it did so. It was established by Osman I who set up a formal government and created the Islamic run superpower. The leader, known as the sultan, had absolute religious and political power.

CE 1300–1399
The Renaissance, Knights Templar arrested and dissolved, Robert the Bruce, the Great Famine, the Hundred Years War, the Black Death, knitting, the Great Schism, the Peasants' Revolt, Geoffrey Chaucer, bank notes

Prior to the 14th century there had not been many advances in art or science, with little regard for learning during this period. However, this changed between the 14th and 17th centuries, a period that came to be known as the Renaissance.

The Renaissance started in Italy with the philosophy of humanism, a way of thinking that placed humans at the centre of their universe, which promoted advances in both arts and science, as well as literature and learning, with a rediscovery of classical Greek philosophy.

Humanism and the Renaissance really gained momentum as a movement in the 15th century.

By the 14th century the Knights Templar, who had settled in France, had become a wealthy and powerful force. This, probably, was the motivation behind their sudden arrest in 1307 by King Philip IV. This created friction with the church and Pope Clement V as the Knights supposedly fell under the authority of the pope, not the king. Under extreme torture during which some died, all except four of 138 Knights confessed to denying Christ, which was heresy. The pope wanted the knights to be tried in Rome not France, in order to provider a fairer trial without torture but in any case disbanded them. In France in March 1314 the Knight's leaders Jacques de Molay and Geoffroi de Charney were executed. [62]

Later that same year both Pope Clement and King Philip IV died, and so ended the Order of the Knights Templar.

In 1314, Robert the Bruce, who had seized power in Scotland following William Wallace's execution in 1305, defeated the English at the Battle of Bannockburn. This event enabled Bruce to convince the English to recognise Scottish independence.

From 1315 through until 1317 bad weather across Northern Europe caused a series of crop failures that resulted in starvation on a huge scale and came to become known as the Great Famine. Most effected were modern-day Britain, Belgium, Holland, France, Scandinavia, Germany, Poland and as far east as Russia. Life expectancy in this period fell from 35 to just 29 and it was estimated that possibly 10% of the population of Europe died in the famine.

In 1337, the Hundred Years War began between England and France. In reality the war was a series of conflicts over land disputes as well as who had the rights to the French throne.

The confiscation in 1337 of Guyenne from the English by the French is seen as the beginning of these conflicts. [63]

The Black Death, also known as the Bubonic Plague, occurred from the mid 1340s to the mid 1350s with the main peak occurring in the 5 years from 1347 and 1352. It was the second great natural disaster to hit Europe after the 1315 famine but was far more acute and deadly, with estimates of 75 million to 200 million dying – possibly 30-60% of Europe's population! It was caused by a bacterium carried by rats.

It was believed that it was during the mid-14th Century, that knitting became popular as a home activity. This is depicted by paintings in the 1350s showing Mary, the mother of Jesus, knitting.[64]

After the first Great Schism of the Christian Church in 1054 when the Eastern Orthodox Church split from the Roman Catholic Church, a second Great Schism occurred in 1378 lasting until 1417.[65] In this schism there was a split between cardinals as to who would be pope and where he would be based. Pope Clement V moved the papacy to Avignon in France, with the split growing stronger after his papacy, with at one stage three separate popes being elected by different cardinals at the same time. The standoff lasted until 1417 when the papacy returned to Rome under a single pope, Pope Martin V.

In 1381 in Essex, England, the Peasants' Revolt occurred. Following the poverty that followed in the aftermath of the Black Death people were becoming increasingly angry at their positions as serfs. Serfdom was the condition whereby a peasant was bound to work on a piece of land for a landlord. A radical priest John Ball preached for greater equality among men and when an unpopular poll tax was levied on the

people, the revolt began. Kent followed Essex in revolt and
the rebels' leader Wat Tyler eventually met the King Richard
II but was killed by the Lord Mayor of London, William
Walworth. To prevent retaliation by the peasants, Richard II
promised to abolish serfdom. This did not occur straight away
with government officials hanging many who had revolted,
but eventually the harsh laws were relaxed.

Born in 1343 and dying in 1400 in England, Geoffrey
Chaucer was one of England's most famous writers and poets,
with his most famous work being *The Canterbury Tales*. He
was the first person to be buried in Westminster Cathedral's
Poet's Corner.

CE 1400-1499
*The Renaissance, the Medici family, Donatello, Gutenberg
Press, Leonardo da Vinci, Michelangelo, Botticelli,
Copernicus, Henry V, the Battle of Agincourt, Beijing
established, Joan of Arc, Machu Pichu, Byzantine Empire,
the Ottoman Empire, the Hundred Years War, the Wars of the
Roses / English Civil Wars, the Spanish Inquisition, the Age
of Exploration, Bartolomeu Dias and the Cape of Good Hope,
Christopher Columbus, Amerigo Vespucci, John Cabot, Vasco
da Gama and India, the Great Wall of China, the slave trade
began*

With the Renaissance having started in the 14th century with
the humanist movement, it really took off in the 15th century, receiving backing from the Medici family through their
financing of the cultural explosion in Florence. Key events and
persons of the Renaissance during the 15th Century included:

The Medici family were a powerful family of bankers and politicians in Florence, Italy, and in 1434 Cosimo de Medici rose to power within the family and strongly supported the arts and humanities, as he wished to see Florence become the centre of the cultural world. His sons and grandsons continued to support cultural activities including those of Leonardo da Vinci and Michelangelo.

One of the earliest Renaissance artists was Donatello, a sculptor, now known as possibly being second only to Michelangelo in his skill. In 1408 Donatello completed his *David*. Whilst both are based on David from the biblical David and Goliath, Donatello's *David* should not be confused with Michelangelo's, which was crafted the following century. Donatello's is more feminine and sculpted in bronze, whilst Michelangelo's is sculpted from marble.[66]

The Gutenberg printing press was invented in 1450 in Germany and this further enhanced the Renaissance with the increased speed of communication through Europe allowing for the spread of ideas.

Leonardo da Vinci was one of the most famous and successful of the Renaissance artists. Born in 1452, his most famous works are *The Last Supper* (painted between 1495 and 1498) which depicts the Passover dinner with Jesus and his Apostles at which Jesus forecasts that one of them will betray him; and *Mona Lisa* (painted between 1503 and 1506). For more information on da Vinci and *Mona Lisa* see 1500–1600 CE.[67]

Michelangelo was born on 1475 in Florence and was spotted for his artistic talent by Cosimo de Medici's grandson Lorenzo de Medici, who gave the young Michelangelo accommodation in his palace where Michelangelo met with, and was inspired by, other intellectuals and artists. His big break came in 1498 when he won a commission to sculpt a statue for St Peter's Basilica in Rome of the Virgin Mary with the body of her dead son Jesus draped across her lap. The sculpture is titled *The Pity* or *La Pieta*. For more information on Michelangelo see 1500–1600 CE.[68]

Sandro Botticelli was born in the 1440s and was a master painter and an integral part of the Renaissance. His finest work is *The Birth of Venus*, painted in his 40s during the 1480s.

Nicolaus Copernicus was born in 1473 in Poland during Poland's "Golden Age" as it too enjoyed unprecedented artistic, cultural and scientific development. Copernicus was Poland's most famous example of this, and his theories are credited as the beginning of modern astronomy. For more information on Copernicus see 1500–1600 CE. It was also during this period that Poland, whilst the rest of Europe was still experiencing religious turmoil, adopted a stance of religious tolerance.[69]

In England, in 1413 Henry V took the throne.

One of England's most famous battles, The Battle of Agincourt (made famous in Shakespeare's *Henry V*) took place in 1415. This victory for England over France was part of the Hundred Years War.

In Beijing, in 1420, the court of the Chinese Emperor of the Ming Dynasty took up occupancy of the completed Forbidden City. Only the Emperor could enter any section of the City, all other people were forbidden to enter at least some parts. Hence the Forbidden City's name. The city was commissioned in 1406, occupied 178 acres, and all the important buildings face south to face the sun.[70]

Joan of Arc, or Jeanne d'Arc, was born in 1412. At age 18 she rose to prominence after she proclaimed she had received visions of the Archangel Michael, as well as St Margaret and St Catherine of Alexandria, urging her to support King Charles VII of France, in the Hundred Years War against the English. This was during a point in the war when the English held the upper hand. King Charles was unanointed at this stage but when he heard of Joan, he sent her to the siege of Orleans. The siege was lifted nine days later, and a number of further victories soon followed which led to Charles' coronation. Joan was considered a heroine by the French, but was captured by some nobles aligned to the English. She was tried and then burned at the stake as a heretic at just 19 years old and declared a martyr 25 years later.

Machu Pichu was constructed around 1450 as an estate for the Inca emperor Pachacuti. Located in southern Peru, this citadel translates as "Old Pyramid" and it is considered that it was built as a retreat for the emperor following a successful military campaign.

In 1453 the Byzantine Empire fell. The Byzantine Empire had been established as the East Roman Empire when the Roman Empire split in 395 CE. The Empire lasted over 1000 years until Mehmed II the Conqueror, leader of the Ottomans, seized control of Constantinople. The Ottoman Empire had been formed by Osman I (Uthman in Arabic) a leader of a Turkish tribe.[71]

In 1453 the Ottoman Empire closed routes with the West and so the famed Silk Road (a network of routes for trade between

East and West) came to an end. This initiated the Age of Discovery, or Age of Exploration, as merchants sourced new routes for trade and so European explorers took to the sea, claiming new lands and introducing new cultures.

In 1453 the English and the French fought the last battle of the Hundred Years' War, although the war continued for another 20 years. This battle was the Battle of Castillon. The English lost land across Bordeaux which resulted in unrest back in England.

In England, this unrest led to the Wars of the Roses, which were also known for a time as the Civil Wars, fought between the Houses of Lancaster and York (each of whom had roses on their badges). (These Civil Wars are not to be confused with the English Civil Wars of the 17th Century (see 1625)).

These Wars of the Roses were fought between 1455 and 1485 as England was ruled by the child king Henry VI whose advisors were extremely unpopular. Henry VI was murdered in 1471 in the Tower of London. Edward IV's sons were in line for the throne but Richard of Gloucester, who was their protector, successfully claimed they were illegitimate, clearing the way for him to become King Richard III. Edward's two sons disappeared, presumed smothered to death. Henry Tudor, who was heir to the House of Lancaster, marched against Richard III and they met in Battle in 1485 where Richard III was killed in the Battle of Bosworth Field in Leicestershire. Henry was crowned Henry VII, and married the heir to the House of York, Elizabeth of York. The War of the Roses were over, and the House of Tudor took the throne.[72]

In Spain, the Spanish Inquisition, which was to last almost 400 years, started. In 1469 Isabella I of Castille and Ferdinand II of Aragon were married, unifying Spain. In 1478 a judicial review was established in order to prevent and punish heresy. Spain had a large numbers of Jews and Muslims and whilst many had converted to Christianity there were large groups who also continued to practice their own faith in secret. The Roman Catholic Church authorised Catholic monarchs to enforce religious unity, and Isabella and Ferdinand used this as an opportunity to consolidate their power. They did so brutally. In 1483 the Pope authorised the Spanish government to establish a grand inquisitor and Tomas de Torquemada was appointed who used torture and punishment to fulfil his duties. Approximately 2000 people were burned at the stake during Torquemada's time, and 160,000 Jews were expelled from Spain.

With The Renaissance causing a newfound quest for knowledge among Europeans, along with their wanting to spread Christianity around the world and discover new routes to Asia to trade spices and other merchandise, including slaves, the period from 1400 –1700 marked a new time of discovery that came to be known as the Age of Exploration, or the Age of Discovery. Prior to this period, any trade with the East had been conducted via overland routes, the famed Spice Road. However due to wars and other attacks on trade caravans, the overland route was becoming more and more difficult.

In 1488 Bartolomeu Dias, a Portuguese explorer was the first person to navigate around the Cape of Good Hope, the point at the southwest point of Africa and sailed eastwards around the southernmost point of Africa, Cape Agulhas and landed at Mossel Bay. He continued a little further eastward until he was sure that it was possible to continue with no further land blocking the way, confirming for himself that he had sailed around the southernmost point of Africa. He then returned to Lisbon to let King John II know as it was the Portuguese King who had commissioned him to find this valuable trade route to the East. Dias originally termed the Cape the 'Cape of Storms' but the King renamed it the 'Cape of Good Hope' due to its giving hope to a new era of trade with the East.[73]

In 1492 Christopher Columbus arrived in North America, by accident. It had been his intention to find a western route around the globe to Asia. His journeys mark the beginning of centuries of European settlement of North America. However, at the time, when he landed on what was North America it was thought by himself and other subsequent explorers that this was still part of Asia.

Columbus was born in Genoa, Italy, and went to sea on a merchant ship in his teens. In his twenties the ship he was on was sunk by Pirates off the Portuguese coast, but Columbus managed to float to shore on a piece of wood. He made his way to Lisbon and studied mathematics, cartography, astronomy and navigation.

Columbus believed that the route to Asia would be shorter by going directly east rather than south around the Cape of Good Hope. He presented his plan to many officials in Portugal and Spain and eventually received a contract from the Spanish Royal Court of Queen Isabella and King Ferdinand. He was to retain 10% of any riches he brought back and, as a devout Catholic, he was also to fulfil the obligation given him by the monarchs to spread Catholicism around the world. Columbus made a total of four voyages west, the other three voyages being in 1493, 1498 and 1502, but it was the first voyage that changed the world. He set sail on this voyage with three ships, *Nina*, *Pinta* and *Santa Maria*. He only made it as far as the Caribbean islands during this trip and even on his last trip he only made it as far as Panama.[74]

A few years after Columbus' famed voyage, another Italian Explorer and Merchant, Amerigo Vespucci undertook at least three voyages west. It is thought these were between 1487 and 1501 but there is no exact proof of the dates. However, what is certain is that it was these voyages that proved that these new lands were completely independent continents, the continents of North and South America, named after Amerigo.[75]

These new continents came to be known as the New World in subsequent times and marked the rapid expansion of European Western culture.

In 1497, inspired by Dias and Columbus, an Italian Explorer born Giovanni Caboto heard of opportunities in England and sailed there where he managed to receive a grant from King Henry VII. Now known as John Cabot, he set sail to the west also believing he would find a shorter route to Asia. He landed in what became Canada and claimed it for the English King.[76]

In 1498, Vasco da Gama, another Portuguese explorer, was the first European to reach India via the new route around the Cape of Good Hope. Departing Portugal in July 1497, da Gama reached Helena Bay in the Atlantic in November, Mossel Bay east of the Cape of Good Hope later in that month, Natal on Christmas day 1497, Mozambique and

Mombasa, Kenya in March and April 1498, before finally arriving in India in May 1498. [77]

Most of The Great Wall that we know today was constructed from 1474 after the Ming dynasty had established its new capital at Beijing.

The slave trade can trace its earliest origins back to the 1480s when Portuguese ships transported slaves from West Africa to their sugar plantations on the Atlantic islands of Madeira and Cape Verde.

Chapter 7. The Early Modern Era and The Renaissance

CE 1500–CE 1699

CE 1500-1599

Spanish settlements in South America and Florida, Aztecs, Maya, Inca, French in Canada, Buenos Aires and Santiago de Chile established, Portuguese Brazil, Michelangelo, Leonardo da Vinci, Copernicus, Machiavelli, the slave trade continues, the Golden Horde ends, Spanish Inquisition, Henry VIII, Goa, Macau, the Reformation, the Ottoman Empire, the Tyndale Bible, William Shakespeare, the Mughal Empire in India, Ming Dynasty, Nostradamus, Sir Francis Drake, the Gregorian Calendar, the Spanish Armada

In 1500 Pedro Alvares Cabral, aiming to follow Vasco da Gama's southern voyage around the Cape of Good Hope, sailed far too far west and reached Brazil, possibly being the first European to do so. The Portuguese claimed Brazil for themselves. It is thought the name Brazil comes from Brasa, the Portuguese name for a dark redwood tree found there. The first trading station was set up in Rio de Janeiro sometime after 1502. Between 1519 and 1522 Ferdinand Magellan became the first man to ever sail around the southern tip of South America as both the Spanish and the Portuguese were searching for new routes for lucrative trades from Asia. The first settlement of Brazil was in 1532 at Sao Vincente and in 1549 Brazil was declared an official colony and a governor was established.

During this 16th Century the Spanish conquistadors continued to explore and open up South America to European influence. This was the beginning of a new age of European nations colonising the so called 'New Worlds', with Spain, Portugal, England, France, Belgium and Holland all vying for control of land across the Americas, Africa, Asia and Oceania.

In 1500 Vincente Pinzon was the first European to sail up the Amazon River and in 1541 Francisco de Orellana sailed up the Amazon to its source, proving it to be a navigable river.

Spain settled in Florida in 1513, fighting with the French who also fought for control of the region until 1565 when a Spanish expedition defeated the French.

In 1519 and 1524, the Spanish conquistadors, Hernan Cortez and Pedro de Alvarado respectively, arrived in South America. Cortez defeated the Aztecs in Mexico, whilst Alvarado defeated the Maya in Guatemala.

Further south in 1532 Francisco Pizarro defeated the Inca in present day Peru. The civilisations of the Aztecs, Mayans and Incas were the ancient civilisations of South America. [78]

In the North, Jacques Cartier claimed Canada for France between 1534 and 1535.

Buenos Aires was first established in 1536. The Spanish explorer Juan Diaz de Solis had navigated his way up the Rio de la Plata in 1516, but it was Pedro de Mendoza who led a latter expedition and established the city. In the beginning it was primarily a trading city.

Pedro de Valdivia, founded the city of Santiago de Chile in 1541.

The Renaissance continued to flourish during the 16th century

After his big break completing *La Pieta*, Michelangelo returned to Florence from Rome and in 1501 he sculpted one of his most famous works, that of *David* from the Old Testament, commissioned to adorn Florence's Duomo

(Cathedral). Michelangelo's *David* can still be seen today and is considered by artistic scholars as "technically perfect". In 1505, he was again requested to return to Rome by the pope for further commissions including, in 1508, the painting of the ceiling of the Sistine Chapel. His painting differed from the original commission to paint the 12 Apostles and instead he painted various scenes from Genesis as well as male prophets and mythical female prophets. He continued to sculpt and paint in Florence and Rome until his death in 1564[79]

Between 1503 and 1505, Leonardo da Vinci painted *Mona Lisa*. It was originally a portrait called *La Gioconda*, thought to be a portrait of the wife of a Florentine merchant Francisco del Giocondo. Situated now at the Louvre in Paris, millions of visitors travel to view her each year. In approximately 1506 da Vinci returned to Milan where he spent seven years before returning to Rome again. Da Vinci was not just an artist, he also studied physics and mechanics and architecture and is also famed for early helicopter designs. He moved to France where he spent his final years, dying there in 1519.[80]

In 1508 Nicolaus Copernicus developed his theory of heliocentricity, in which the sun is at the centre of our galaxy, not the earth. This theory stated that we circle the sun, rather than the sun circling earth. He published his findings in 1514 but his book received little response. He conducted further research and in 1534 published a second book *The Revolutions of Heavenly Spheres* which was banned by the Roman Catholic church. Copernicus died a year later so never got to learn how his theories revolutionised astronomy.

Niccolo Machiavelli wrote his famed work *The Prince* in 1513 after being expelled from political life in Florence. *The Prince* outlined a theme that is known now as "the end always justifies the means", any means. This was not Machiavelli's personal way of living, but a view he expressed in the book as to how leaders could be effective, with the belief that it was such a leader that Florence required to return it to its former glory. *The Prince* was only published in 1532, five years after Machiavelli died.[81]

The slave trade also continued to grow during this century. In 1502 the Spanish conquistadors (conquerors), as well as the Portuguese who had started the trade, transported slaves from Africa through to the Caribbean, but it was the Portuguese who dominated the trade. The slaves at this stage were taken mainly from West Africa, from countries including Congo and Angola.

In 1502, after 250 years, the Golden Horde of Mongolia finally came to an end. (See CE1200–1300 for information on the beginning of the Golden Horde). They had ruled from Mongolia, across Russia and through to Bulgaria, but for the last century they had not been the power they once were. The Ottomans backed the Khanate from Crimea who took control of the Horde's capital of Sarai (on the Volga in modern-day Russia), and the Golden Horde were no longer.

Meanwhile, in Spain in 1507 Cardinal Francisco Jiminez de Cisneros took over as grand inquisitor from his predecessor Torquemada in the Spanish Inquisition. Whilst the Jews had been Torquemada's main target, Jiminez took aim at the Muslims and sought for their public conversion to Christianity.

In 1509 in England King Henry VIII took to the throne. He soon married his first wife Catherine of Aragon but by 1527 they had only one daughter (the future Queen Mary I), and no sons. Henry, believing the lack of a son, and Catherine's many stillbirths, proved his first marriage was against God's wishes, requested an annulment of the marriage from Pope Clement VII in Rome. This was refused by the pope but Henry then divorced Catherine anyway, and married his mistress, Anne Boleyn, in 1533. This led to Henry being excommunicated by the Roman Catholic Church and he became sole Head of the Church of England in 1534. Henry's schism with the Catholic Church and his ascension to the Head of the Church of England became known as the English Reformation.

Whilst Anne Boleyn gave Henry another daughter (Elizabeth I), he had his wife executed in 1536 for infidelity. Henry took his third wife, Jane Seymour, who finally provided him with a son, Edward VI. Jane Seymour died in childbirth. In a political move to bring England and Germany closer, Henry then married Anne of Cleves, but Henry did not like her and divorced her after only six months. Henry went on to marry twice more, Katherine Howard who was also executed for infidelity, and finally Katherine Parr who outlived the King. Henry VIII died at age 55 in 1547 and his son Edward VI took to the throne.

In 1510 Goa became the capital of Portugal's Asian Empire when Afonso de Albuquerque captured the city from the Muslim king Yusuf Adil Khan. Goa was previously an ancient Hindu city but it remained Portuguese through until 1961, when India invaded and it once again became Indian territory.[82] The first Portuguese ship to land in Macau did so in 1513 and, although the Chinese did not recognise it, by 1553 it became a Portuguese territory and their main Asian trading port.

In 1517, and before England's 1534 Reformation, THE Reformation swept through Europe. This occurred after Martin Luther, a German monk and teacher, published his 95 Theses, a series of ideas that he thought would make the (Catholic) Church better, but were seen as a revolt against some of the material elements of Catholicism, such as the ability to purchase forgiveness.

> Legend has it that Luther nailed his theses to the door of the castle church in Wittenberg, Germany. However, it is more likely that the door was used as a notice board for many notices and Luther's attaching his theses to the door was probably more of a means of publicising his thesis than a dramatic act of defiance (if in fact it was even put on the door in the first place).[83]

> The Reformation was the collective term given to the separation of many religious groups from the Catholic Church during the 16th Century. These various groups went on to become a new branch of Christianity called Protestantism, with each Protestant Church holding their own individual doctrines.

The Ottoman Empire had reached its peak between 1520 and 1566 under Suleiman the Magnificent (see CE 1200–1300 and CE 1400–1500 for more information on the Ottoman Empire). At its peak it controlled most of Turkey, Greece, Bulgaria, Hungary, Macedonia, Romania, Jordan, Palestine, Lebanon, Egypt and parts of Arabia and North Africa. During this period the Ottomans established the rule of law and expanded art and literature, with Istanbul considered an artistic hub with beautiful architecture and construction created during this time.

The Renaissance continued to thrive throughout the remainder of the century.

Between 1522 and 1536 Willian Tyndale was the first person to translate parts of the Hebrew Bible into English. He was refused permission to do so and when he did the translations were banned by Catholic officials and Tyndale was strangled to death and burnt at the stake in 1536.

Also in England, whilst the exact date of his birth is unknown, William Shakespeare was christened in Stratford-upon-Avon in 1564 and married Anne Hathaway in 1582.[84] It is believed he moved to London in the mid-1580s and the 1590s' records show he was the managing partner in a London acting company called the Lord Chamberlain's Men, later to be called the King's Men. By 1597 Shakespeare had published 15 of his 37 plays and by 1599 he and his partners had built their own theatre, The Globe, on the South Bank of the Thames. By 1613 Shakespeare had completed 37 plays across three categories. These were History, Tragedy and Comedy.

The 37 plays were:

Histories	Tragedies	Comedies
Henry IV part I	Romeo & Juliet	A Midsummer Night's Dream
Henry IV part II	Julius Caesar	The Comedy of Errors
Henry V	Hamlet	All's Well That Ends Well
Henry VI part I	King Lear	Much Ado About Nothing
Henry VI part II	Macbeth	As You Like It
Henry VI part III	Antony & Cleopatra	The Merchant of Venice

Henry VIII	Coriolanus	The Merry Wives of Windsor
Richard II	Cymbeline	Twelfth Night
Richard III	Othello	The Taming of The Shrew
King John	Timon of Athens	The Tempest
Pericles, Prince of Tyre	Titus Andronicus	The Two Gentlemen of Verona
Troilus and Cressida	The Winter's Tale	
Love's Labour's Lost		
Measure for Measure		

In India, in the 16th Century, the Mughal Empire took power. Throughout Medieval times much of India had been developed by Islamic kingdoms with a number of different kingdoms and dynasties ruling different areas at different times. But the Mughals, also Muslims, finally united India under one monarch. The first of the Mughal Kings was Babur who was succeeded by Humayun and then in 1556 by Akbar. Under these Mughal Kings, public administration was set up and infrastructure and the arts were developed.

During the 1550s in China, under the ruling Ming Dynasty, trade increased, especially the exports of silk and porcelain. European merchants entered China, and for the first time Chinese merchants emigrated to pursue trade.

In 1555 Nostradamus published *Les Propheties*, a collection of 942 prophetic stanzas. He was both a writer and an astronomer and in the centuries since *Les Propheties* many supporters claim his prophecies were accurate and have come true. However, other analysts claim his writings were far too vague to be accurately translated, and any similarities between real events and what he wrote were from misinterpretations, or incorrect translations.

After 200 years, England lost their last land on continental Europe, Calais. Since 1347 the port had been under English control and had been their main port for exporting goods, mainly English wool into Europe. In 1558, Mary Tudor, Queen of England was at war with France. Knowing that France was to invade Calais, England sent reinforcements but as they were in the midst of a flu pandemic, this was difficult to achieve. By the time the reinforcements had arrived the French had already taken control of the city, reclaiming it as their own. [85]

In 1580 Sir Francis Drake arrived back in England having become the first Englishman to circumnavigate the globe. He had left in 1577 with five ships but only one, *The Golden Hind*, remained by the end of the voyage. Drake had plundered Spanish ports in South America on his journey, and crossed the Pacific and Indian oceans, before he rounded the Cape of Good Hope and returned laden with spices and Spanish treasure.

In 1582, Pope Gregory VIII introduced the Gregorian calendar (replacing the Julian calendar), which was thought out by Luigi Lilio an Italian astronomer, who died six years prior to his calendar being introduced. [86]

The Gregorian calendar is more accurate in its judgement of how long a year is, as the timing of leap years is more accurate. In the Julian system, there is a leap year every four years without exception, whilst there are exceptions to this rule with the Gregorian calendar which states that century years (1900, 2000, 2100 etc,) can only be a leap year if they are also divisible by 400. The small inaccuracies provided by the Julian calendar meant that by the time the Gregorian calendar was introduced it was out of sync with annual equinoxes.

In 1588 the Spanish Armada, a fleet of 130 naval ships, left Spain planning to invade England following years of hostilities between the two countries. After Sir Francis Drake had plundered Spanish ports in South America, tensions were already stretched, but in 1585 the English signed a treaty of support for Dutch rebels in the Spanish controlled Netherlands (an area similar to modern-day Belgium). The incensed Spanish king decided to attack, wanting to dethrone the English queen, Elizabeth I, and restore England to a Roman Catholic, rather than a Protestant, state. Elizabeth, aware of the planned invasion, authorised Drake to launch a surprise attack with a small hidden fleet destroying part of the Armada and a large number of supplies, which delayed the Armada's planned invasion. When the Armada did eventually set sail, the Royal Navy, led by Drake and Lord Charles Howard, counterattacked armed with better long-range naval guns than the Spanish. The English enjoyed some initial success with these long-range guns but found it difficult to properly penetrate the Spanish half circle defensive formation. The English then set eight ships ablaze and sailed them directly to the Spanish, who panicked and broke formation allowing the English to gain the upper hand through repeated attacks of gunfire, in what was known of the Battle of Gravelines. Strong winds and poor weather then pushed the Armada north and with supplies running out, the Spanish Armada was forced to round Scotland and Ireland in order to return to Spain. Terrible weather then set in and by the time they returned to Spain the flotilla had lost almost 60 of its 130 ships, and 15,000 men.[87]

CE 1600-1699

Ottoman Empire loses its power, Russia's worst famine, Dutch East India Company is formed, Spanish Inquisition bans Islam, the last century of the Renaissance, Hans Lipperhey, Galileo Galilei, Johannes Kepler, Rene Descartes, John Milton, Isaac Newton, Europeans continue to colonise the Americas, Walter Raleigh, Pocahontas, New York, Salem Witch Hunt, the slave trade continues, the Qing Dynasty takes control from the Ming Dynasty, English Civil War, Oliver Cromwell, St Peter's Basilica is completed, Shah Jahan takes power in India and builds the Taj Mahal, Mount Vesuvius erupts again, Abel Tasman the first European in New Zealand, Peace of Westphalia signed, Tsar Peter the Great travels Europe, Jan van Riebeeck settles at Cape Town, the Anglo-Dutch Wars, William of Orange, Christian Huygens invents the Pendulum Clock, Treaty of Copenhagen, Robert Hooke discovers cells, Great Plague of London, Great Fire of London, Bank of England incorporated, Great Famine in France

In the 1600s the Ottoman Empire (formed in 1453, see 1400–1500) began to lose is power, both militarily and economically. It had previously controlled trade routes from the East, but with the Renaissance and Age of Discovery it now had to compete with trade from the Americas and India coming via sea routes, not the famed land-based spice route.

In 1653 the Ottomans lost the Battle of Vienna against the Holy Roman Empire, after they had besieged Vienna for two months. The battle included the largest cavalry charge in history with 18,000 horses used. This battle is thought to mark the decline in the strength of the Ottoman Empire from its peak in the 16th Century.

Between 1601 and 1603 approximately 2 million people, or 30% of Russia's population, perished in their worst ever famine. The famine resulted from a series of record winters, later linked to a volcanic eruption in Peru which created climate disruptions.

In 1602, the Dutch East India company (in Holland it was known as the Vereenigde Oostindische Compagnie, or VOC) was founded as a private merchant company and granted a 20-year monopoly by the Dutch government for trading spices from the Dutch East Indies (modern-day Indonesia). Over 1 million voyages were undertaken, many ships and men perished, and over 70,000 people were employed by the company. The VOC lasted until 1800 and held such power over the spice trade that it acted like a government. It was instrumental in the slave trade, and established colonies of Indonesian islands, and set up an outpost in the Cape of Good Hope called the Cape Colony, followed by outposts from Persia to Taiwan. It was also the first ever company to issue shares and at the height of the Tulip Bubble the company was thought to be worth USD$7.9 trillion in today's terms![88]

Tulips had arrived in Holland along with spices from the Far East and became a luxury object of desire. The tulip bulbs became highly traded and sort after with rarer different varieties trading at amounts far higher than an average person's annual salary at the time.[89] The world's first economic bubble was created, which burst in 1637.

The Dutch East India company eventually lost its command of the spice trade but over the previous two centuries it had been instrumental in expanding European expansion and increasing Europe's wealth, as well as taking European technologies and ideas to Asia.

The Spanish Inquisition continued throughout the 1600s, and in 1609 Islam was banned in Spain by Phillip III, and within five years 300,000 Spanish Muslims were thrown out of Spain with thousands more executed.

This 17th century was the last century of the Renaissance which then gave way to the Age of Enlightenment, or Age of Reason, in the following century.

In 1608 Hans Lipperhey from Holland patented the first telescope.

In 1609, Galileo Galilei, who had been Chair of Mathematics at the Universities of Pisa and then Padua, built his first telescope, improving on the Dutch telescope's design. It is said that Galileo was the first person to use a telescope to observe the stars and in doing so he discovered four new stars and made new observations of the moon's surface as well as numerous new stars within the Milky Way. He then successfully published *The Starry Messenger* in which his observations of these stars and their orbits contradicted the Catholic Church's stance that all stars, planets and the sun revolved around Earth, and instead supported Copernicus's previously published theory of heliocentricity. In 1633 Galileo was convicted of "suspicion of heresy" and forced to apologise. He died aged 70, but his laws of motion went on to pave the way for further scientific advances under Isaac Newton, and history judged him as the first person to correctly verify Copernicus's heliocentricity and establish this as the true law of our galaxy.[90]

In 1609, Galileo also perfected the first microscope, again with initial work done by the Dutchman Hans Lipperhey and fellow Dutchman Zacharias Janssen.

Johannes Kepler who had studied Copernicus, the Danish astronomer Tycho Brahe, and Galileo, published his laws of planetary motion and improved upon Galileo's telescope design. His theories of planetary motion were the first to describe how the planets move around the sun in ellipses, not circles.

In 1637 Rene Descartes, the French philosopher who went on to become considered as the father of modern philosophy, published *Discourse on the Method* in which he wrote his most famous quote, "I think, therefore I am". The premise for this was to start completely afresh in philosophical thinking and this quote was meant as a statement of the single first truth that "I exist" from which all other things can then be considered.[91] He went on to publish *Meditations on First Philosophy* and *Principles of Philosophy*.

In 1667 John Milton published England's most famous poem, *Paradise Lost*, cementing his place as one of England's finest writers. *Paradise Lost* is the story of Satan tempting Adam and Eve in the Garden of Eden.

In 1667 Isaac Newton was elected a fellow at Cambridge and became Lucasian Professor of Mathematics. In 1687 he published his *Principia Mathematica* in which he explained the three laws of motion, and the law of universal gravity. The three laws of motion are:

Whether at rest or in motion an object will remain like that unless acted upon by another, external, force

The force of an object equals its mass times by its acceleration

When one object meets another, for every action with one object, there is an equal and opposite reaction with the second object.

Newton became master of The Royal Mint in the late 1690s where he moved the English pound sterling from the Silver Standard to the Gold Standard, and became chair of The Royal Society in 1703. He was knighted in 1705 and died in 1727.

In 1752 William Stukeley published memoirs of *Sir Isaac Newton's Life* in which he relayed the story that Newton had told him, of when he had sat under the shade of an apple tree and when an apple fell to the ground it made Newton ponder as to why apples always fell "perpendicularly to the ground". It was this story that gave ground to the famous story that an apple had hit Newton on the head, and this gave him his Eureka moment of discovering gravity.[92]

During this 17th century the European nations continued to arrive and colonise the Americas.

Queen Elizabeth I tasked Sir Walter Raleigh with the job of sending expeditions to the Americas to settle there and send back goods to England. A short-lived English colony was established at Maine but failed to establish sufficient crops to outlast winter. The first permanent colony to settle in North America was at Jamestown in 1607 lead by Christopher Newport and Captain John Smith and funded by the Virginia Company of London, so called because Raleigh had named the area they had mapped out in North America "Virginia", after Elizabeth I, the Virgin Queen. John Rolfe, Sir Thomas Gates and Thomas West,

Lord de La Warr arrived the following years to help establish the colony.

Captain John Smith took over managing the organisational duties of the settlers but struggled to build relationships with the local Powhatan tribes. Myth has it that he had a romantic relationship with Pocahontas, a young Powhatan girl sent by her father to negotiate the release of some Powhatans captured by the settlers. The story goes that Pocahontas intervened to save Smith's life when he was in turn captured by the Powhatans, but newer scholars believe this is just a myth and that in reality Smith had undergone a ritual in which he would be ritually killed in spirit only, and reborn as a member of the Powhatans.

It was tobacco, introduced by John Rolfe, that first brought commercial success to Jamestown and Rolfe then married Pocahontas and took her to England where she became a celebrity.

During these initial years of settlement there were a series of wars between the settlers and the Powhatans between 1610 and 1646, the most famous of which was the Jamestown Massacre of 1622, also known as the Indian Massacre, in which over 300 settlers were killed. A truce was formed in 1626.

Separate to Sir Walter Raleigh's efforts to send out expeditions to settle in the Americas, a group of religious separatists called Puritans also sailed across the Atlantic. These Puritans did not want to reform the Catholic Church as the Protestants did in the Reformation, but wanted to be pure to their own faith, completely separate from the tainted Catholic Church. These Puritans had already left England and were living in Leiden in Holland before departing for America. They were transported there on the *Mayflower* which arrived in November 1620 as winter set in, landing at Plymouth Rock (named so by John Smith, after Plymouth in England).

> These Puritans came to be known as Pilgrims, and their settlement known as the Plymouth Colony. Under John Carver, Edward Winslow and William Bradford these Pilgrims signed a pact that bound them all to follow the rules of their group for the good of the group. The Pilgrims would not have survived the first winter were it not for the help of the Native American Patuxet and Abenaki people, and a year after their arrival they held a feast to give thanks for their survival.

> This feast is now the annual Thanksgiving feast held in November every year celebrated throughout the USA.

The first explorer to reach present day New York was an Italian explorer Giovanni da Verrazzano who was commissioned to explore on behalf of the French crown. However, it was the second explorer, Henry Hudson, an English explorer who was commissioned by the Dutch East India company, who really explored the area and sailed up the Hudson River, later named after him. This exploration by Hudson laid the framework for European settlement of the area and in 1626 Peter Minuit the Governor of the Dutch West India company (a separate Dutch company) bought the island of Manhattan from the native Americans in the area for $24. A Dutch colony then settled there naming the area New Amsterdam with Peter Stuyvesant installed as governor.[93]

Back in Europe, the English, French and Dutch were warring with each other and in 1674 the English and Dutch signed the Treaty of Westminster, in which part of the agreement passed ownership of New Amsterdam to the English. At the same time, a Colonel Nicolls who was in the service of James, Duke of York during the English Civil Wars, set sail for New Amsterdam as the new King of England, Charles II, had decided he wished to take ownership of the Dutch colony. Nicolls blockaded New Amsterdam and Peter Stuyvesant surrendered the city. Nicolls became the new governor, renaming it New York after the Duke of York.[94]

In 1692, in Salem Massachusetts, a great witch hunt took place and 20 people were convicted and hanged for witchcraft.

During this 17th century the slave trade continued to grow, with the cooperation of African kings and merchants. The reason for the slave trade was financial, with the Triangular Trade being composed of slaves from Africa being shipped to the Americas where they were forced to work on plantations. The second leg of the Triangular Trade was the produce of these plantations including sugar, tobacco, cotton and rum being sold back to Europe. The final piece of the triangle was then manufactured goods from Europe such as cloth and guns being used to acquire more slaves from Africa.

Brazil was the largest importer of slaves during this century as Brazilian sugar production was at its peak, and it is estimated that up to one third of all slaves traded during the whole transatlantic slave trade were done so by the Portuguese, either for Brazil or for onward sale to other colonies.

In China, between 1618 and 1683, a major transition occurred between two dynasties as the Qing Dynasty took over from the Ming Dynasty. The Qing were established in northern China by the Manchu clan at a time when the Ming, who were mainly Han Chinese (the dominant people of China), were fighting peasant revolts during a time of drought and famine as well as deteriorating relations between the ruling royalty and their military leaders. The last Ming emperor hanged himself from a tree near the Forbidden Palace.

Once in power the Qing introduced elements of Manchu culture into Chinese society including the Manchu queue hairstyle which included a high shaven forehead and pony-tail among males which was seen as an act of obedience towards the new Qing, and to not have one was seen as rebellion. The queue remained a sign of Qing oppression until the 1911 rebellion.[95]

In 1624 and 1626 the Dutch and the Spanish arrived in Taiwan, which had for centuries been home to nine tribes. It was sulphur and gold which lead to the Dutch and Spanish in Taiwan. The Dutch fought off the Spanish over gold and then in 1662, the Ming, retreating from the Qing in mainland China, threw out the Dutch. The Qing then brought Taiwan under their control in 1683.[96]

In England in 1625, Charles I took the throne. His view, that royalty had a divine right to rule, soon clashed with parliament. Charles started bypassing parliament to get funding, imposing outdated taxes and angering the population, resulting in battles between Charles and the Scots and between Charles and parliament. During 1642 society began to align with either Charles (the Royalists or Cavaliers) or with parliament (the Parliamentarians, or the Roundheads after their round-headed haircuts), and in October 1642 the Battle of Edgehill occurred. This was the first Battle in the English Civil Wars. This battle was indecisive.

Parliament and Scotland then created an alliance, and their forces won a victory at the Battle of Marston Moor at which Oliver Cromwell emerged as a key figure for the Parliamentarians. Following this victory, parliament went on to form the New Model Army lead by Thomas Fairfax and Oliver Cromwell. Further defeats occurred for Charles who eventually fled north and was captured by the Scots who turned him over to parliament. This was the end of the first English Civil War.

During ongoing negotiations between parliament and the Scots, Charles signed an agreement with the Scots that if they supported him and invaded England, he would allow Presbyterianism in Scotland. So started the Second English Civil War. However, in the ensuing invasion, Cromwell, with the support of John Lambert, defeated the Scots, and Fairfax put down further rebellions. Parliament was cleared of all those who still supported Charles and the remaining parliament, called a Rump Parliament (Rump in this case meaning remnants) pushed for Charles to be tried for treason. He was beheaded in 1649.

In the Third Civil War, further rebellions occurred in Ireland and Scotland, with those in Scotland headed by Charles I's son, Charles II. Cromwell put down these rebellions and defeated Charles II at Worcester, forcing Charles II to flee for France, where he went into exile.

In 1653 Cromwell was appointed Lord Protector, ruling until his death in 1658. A Rump Parliament again took control of Parliament and negotiations with Charles II saw Charles return to England where he was crowned in 1661. This event was known as the Restoration as it restored a monarchy to England, Scotland and Ireland, but the main outcome of these wars was that the monarchy could now only govern with the consent of parliament.[97]

In 1626, 120 years after it was started, St Peter's Basilica in the Vatican City, Rome was completed. Not only is it one of the holiest Christian buildings in the world but it is also one of the largest buildings in the world. A number of architects were involved in its design including Michelangelo, Donato Bramante and Carlo Maderno.

In India during this century Shah Jahan took over from his father Jahangir as Mughal Emperor and ruled from 1628 through until 1658. During this period Shah Jahan transferred his capital from Agra to Delhi in 1648.

Jahan was passionate about building, and besides two great mosques in Agra he also built the Taj Mahal in memory of his wife Mumtaz Mahal. During this period there was also great expansion of art and literature specifically painting and calligraphy.

In 1657 Jahan fell ill and after a war between his three sons, Aurangzeb took over, who reigned from 1658 through until 1707.

During this time, in the west of India however, the Maratha Empire was founded by Chhatrapati Shivaji Maharaj a renowned warrior, who wrestled this part of India away from the Mughal Empire.[98]

In 1631 Mount Vesuvius erupted again killing an estimated 3000 to 6000 people from the surrounding towns and villages. Vesuvius had erupted since the famous CE 79 eruption that covered Pompeii (see the Chapter covering CE 80–99) but this was the most devastating.

In 1642 the first European, a Dutchman named Abel Tasman, arrived in New Zealand, which had been settled by Polynesians since between CE 1200 and 1300. Tasman was employed by the Dutch East India company and his expedition was to discover a mythical landmass which was purported to have plenty of gold. He landed at Mauritius and Tasmania before becoming the first European to arrive in New Zealand. Lacking the hoped-for gold, the voyage was considered a disappointment and it was over a century before Europeans revisited the islands.

In 1648 the Peace of Westphalia was signed, which ended the Thirty Years War between the Catholics and Protestants in Germany which had spread into Austria, France, Spain, Sweden and other European nations. The Holy Roman Emperor, and representatives of France and Sweden were also party to the negotiations. This document is now credited as being the first recognition of the sovereignty and foundation of the modern state with the states present being allocated ownership of various lands and seas that make up their modern-day territories. Alongside these territorial agreements the Peace of Westphalia also recognized the different state's rights to religious beliefs by agreeing to religious tolerance.

In Russia in 1649 slavery was replaced with serfdom, a system in which while people themselves could not be owned, they were tied to the land and were not allowed to leave the lands on which they worked, thus in any case severely restricting their human rights.

Peter the Great, from the House of Romanov, ruled the Russian Empire as tsar from 1682. Peter's reign was marked by his sweeping reforms of Russia. These were based on his seeking European allies against the Ottoman Empire. Peter travelled incognito as part of a Russian diplomatic mission called the Grand Embassy. As far as gaining allies went, the mission failed but Peter learned much about Europe and decided to modernise Russia, including reorganising the army, ending arranged marriages in Russia and changing the date of the New Year from September 01 to January 01. His modernisation also led to the establishment of St Petersburg (see 1703).

In 1652, Jan van Riebeeck, on behalf of the Dutch East India company, set up a supply settlement at the site of modern-day Cape Town's Table Bay. Bartolomeu Dias had rounded the Cape of Good Hope in 1488 (see Chapter on 1400) and since that time a number of minor settlements were set up by Portuguese fishermen over the next two centuries, but none were permanent, until van Riebeck's.

After van Riebeeck set up the permanent base, over the next 200 years the settlement belonged to the Dutch who occasionally battled with the local Xhosa people as more and more Dutch arrived to farm.

During this century, three Anglo-Dutch wars occurred. The first from 1652 to 1654, the second from 1665 to 1667, and the third in 1672. The wars were naval wars fought over trading rights and territories. The Dutch were the major power in the East and the English were closely guarding their American interests.

In Holland, in 1672, William (later William of Orange) came to power. He was nephew to England's Charles II. In 1674 he made peace with the English and was then persuaded by a group of English, who were against Catholic rule in England, to overthrow the English king, James II & VII (James was James II in England but James VII in Scotland so is known as James II & VII). William did so, becoming king of England in 1689, jointly sharing the monarchy with his English wife Mary, James II's niece. The Anglo-Dutch Wars were resolved, and the English and Dutch became allies.

James tried unsuccessfully to regain the monarchy with his supporters the Jacobites (Jacob is Latin for James), with the decisive battle being the Battle of the Boyne, which William won. It is seen as a key moment in British history in that it marks the crucial moment in the struggle England fought to become a Protestant nation, rather than a Catholic one. William's conquest of England, and the Catholic movement, was known as the Glorious Revolution and during his negotiations with parliament to allow him to share the monarchy with Mary, William had to cede a number of powers to parliament.

The new joint king and queen both had to sign a Declaration of Rights, which became known as the Bill of Rights, and this agreement fundamentally shifted power away from the monarchy and changed the way Britain was governed and is seen as the first step towards a constitutional monarchy, whereby the monarchy has to make decisions based on the constitution.

In 1656 Christian Huygens, from Holland, invented the first pendulum clock. Until this point there had been a step by step development of various timekeeping pieces after the first one had been invented in 1504 by a German, Peter Henlein, but these were not very accurate. Huygens' pendulum clock brought a far higher degree of accuracy to timekeeping from then on.

In 1658 the Treaty of Roskilde, and later the Treaty of Copenhagen, were signed between Sweden and Denmark-Norway (at that time a union between the 2 kingdoms of Denmark and Norway), ending a generation of warfare between the countries, and setting the boundaries between the three countries.

In 1665 Robert Hooke, an English scientist, published *Micrographia* in which he detailed the idea of cells, the smallest complete part of any organism. He was only able to do this after observing the cells of a cork under the newly invented microscope (see 1609). Until that time, it was thought that life was created spontaneously, but Hooke's discoveries of cells helped establish that cells were created from pre-existing cells. Hooke gave cells their name as under the microscope he thought they looked like the small cell-like rooms found in monasteries.[99]

Although there had been other outbreaks of plague since the Black Death/Bubonic Plague of 1346–1353, the largest outbreak since then occurred from 1665 to 1666 and became known as the Great Plague of London. Of an estimated population of 400,000, as many as 100,000 Londoners died. It was the last great outbreak of the Plague and, as with other plagues, was caused by a bacterium carried by rats called Yersinia pestis.

Just as Londoners were getting through the final stages of the Great Plague, the Great Fire of London broke out. Started at a bakery in Pudding Lane on Sunday, 02 September 1666, it lasted until Thursday, 06 September, sweeping through the medieval city inside the Roman Wall destroying almost the whole city including St Paul's Cathedral. Although there was substantial damage and destruction to homes and buildings, resulting in large losses of homes, the actual deaths from the fire were relatively few, with six deaths given as the estimated figure.

In 1694 the Bank of England was incorporated specifically to try and raise capital to fund war against the French.

In France, approximately 1.3 million people died during the Grand Famine of 1693–1694, caused by a terrible winter in 1692 and the subsequent poor harvest.

Chapter 8.   The Modern Era

CE 1700–1899

CE 1700-1799

Invention of the piano, Vivaldi, Handel, Mozart, Beethoven, the Great Northern War, War of Spanish Succession, the slave trade continues, the Camisard Rebellion, Seven Years War, American Revolution/War of Independence, New Orleans and Los Angeles founded, Peter the Great established St. Petersburg, Catherine the Great ruled Russia, Mughals expanded their Empire in India, Britain – via the British East India Company – established a power base in India, steam engine invented, rubber discovered, Fahrenheit and Celsius, the Freemasons, Drapier's Letters, the First Saudi state, Age of Enlightenment or Reason, the Longitude Act and John Harrison's watch, photosynthesis, Industrial Revolution, Luddites, the Great Lisbon Earthquake, Captain James Cook and New Zealand and Australia settled, China flourishes under Qing Dynasty, the Illuminati are formed, Tay Son Dynasty takes control in Vietnam, French Revolution, Robespierre, Napoleon, the Rosetta Stone, the British take control of the Cape of Good Hope, Wall Street and the New York Stock Exchange formed, First vaccine developed, the Irish Rebellion

In 1700 Bartolomeo Cristofori, an Italian who was unhappy with the harpsichord's volume, changed the internal mechanism from one of plucking to that of a hammer, resulting in the invention of the piano, known initially as the "clavicembalo col piano e forte".[100]

This led to an incredible age for music composition:

Antonio Vivaldi composed the *Four Seasons* between 1718 and 1720.

George Frideric Handel, born in Germany but naturalised as British composed *Zadok the Priest* in 1727 (which has been played at every British Coronation since then) and *Messiah* in 1742.

Wolfgang Amadeus Mozart, from Salzburg, Austria, only lived from 1756 to 1791, but composed over 800 works. His death remains a mystery, probably an illness, but rumours remain to this day that he was poisoned over time by his arch-rival Antonio Salieri, a rumour that first arose six years after his death in a play by the Russian writer Pushkin. Mozart's most famous works include:

Serenade No. 13 *'Eine kleine Nachtmusic'.*

The Operas, *The Magic Flute*, *Don Giovanni* and *The Marriage Figaro*.

Requiem.

Ludwig van Beethoven was born in 1770 and over the next 57 years until his death composed some of the most iconic works of all time including:

Symphony No 9, also known as the *Choral Symphony.*

Fidelio.

Bagatelle No. 25 commonly known as *Fur Elise.*

Between 1700 and 1721 the Great Northern War occurred as Russia and her allies rejected Swedish supremacy in the region. Throughout the two previous centuries, Sweden had established herself as the major force in the region and antagonised Russia who were blocked access to the Baltic Sea. Separately

Denmark and Norway were also unhappy with Sweden's dominance as both had lost territories to Sweden and in the south both Poland and parts of Germany (Saxony) had disputes with Sweden over land and power. In 1700 war began as Sweden was attacked from the south by the Poles, the Danish and Norwegians, and from the east by the Russians. In 1718, Charles, King of Sweden, was killed in fighting and with no heir to his throne, peace was negotiated and in the Treaties of Stockholm and Nystad, the land disputes were agreed, and Russia emerged as a stronger force in the region.

Also in 1700, the War of Spanish Succession broke out as the childless Spanish King, Charles II, died leaving his throne to Philip, the grandson of Louis XIV of France. A union was formed between Spain and France which ignited tensions with England, Holland, Prussia and Austria, who were unhappy with the new balance of power. This opposing contingent, which was called the Grand Alliance, defeated the French and Spanish in four major battles. However, these battles were costly and put England under pressure to negotiate for peace. Simultaneously, the Austrian archduke, Charles, who was the Grand Alliance's favourite to take over the Spanish throne if they won the war, succeeded Joseph I of Austria. This resulted in the Grand Alliance deciding they no longer favoured him as leader of both Spain and Austria, and Philip was allowed to remain on the throne in Spain so long as Spain and France agreed to never unite. In the resulting Treaty of Utrecht (1713) and Peace of Rastatt (1714) Britain received the territories of Gibraltar, Nova Scotia, Newfoundland and other territories and garnered a monopoly on the ongoing slave trade.[101]

It was thus this agreement signed between Spain and England in 1713 that granted the British the right to supply almost

150,000 slaves to the Spanish colonies over 30 years. The French and English therefore controlled about half of the transatlantic slave trade, surpassing the Portuguese (early 1600s) and Dutch (later 1600s).

It was during this 18th century that the most slaves were traded, with nearly 60% of all slaves transported during this time.

In 1787 however, a meeting took place in London for the abolishment of the slave trade and high-profile figures such as William Wilberforce (MP) advocated for its abolishment. However, it took a further 20 years for this to occur (see 1800–1900).

In 1702 Protestant rebels in France known as Camisards rose up against Louis XIV's persecution of Protestantism. In 1675, at the Edict of Nantes, Louis ended religious tolerance and tried to force Catholicism on the French. A terrorist war broke out, with the Camisards using ambush tactics. The war continued for some years but ran out of steam by 1710.

In this century the Spanish continued to dominate the colonial landscape across the Americas. With the exception of Portuguese Brazil, they controlled all of South America, Central America and Florida, New Mexico and California, with the French controlling Nova Scotia and Quebec, and the English in Jamestown, Bermuda and modern-day Virginia and Massachusetts.

In 1722 a young Benjamin Franklin wrote a series of essays on morals called the Dogood Papers for a Boston journal, before going on to write and publish the Pennsylvania

Gazette and set up the Library Company of Philadelphia. Franklin also developed an interest in electricity and spent ten years conducting various experiments, the most famous being in 1753 when he flew a kite with a wire attached into a thunderstorm to demonstrate the fact that lightning contained electricity. The kite collected ambient electricity from the storm around it and the electrical charge travelled down the wire through a wet hemp string (Franklin saw the wet hemp hairs stand up so he knew then the electricity was travelling through the string) and into a Leyden jar that Franklin had attached to the hemp string. A Leydan jar is a device used to store electricity. Franklin's electrical experiments also involved him originating the words battery, electrician and conductor. [102]

In 1752 and around Ohio, France and England engaged in a series of battles for control of land, where George Washington, a young Virginia farmer, and a trained surveyor, was sent by the Governor of Virginia to encourage the French to withdraw. A battle ensued and ten Frenchmen were killed, and Washington was later captured by the French. This was the start of what came to be called the French–Indian War where the French and their Native American allies fought against Britain and the Anglo-American colonists.

The French–Indian War was actually part of a larger international conflict, the Seven Years War, from 1756–1763. This war pitted Britain, Prussia (a kingdom which is now part of modern-day Poland and Germany) and Hanover (part of modern-day Germany), against France, Austria, Saxony (also part of modern-day Germany), Sweden, and Russia, but in essence it was a power and land struggle between Britain and France and their respective allies.[103] The war was ended with the signing of two treaties. The Treaty of Hubertusburg granted Silesia (part of modern-day Poland) to Prussia, and the Treaty of Paris laid out colonial boundaries in Britain's favour, with them gaining Canada, Louisiana (from France) and Florida (from the Spanish). With the war out of the way Britain could proceed with expanding North America westwards. Although Britain gained enormous territories, the expenses for this war, and the subsequent taxes, created disquiet amongst the colonialists which eventually lead to the American Revolution (War of Independence).

In 1764 and 1765 Britain passed the Sugar Act and then the Stamp Act, taxing sugar, wine and textiles imported into America, and legal taxes in these American colonies. Various protests occurred including one in Boston in which the British fired into a crowd and five people were killed. Britain then removed taxes on all commodities except tea.

In 1773, 50 colonialists dressed as native Indians, tipped a cargo of tea into Boston Harbour as a protest against this remaining British tax. Whilst it was an extremely expensive cargo of tea, the message was of greater importance. The message was clear that there was disquiet amongst the people tired of Britain's dictatorial attitude. This event came to be known as the Boston Tea Party.

As the disquiet grew, colonialists in Concord started to amass weapons, and the British sent troops to try to seize these weapons. Paul Revere, a US rider tried to ride through to Concord to provide a warning but was captured en-route. In 1775, in Lexington, on the road to Concord, colonial militia encountered the British Red Coats and the first shots of what were to be the American Revolution, also known as the American War of Independence, were fired. (In 1837

Ralph Waldo Emerson described in a poem the first shot fired as, "the shot that was heard round the world"). [104]

The rebels elected George Washington as their commander in chief and by 1776 rebels across all 13 British colonial states were at full scale war against the British. "Yankee Doodle" became the popular revolutionary song among the rebel army and George Washington raised a new American flag on Prospect Hill, one with 13 stars on it, one for each state.

At the rebel leaders Congress in 1775 George Washington, Benjamin Franklin and other delegates from the 13 states met. Included at this congress was Thomas Jefferson, a Virginia lawyer, who was a talented writer as well. By 1776 Jefferson had written the text for the Declaration of Independence which was accepted by Congress on the 4th of July 1776, with John Hancock the first to sign it. This was the first time a nation under British control made a unilateral decision to become independent and choose their own government. (The only time in history this occurred again was Rhodesia in 1965.) In 1777 Congress adopted a revised independent flag, the Stars and the Stripes.

In 1778 after persuasion from Benjamin Franklin, France entered the war on the side of the rebels and by 1781 Maryland ratified the Articles of the Confederation, becoming the final state to do so. At fighting in Yorktown, the British general, Charles Cornwallis, found himself isolated and was forced to surrender. The British had effectively lost the war and by 1783 they, the British, recognised US Independence at The Treaty of Paris.

In 1789 George Washington was elected the first president of the United States of America and in 1790 a new site for a capital was agreed on the banks of the Potomac River. This new city was named after Washington himself. Washington's second term as President ended in 1796, and John Adams became the second US president, and in 1800 he moved into a new house for the president, the White House.

Also in America, New Orleans, was founded in 1718 on the banks of the Mississippi and in 1723 became the capital of French Louisiana, which became Spanish shortly thereafter as a result of the French Indian war, and was then passed back to France in 1800, only for Napoleon to sell it to the United States in 1803.

Further north, in 1781, the Town of the Queen of the Angels, El Pueblo de la Reina de Los Angeles, now known simply as Los Angeles, was founded. It was settled as part of the continued colonisation of California by Spain,

In 1703, Tsar Peter the Great established a fortress on the banks of the Neva River. This was the beginning of the new capital of Russia that Peter envisioned, St Petersburg. In 1712 the capital was moved from Moscow. A number of European architects were involved in its construction and in 1724 Peter established a university, Academy of Sciences and Academic Gymnasium there. It is still today Russia's most European city, but it lost its status as capital, which returned to Moscow in 1918 on the orders of Lenin.

Also in Russia, in 1762 Catherine the Great, a German born Empress, took the reins in Russia, having forced her weak husband Peter III to abdicate. She ruled for 34 years until 1796, supported by her lover Grigory Potemkin, Count Orlov, during which she led Russia into far greater participation in Europe, both culturally and politically. She also increased Russian territory through the 1768–1774 Russo–Turkish War where Russia took Crimea as its own. Up until this point Crimea had been a part of Ottoman Turkey since 1475 (having previously changed hands from Kievan Rus' (see 800–900 and 1100–1200) to the Venetians, to the Mongols. After the Russian Turkish war Crimea was briefly declared independent of Turkey but was then annexed by Russia in 1783 which built Sevastopol and Simferopol in 1784. A second Russo–Turkish War occurred from 1787–1791, which resulted in Turkey officially recognising Crimea as Russian.

In India during this 18th century Aurangzeb expanded the Indian Empire under the Mughals to its greatest size, but his dictatorial tendencies also enabled its decline. Hindis were omitted from public office and he destroyed their schools and temples, and Sikhs were persecuted.

By the time of his death in 1707 rebellions were brewing with many groups questioning his authority. These rebellions continued under the new Emperor Bahadur Shah I who ruled until 1712, and Farrukhsiyar who ruled until 1719. The Mughal Empire then began to break up during the reign of Muhammad Shah who ruled from 1719 to 1748. After that the Mughals were confined to an area around Delhi as the Marathas overran most of the remainder of India.

It was also about this time that the British, looking for fortification and replenishment posts for their trading vessels entrusted this to the British East India Company in India.

This company soon started flexing its muscles and overthrew the Mughal Nawab (leader) of Bengal and installed its own leader. British Parliament then started regulating the British East India Company meaning that effectively The British Government took charge of Bengal.

During the remainder of this century the British Government, via The British East India Company, took over control of more and more of India.

In 1706 and 1707 England and Scotland respectively passed the Union with Scotland Act and the Union with England Act which effectively ended their existence as separate states (under one monarch) and created a single state, the Kingdom of Great Britain.

In 1712 Englishman Thomas Newcomen from Dartmouth in Devon invented the steam train. This was not used for transport, but rather as a means to pump water out of tin and coal mines that often flooded. An earlier invention by another Englishman from Devon, Thomas Savery, had used steam condensed in an empty chamber to create a vacuum that sucked water up. Newcomen revised this invention to use the vacuum created to rather power a piston that in turn moved a central beam on a fulcrum, that in turn powered a pump. Newcomen's engine remained relatively unchanged for 75 years until James Watt improved it greatly.

Between 1714 and 1742 our two modern-day methods for measuring temperature were invented. In 1714 the Polish born Dutchman Daniel Fahrenheit invented the glass thermometer containing mercury, which was the first practical accurate thermometer, and the Fahrenheit scale as a means for measuring temperature which showed water froze at 32 degrees

Fahrenheit. Then in 1742 Swede Anders Celsius invented the Centigrade scale. The name Centigrade originated from the Latin Centum (100) and Grade (Steps) and the scale divided the two points of when water becomes ice (zero degrees) and when it boils and becomes steam (100 degrees), into 100 different grades or degrees. In 1948 the Centigrade scale was renamed Celsius in the inventor's honour.

In 1717 the first Grand Lodge of England was formed. The Freemasons had been in existence since the 13th century and had formed a regulatory body for stonemasons and other craftsmen. Over the centuries various Lodges (placed where local groups of Freemasons met) were established, and members had to be "of good repute", and "believe in a supreme being", and in each lodge a Bible had to be present, women were not allowed, and no religious or political discussions were allowed.

In Ireland, between 1724 and 1725, the Dean of St Patrick's Church in Dublin, Jonathan Swift, published a series of pamphlets against what he saw as the corrupt introduction of new coins by William Wood, who had been given the right to do so by the Irish government, who were supported by the British. As it was politically unsafe to openly write against the government Swift wrote under the name Drapier. These letters became known as *Drapier's Letters*, and were well received by the public and the government was forced to backtrack on the coins. More than this however, the *Letters* were seen as the first open defiance of Britain and argument for independence from Britain. Swift was also the author of *Gulliver's Travels*, which has become a classic of English Literature.

In 1730 the Bank of England moved to its present-day position on Threadneedle Street. It was by now the largest financial institution in England and became the banker to other banks. It remained a private bank until 1946 when it was nationalised.

In 1736 Charles Marie de la Condamine, a French explorer, was the first European to discover and document rubber, which he encountered whilst exploring Ecuador. He sent samples back to the Academie Royale des Sciences in France, and published the first scientific paper on rubber in 1755.

In approximately 1744 or 1745 a reformist Muslim scholar Shaikh Muhammad bin Abdul Wahhab and Muhammad bin Saud, who ruled a town called Diriyah, formed an alliance to teach Islam to the Muslim communities, and in doing so formed the first Saudi state which expanded rapidly until besieged in 1818 (see 1818).

The period from the mid-17th century through to the mid-19th century came to be known as the Age of Enlightenment or Age of Reason as thinkers throughout Britain and France came to question traditional authority. It was a natural progression from the Renaissance.

In 1765, the Board of Commissioners of the Longitude Act finally agreed that a new watch by English carpenter and self-taught watchmaker, John Harrison, had solved the longitude problem. The longitude problem had been formally recognised in 1714 when the Longitude Act was passed which offered a financial reward to anyone who could accurately measure a ship's longitude at sea. Without this accurate measurement ships continually missed their bearings, often resulting in tragic sinkings. Because latitude was a north–south measurement it related to the physical equator and it could therefore be accurately measured by the position of the sun, longitude (which was an east–west measurement), was more difficult. To measure longitude, one needed to know exactly what time it was at one's departure point, and what time it was at one's present location, then one could determine how many degrees east or west one had travelled. The problem was that until John Harrison's timepiece was invented, time was not measured accurately enough, so ships could not accurately measure how far east or west of their departure point they were.[105]

In Yorkshire, England, Dutch born British biologist Jan Ingenhousz discovered photosynthesis in plants. He had previously met English scientist Joseph Priestley who had already discovered that plants produce and absorb gases. In 1779 Ingenhousz discovered that plants give off oxygen from their green sections and this gaseous production slows or stops in the shade, whilst at night the plants give off carbon dioxide.

This century was also the century of the Industrial Revolution which began in the 1760s and lasted through to the 1830s as Britain's economy transitioned from one largely dependent on agriculture and home crafts, to one more focussed on mechanisation and manufacturing.

As already highlighted, in 1712 Thomas Newcomen invented the steam engine which was refined and improved in the 1760s by Scotsman James Watt. Then in 1733 John Kay invented the Flying Shuttle which sped up the weaving of cloth, and in 1770 James Hargreaves patented the Spinning Jenny for spinning wool and cotton. This industrialisation also resulted in the industry's labour forces being organised into working within factories which improved and increased both the speed and quantity of production of goods.[106] Later, in the following century, advances in electricity and the internal combustion engine fuelled further growth with new power sources for production.

Not everyone was happy with progress however and in 1779 a young apprentice Ned Ludd destroyed a textile machine. The term Luddites was born to identify those opposed to technological advances, (and the term is still in use today). These people were mainly trained artisans who were concerned with the way machinery was taking away or changing their livelihoods.

In 1755 the Great Lisbon Earthquake occurred, estimated at 7.7 on the Richter Scale, and which almost completely destroyed Lisbon. Whilst it curtailed Portugal's colonial ambitions, it also led to the serious scientific study of earthquakes, eventually leading to the study of seismology.

After Abel Tasman was the first European to set foot in New Zealand in 1642 it wasn't until 1769 that it was revisited, this time by Englishman Captain James Cook, which then lead to more regular visits from whalers, sealers and traders.

In 1770 Cook spent four months exploring a new territory, the East Coast of Australia. Previous Dutch explorers had visited but hadn't found anything worth trading. Cook however decided it was fertile land and in 1779 Joseph Banks from the Royal Society, who accompanied Cook on the voyage, recommended Botany Bay, named after the prolific number of new plants found there, a suitable site for a penal colony. The British were looking at the time for a new site to transport convicts to, after losing their states in America after that War of Independence. In 1786 the British government adopted Banks' recommendation and the first convicts arrived in January 1788. On 26 January 1788 Captain Arthur Phillip of the Royal Navy raised the British Flag at Sydney Cove. January 26 is celebrated each year as Australia Day.

During the 1700s the Qing were firmly in control in China, with political stability and strong agricultural production. International trade flourished and the people flourished and there were social and economic reforms. Rice production was improved, and corn began to be imported, whilst there were also advances in arts and culture.

By 1773 the British had started the opium trade to China. Up until this point the drug, indigenous to Turkey, had mainly been used for medicinal purposes in China. As tobacco smoking became more popular, so did opium usage, and addiction increased. The British East India company imported it from Bengal, India (where they cultivated it) at considerable profit, even though the Chinese Emperor had banned its importation. This trade allowed The British to finance their purchases of tea, silk and porcelain.[107] This trade flourished well into the following century (see 1838).

In 1776 a German Professor of Law and a Philosopher, Adam Weishaupt, founded the Illuminati in Bavaria. It was supposed to be for enlightened individuals to meet but over the years since has been controversial with some believing the groups aims are to promote freedom and equality, whilst others state its goal is to combat religion and replace religious views with rational ones.

In 1776 Adam Smith published *An Inquiry into the Nature and Causes of the Wealth of Nations* which has come to be known as *The Wealth of Nations*. The publication has led Smith to become known as the Father of Economics and his theory of the Invisible Hand describes how free market economies fare better in providing for the needs of their people than a controlled state does. He believed that governments should only conduct three activities, namely: protect their borders, maintain civil law and conduct public works including education.

In Vietnam, after 200 years of conflict, the three Tay Son brothers unified the country and created the Tay Son Dynasty leading to a period of relative peace and prosperity.

France, in the 1770s, was undergoing a financial crisis. The economy was spiralling downwards and the tax system was badly in need of an overhaul. The King, Louis XVI, had brought in a number of advisors who had all given the same opinions, that the tax system needed change, and so, in 1783 Louis appointed Charles de Calonne as his new head of finance. Calonne's suggestions included one that would mean the nobility would, for the first time, be taxed too. With the nobility refusing to accept this, in 1779 Louis convened an old assembly of Three Estates – called the Estates General – the clergy, the nobility and the general public, to try and reach an agreement. With the clergy and the nobility both being tax exempt, this set these two arms of the Estates General off against the general public.[108]

> At this point the general public broke away to unilaterally form a National Assembly and swore the Tennis Court Oath (sworn at a meeting held on a tennis court in Versailles as they had been locked out of their meeting room) that they would not rest until they formed a new constitution. The Public rallied behind them and in Paris the public stormed the Bastille, Paris' main prison, to take up arms.

The year was 1779 and marked the start of the French Revolution. In the country the peasants attacked the manors and estates of their landlords creating an environment known as the Great Fear. The peasants were freed of their harsh work contracts in the August Decrees and soon after that, the National Assembly produced the Declaration of the Rights of Man and of the Citizen, which provided legal rights and autonomy to the French people. The King refused to accept it and the people marched against him. In 1791 he tried to flee but was prevented from doing so. A new constitution was adopted but it was too much of a compromise for the likes of Maximilien de Robespierre, one of the leaders of the radical revolutionaries.

Meanwhile in neighbouring counties of Austria, Switzerland, Germany, Belgium and England those who wanted change took faith in the events in France and began to line up against France. Certain nobles from France had also emigrated and re-formed across the borders looking for support from foreign nobility. In 1792 France declared war on Austria. The revolutionaries in the Legislative Assembly believed it was to fight off counterrevolutionaries coming in from across the border, and Louis XVI, thinking war may act in his favour was also pro-war, hoping foreign powers would come to his rescue. The war did not go well for the French and in 1792 an Austrian Prussian Army crossed the border.

The French revolutionaries in Paris, in particular the radical Jacobins (a revolutionary group named after the Jacobin monastery in which they had formed), thinking their revolution may be at risk, arrested King Louis XVI and his queen, Marie Antoinette. The Legislative Assembly was replaced by the National Convention, which then abolished the monarchy. In 1793, first the king and then nine months later, Marie-Antoinette, were convicted of treason, and were executed by guillotine.

Interestingly, although Marie Antoinette is famously attributed as saying "Let them eat cake", it is probably not true that she said the words. The meaning behind the saying is to suggest that she was so out of touch with reality that when she learned the people could not buy bread, she said they should just eat cake instead. However, the true quote translation would be "Let them eat brioche", which is a cake-like bread mixture, and also, this saying was already in place prior to the Revolution, having been used in Germany and by French philosopher Jean-Jacques Rousseau. However, there is no proof she ever actually uttered the words.

From 1793–1794 Robespierre went on an anti-counterrevolutionary rampage and had over 15,000 people executed as he tried to wipe out any form of counterrevolution. He was overthrown in 1794 and he himself was then executed, also by guillotine.

The following period was known as the Thermidorian Reaction (Thermidor being a date then in the French Republican calendar) and the French Army took control and in 1795 a new constitution was formed. In 1795 "La Marseillaise" was adopted as the French National Anthem. A new group was created to restore order and this was called The Directory but they soon also became dictatorial in the extreme.

At the same time, the French Army was now enjoying success abroad, mainly due to a new young general, Napoleon

Bonaparte. Finally defeated in Egypt, Napoleon returned to France where he promptly took control of the situation and removed The Directory in a coup and named himself First Consul.

The Revolution was finally over, and Napoleon was in charge.

Though the Revolution was over, French troops continued fighting abroad and in Egypt in 1799 French Officer Pierre-Francois Bouchard discovered the Rosetta Stone, near the town of Rashid (Rosetta). The stone had three inscriptions, two in hieroglyphic and demotic scripts (both Ancient Egyptian), and a third in Ancient Greek, which then allowed scholars to finally decipher hieroglyphics.

Since 1652 the settlement around Cape Town, the Cape of Good Hope, had belonged to the Dutch, but in 1797 the British seized it as they wanted to have Cape Town as a stop for their ships en-route to Australia and India. The Dutch had been battling the Xhosa as they had expanded agriculture inland away from the Coast, and the British then continued with these ongoing fights against the Xhosa.

In 1792 the Buttonwood Agreement (apparently signed under a Buttonwood tree) was signed between 24 stockbrokers on Wall Street, New York, who agreed that brokers and merchants would only trade with each other within the devised system, for set commissions. This was the formation of the New York Stock Exchange and the Wall Street Investment Community.

In 1796 a British Doctor, Edward Jenner, produced the first vaccine to be developed against a contagious disease, the smallpox vaccine. He demonstrated that being infected with a small amount of a virus brought about immunity to that disease. Against smallpox, Jenner administered the cowpox virus to counter the smallpox, and the word vaccine comes from the Latin word for cow because of this.

Since 1169 the English had been in control in Ireland (see 1169) and in 1798 there was a major uprising against this British rule. It was launched by the United Irishmen who aimed to establish a Republic of Ireland, completely Independent of Britain.

> The rebellion failed to create a nationwide uprising and was brutally put down by the British, with many leaders, including Wolfe Tone, killed. As a result, the Irish Parliament was dissolved by the British and control was moved directly to London under the Act of Union of 1800.

CE 1800–1899

Napoleon Bonaparte and the Napoleonic Wars, Act of Union of United Kingdom of Great Britain and Ireland, Russo-Persian Wars, Franz Joseph and the Austrian and Austro-Hungarian Empires, Lewis and Clark, the War of 1812, the Battle of the Alamo, the Mexican-American War, the California Gold Rush and the Pennsylvania Oil Rush, American Civil War, Abraham Lincoln assassinated, Custer's Last Stand, Alaska bought by America from Russia, Brooklyn Bridge and Statue of Liberty built in New York, Coca-Cola invented, the Spanish-American War, Latin American Countries independence, the Paraguayan War, the War of the Pacific, Britain Annexes the Cape Colony, the Anglo-Zulu War, Battle of Isandlwana, Battle of Rorke's Drift, the Boer Wars, David Livingstone, Victoria Falls, Henry

*Stanley, Lobengula and the Ndebeles, French Algeria, Tunisia
and Morocco, Kenya and Joseph Thomson, King Leopold
and the Congo Free State, Ghana colonised, Egypt invaded
by the British, the Suez Canal, French West Africa, the Berlin
Conference, the First Italo-Ethiopian War, slave trade abolished,
Decline of the Ottoman Empire, Riyadh becomes Capital of
reclaimed Saudi State, Modern Singapore established, Antarctica
discovered, Trafalgar Square built, internal combustion engine
patented, London Metropolitan Police formed, Discovery
that Electricity can be created , Edison patents the modern
lightbulb, Spanish Inquisition abolished, Chinese Opium Wars,
Hong Kong ceded to the British, Empress Dowager Cixi takes
power in China, the Sino-French War, the First Sino-Japanese
War, Britain's Victorian Era, classical cell theory, New Zealand
established as British Colony, Tchaikovsky born, the Irish Potato
Famine, Switzerland becomes a Federal State, the Communist
Manifesto published, the Great Exhibition at Crystal Palace,
telegraphy and morse code established, the Crimean War, the
Charge of the Light Brigade, Florence Nightingale, the Telegraph
Newspaper Launched, the birth of the steel industry, Charles
Schwab and Andrew Carnegie, the end of the Mughal Empire
in India, Establishment of the East India Company, the Indian
Sepoy Mutiny, British Colonisation of India, the Aga Khan,
France colonises Vietnam, Big Ben built in London, Charles
Darwin publishes The Origin of Species, Emancipation of
Russian serfs, Alexander II assassinated, Russian pogroms,
Louis Pasteur and pasteurisation, Revolution in Spain dethrones
Queen Isabella II, Extinction of the Quagga, Eiffel Tower
completed, Japan's first written constitution, Tower Bridge
completed, Invention of the x-ray, the first Modern Olympics,
the Spanish-American War*

Early in this 19th century Napoleon first healed the rift with
the Church at home in France, then signed the Peace of

Amiens with the British. Next, he sold Louisiana, the French owned state in America, and then in 1804 established a new legal code for France, the Napoleonic Code, before crowning himself Emperor of France.

In 1805 he defeated the Austrian and Russian forces and expanded his empire into Germany and Poland.

His Peace Treaty with Britain proved temporary and in in 1805 the Battle of Trafalgar was fought off the Cape of Trafalgar, Spain, between the British Royal Navy, under Horatio Nelson with a fleet of 27 ships, against a combined French–Spanish force of 33 ships, under Pierre de Villeneuve. The British won the battle decisively with Villeneuve captured. Nelson, however, died in battle after being shot, but not before he received news of the victory. The battle ended any hopes Napoleon had of invading England and established Britain's naval supremacy for the remainder of the century.

In 1810 Napoleon had his marriage to Josephine annulled as they had not managed to have any children, and remarried Marie-Louise, who gave birth to a son in 1811.

In 1812 Napoleon went to war against the Russians who had retreated from the Continental System that Napoleon had set up which banned British shipments in Europe. Napoleon had set up the Code in order to weaken Britain economically, but this failed. The war against Russia was fought at enormous cost to his troops who suffered terribly in the deadly Russian winter.

He then further lost a Battle at Leipzig in 1813 by a coalition of European forces. Napoleon was defeated and exiled to Elba. However, he escaped and managed to raise an army. A final battle was fought at Waterloo (modern-day Belgium) against British forces lead by the Duke of Wellington and Prussian forces lead by Field Marshal von Blucher. Wellington described it as an incredibly tight battle, but Napoleon was defeated.

Napoleon was exiled to Saint Helena where he died in 1821, and a period of peace ensued between Britain and Europe, known as Pax Britannia.

In 1801 the Act of Union occurred between Great Britain (England and Scotland) with Ireland, creating the United Kingdom of Great Britain. This followed the previous Acts of Union between England and Scotland in 1707 when Great Britain (see 1707) was formed, and which had brought the two nations together as one state, under one monarch. With the Irish rebellion having occurred in 1798, William Pitt the Younger, who was Britain's prime minister at the time, decided that a Union with Ireland was the way to prevent further dissent. The parliament in Ireland was done away with and instead Ireland was represented by peers and members in parliament in Westminster, London.

In 1804 a territorial dispute between Russia and Persia broke out into war that lasted until 1813, the Russo-Persian War. As a result, most of modern-day Azerbaijan and Georgia and Dagestan became Russian territory. A second Russo-Persian war broke out in 1826 and lasted until 1828 when Persia tried to reclaim these territories, which again Russia won and took over further territories, comprising most of modern-day Armenia.

In 1804 Francis II of the Holy Roman Empire declared

himself Emperor of Austria, Francis I, and formed the Austrian Empire. He did this in response to Napoleon's formation of the French Empire. This Empire united the various Hapsburg monarchies into one Empire. After Napoleon's downfall, Austria lead the German states until war broke out with one of the German kingdoms (Prussia) in 1866, the Austro-Prussian war.

Austria was defeated but the Emperor Franz Joseph then created the Austro-Hungarian Empire. Franz Joseph was then King of Hungary as well as Emperor of Austria and held these titles until his death in 1916.

This century saw major developments in the United States of America.

In 1805 an expedition to explore the west of the country resulted in 33 explorers under Commanders Lewis and Clark reached the Pacific Ocean, linking the east coast of the country to the west coast.

In 1812 war broke out between Britain and the United States. As Britain was concurrently fighting the Napoleonic wars for control of Europe, their navy was heavily undermanned. They seized American merchant ships and their cargo and forced the men from these ships into serving in the British Navy. This, and the fact that Britain was encroaching into American waters, caused the young United States to declare war on Britain. America tried to invade the British territory of Canada but failed. After a sustained war on land and sea eventually a peace treaty was signed in 1814 in Belgium, the Treaty of Ghent. Canada was retained by the British, leading to it becoming an independent nation from America, but America could claim they had not been defeated on their own land thus establishing the young country as a new force to be reckoned with.

Incidentally, during this war a meat packer from New York called Sam Wilson supplied beef to the United States Army and the barrels containing the food were labelled with his name. The Army soldiers gave the food the nickname 'Uncle Sam's' and the name caught on and eventually came to represent America as a whole, 'Uncle Sam'.[109]

Another result of this war was the "Star-Spangled Banner". It was originally a poem written by Francis Scott Key in 1814 called "The Defence of Fort M'Henry" after he witnessed the bombardment of Maryland by the British and saw a single US flag flying over the Fort at daybreak. The poem was later put to music and eventually became the American national anthem in 1913.

In 1836 Texas declared itself independent from Mexico. At the Battle of the Alamo, Mexico sought to take back control of Texas but this galvanised Texans to fight back and win independence. The Alamo itself was a fort used by the Texan soldiers having converted it from a Mission.

America then sought to make Texas part of the United States. The Mexicans saw this annexure of Texas by America as an act of war and in 1846 war broke out between the two nations, the Mexican-American War. After two years of warfare America gained control of Texas and the Treaty of Guadalupe Hidalgo was signed in 1848. Whilst Mexico received $18 million in compensation in the treaty, Texas, California, Arizona, Colorado, Nevada, Utah, Oklahoma, Kansas, Wyoming and New Mexico all became United States territory.

In January 1848 James W. Marshall found gold on his land in California. News spread quickly and within a matter of a few years over 300,000 people arrived in California from as far afield as Europe and China. Many arrived in 1849 and became known as the "49ers" (hence the name of the San Francisco 49ers American football team). The rush peaked in 1852, but by then California had developed rapidly and become a State in 1850.

In 1859 a tenacious driller by the name of Edwin "Crazy" Drake struck oil in Pennsylvania after most of his investors had given up on the idea. The Pennsylvania oil rush began thereafter, leading an oil refiner by the name of John D. Rockefeller to build his fortune.

In 1860 Abraham Lincoln was elected president of the United States. The southern states had only recently joined the Confederation and they were alarmed at Lincoln's anti-slavery stance and at the movement against slavery taking place in both the other American states and Britain. First seven and then eleven southern states withdrew from the United States. Lincoln refused to recognize these states as an independent nation and in 1861 the American Civil War started. The northern states were known as the United States of America and were led by Lincoln, while the southern states were called the Confederate States of America and were led by Jefferson Davis. After four years of war, the United States prevailed and the rebellious states were readmitted into the United States. In 1863 Lincoln had signed the Emancipation Proclamation freeing all slaves, and the southern states then had to comply with this proclamation. Slavery was abolished throughout the United States.

The bloodiest battle of this bloody war was the Battle of Gettysburg, Pennsylvania in 1863. Robert E. Lee of the Confederate States launched a raid to gather vital supplies from the north. Over a three-day battle, 51,000 men were killed or wounded. The battle was won by the United States under General George G. Meade. Soon after, Lincoln visited Gettysburg and read out the famous Gettysburg Address speech which confirmed his commitment to preserving the Union of the United States. [110]

Whilst Robert. E. Lee was the most famous and successful Confederate General, the North had Ulysses S. Grant who engaged Lee in a continuous series of battles, until Lee surrendered in 1865. [111]

Another famous general to emerge from the Civil War was George Armstrong Custer who played an important role in the Battle of Gettysburg as well as the final battle of the war, the Battle of Appomattox Court House. After the war Custer arrived in Kansas in 1866 were he engaged in battles with the Sioux and Cheyenne Native Americans and by 1874 one of Custers Expeditions discovered gold in the region of Wyoming. The Government wanted to permanently remove the Native Americans from the region and this set off strong resistance, led mainly by a Native American Chief, Sitting Bull. An estimated 2000 members of Sioux, Cheyenne and Arapaho tribes joined with Sitting Bull and Crazy Horse, another famous Sioux. In June 1874 after a long trek, Custer attacked this tribal army, separating his troops into three sections. Custer, along with just 210 men headed north into the Battle of Little Bighorn. They were massacred in what became known as Custer's Last Stand.[112]

Towards the end of the Civil War, in April 1865, Abraham Lincoln was assassinated by John Wilkes Booth whilst he attended a play at the Ford's Theatre in Washington D.C.. Booth and fellow conspirators aimed to assassinate the President, the Vice President and the Secretary of State in order to revive the Confederate Civil War. The Secretary of State was wounded and the Vice President unharmed. Booth was tracked down and killed, whilst four conspirators were hanged.

In 1867 Alaska was purchased from Russia by the United States. Russia had previously acquired it as its most western point, but the Russian Tsar Alexander II realised it would be too difficult to defend and decided to dispose of it. The American Secretary of State William Seward, who had been wounded when Lincoln was assassinated, negotiated the purchase for USD $7.2 million. Initially a department and then a territory, Alaska became a full state in 1959.

During this century New York emerged as one of the country's most important ports. Brooklyn Bridge was completed in 1883 linking the city's two boroughs of Manhattan and Brooklyn, and in 1886 the Statue of Liberty was completed. The statue was a gift from France as a symbol of America's freedom.

In 1886 a pharmacist in Atlanta, John Stith Pemberton developed a syrup, which he then mixed with carbonated water, and placed it on sale as a soda drink. His bookkeeper suggested the name Coca-Cola. Pemberton had originally intended it to be a tonic for various ailments and both cocaine and caffeine were included in the original recipe, which was later revised and cocaine removed.

This 19th century also saw great changes in South America. With Spain involved in the Napoleonic Wars, the countries of South America each looked to gain their independence from Spain, whose attention was elsewhere.

By the 1820's Mexico and Columbia and Argentina had gained their independence and then Brazil took its independence from Portugal. By the end of the century almost the whole continent was independent with the exceptions of French Guiana, Guyana, Belize, Panama and Suriname, with Cuba administered by America after its independence from Spain in 1898 through until 1902.

Between 1864 and 1870 the Paraguayan War, also known as the War of the Triple Alliance, broke out with Brazil, Argentina and Uruguay on the one hand, and Paraguay on the other. Paraguay lost extensive lands as an outcome.

Another war, the War of the Pacific, broke out from 1879–1884 between Chile and Bolivia over disputed land. Chile emerged victorious and took the land under dispute, leaving Bolivia forever landlocked.

This century also saw the European powers vying for power and control of Africa.

In 1806 Britain annexed the Cape Colony after the Dutch East Africa Company declared bankruptcy. They had already seized it from the Dutch in 1797 and then handed it back to them in 1803. However, with the Dutch East Africa Company out of the way, in 1806 they reclaimed it fully as their own, which was ratified by a treaty in 1814, and in the 1820s the first British Settlers started arriving.

The Dutch settlers, Boers, resented the British rule and began migrating north looking for farmland. The Great Trek, a mass migration of Boers, began in 1835. Meanwhile this was at a similar time that a strong Zulu leader, Shaka, established his own Zulu kingdom over a vast area in South Africa. Shaka was replaced by his half-brother Dingaan and the Boers and Zulus started clashing, culminating with the Battle of Blood River. Eventually the Boers settled in two areas, Orange Free State and Transvaal.

Between 1860 and 1880 diamonds and gold were discovered in the Northern Cape, Kimberley and Transvaal and this intensified the competition between the British, the Boers and the Zulus as the British also moved northwards. The Anglo-Zulu war occurred during 1879 with two notable battles being the Battle of Isandlwana won by the Zulus and the Battle of Rorke's Drift, won by the British. The British eventually won the war.

The British then moved on towards their goal of a united South Africa with the two Boer republics under their control. An initial conflict, known as the First Boer War, or the Transvaal War, occurred between the British and the Boers between 1880 and 1881 after the British tried to annexe Transvaal. The Boers won this war but tensions erupted again in 1899 with the Second Boer War.

In 1886 the SA Prime Minister Cecil John Rhodes plotted to overthrow the Government of Paul Kruger, the President of Transvaal, and a raid on Transvaal lead by Leander Starr Jameson was defeated by the Boers. Tensions grew until 1899 when war broke out in full. For further details on The Second Boer War, see 1900.

Whilst all this was occurring in South Africa, further north exploration and developments were also occurring.

The missionary David Livingstone, a Scotsman, had by 1842 ventured further north than any other European in his quest to spread Christianity. In 1855 he was the first European to come across the Victoria Falls and in 1856 was the first European to traverse the continent west to east. He returned to Britain a national hero as his exploits were well publicised. He returned to Africa two further times exploring the continent as far as the Lakes Malawi and Tanganyika, searching for the source of the Nile and writing home exposing the horrors of the slave trade. In his final expedition he went missing for some years resulting in an American journalist, Henry Stanley, mounting his own expedition to find Livingstone. He succeeded in 1871 uttering the immortal words, "Dr Livingstone, I presume" after tracking the missionary to Lake Tanganyika. He resupplied Livingstone who continued his expedition until 1873 when he died of Malaria. Livingstone was returned to England a hero and buried in Westminster Abbey.

In the area immediately North of South Africa, over the Limpopo River, the Rozvi Kingdom, which had succeeded the Kingdom of Mutapa, which in turn had taken over from the Kingdom of Zimbabwe (see 1200–1300), was in decline. [113]

Regional migrations called Mfecane had weakened the Rozvi, specifically the arrival of the more warlike Ndebele people who had arrived in the 1830s and 1840. The Ndebele had descended from Shaka's Zulus from South Africa and fled north when their leader Mzilikazi fell out with Shaka. When Mzilikazi died in 1838 he was succeeded by his son Lobengula. At this time the colonial powers were arriving in the region and the British and Portuguese started making incursions into the area. In 1888 Lobengula approved the Rudd Concession which provided Cecil Rhodes exclusive mineral rights for the area. Rhodes used this concession to have a Royal Charter approved by the British monarchy giving him the rights and power to form the British South Africa (BSA) Company in 1889.

Lobengula had received arms and ammunition in return for these mineral rights, whilst simultaneously the Portuguese had been arming other local chiefs, including the Shona, who controlled areas north east of Lobengula. This created friction between the Ndebele and the Shona who battled in 1893 near another British settlement called Fort Victoria. The British intervened and insisted the Ndebele leave. The Ndebele refused and the Matabele War began between the Ndebele (Matabeleland was the name given to the land ruled by the Ndebele) and the British. The British, with superior firepower, advanced to take Lobengula's capital at Bulawayo. Lobengula fled and the British chased him north. At Shangani the Ndebele ambushed a British patrol headed by Alan Wilson and killed him and 34 soldiers. This however was a limited victory for the Ndebele and in 1894, when Lobengula died of an illness, they were a weakened force. By 1895 the whole area was a British colony and named Rhodesia after Cecil John Rhodes, who had been instrumental in its creation. In 1889 the British granted Rhodes' company, the British South Africa company, the right to govern the new colony.

Whilst these developments were occurring in Southern Africa, North and East and West Africa were also being colonised.

In 1830 the French invaded Algiers and by 1848 the country had been incorporated into France as French Algeria. The French then moved to establish a greater presence in the region and in 1881 established the French protectorate of Tunisia followed by the French protectorate of Morocco in 1912.

East Africa was also opening up. In 1878 Joseph Thomson was appointed geologist on a Royal Geographic Society expedition to venture inland from Dar Es Salaam, a trading port on the East Coast of Africa (in present day Tanzania). He was reappointed on another expedition in 1883, this time tasked with developing trading routes up to Lake Victoria. In 1887 Britain then granted the Imperial British East Africa Company the rights to administer what is present day Kenya. By 1895 the British government took over the administration and control and began building a railway there between 1895 and 1901.

Over to the Central West of Africa, interest had grown in the area we now know as the Democratic Republic of Congo. Henry Stanley, who had famously found Livingstone, had explored the Congo River between 1874 and 1877 and shed light on the area and its potential. A group of investors, led by the Belgian King Leopold II, employed Stanley to negotiate with the regional chiefs, and by 1884 the group of investors began governing the area having signed treaties with various local chiefs, naming the new territory the Congo Free State.

The Congo Free State differed from other colonial territories in that it was the personal territory of Leopold and his investors. A brutal regime was put in place by the group to such an extent that pressure was exerted on the Belgian King by Britain and in 1908 he had to abolish the Congo as his personal possession and hand it over to the Belgian government. In 1899 Joseph Conrad's novel *The Heart of Darkness* was first published, an insight into the brutality of the Belgian King's control in the Congo.

In 1874 Britain also colonised Ghana, renaming it the Gold Coast as a British crown colony.

In Egypt, after Napoleon had been defeated by the British at sea, a brief power struggle ensued with Mohammed Ali winning control. After Ali's death in 1849 Khedive Ismail took over. In 1856 work began on the Suez Canal as Ismail tried to modernise the country and bring in investors. The cost of this proved high and put pressure on the population which revolted in 1882. The British, worried about their investments including the Suez Canal, invaded and occupied the country from 1882 to 1919.

Germany too embarked on a programme of colonisation. Germany had undertaken its own industrial revolution in 1871 and now required raw materials. In 1884 it annexed South West Africa (now Namibia) and then annexed German Cameroon and Togo. Germany then backed the German East Africa Company which embarked on a number of expeditions to sign treaties with various African leaders and by 1889 the Germans controlled Tanganyika as well as Rwanda and Burundi.

By 1890 France had signed treaties with a number of West African leaders, negotiated from a strong military position on the side of the French. Fort by fort they increased their presence in the region until by the end of the century most of Senegal, Burkina Faso, Niger, Benin, Guinea and Ivory Coast were theirs.

With all this activity occurring across Africa, in 1895 European leaders met in Berlin. Here they agreed which territories would belong to which European power, in what has since become known as the Berlin Conference.

Among other agreements:

Britain received modern-day Malawi, Zambia, Zimbabwe, South Africa, Kenya, Uganda, and Egypt.

Germany received Tanzania and Namibia

Portugal received Angola and Mozambique

Belgium received the Democratic Republic of Congo

France received much of West Africa including Mali, Ivory Coast, Mauritania, Niger, Senegal and Burkina Faso.

In 1889 the Ethiopians and Italians signed The Treaty of Wuchale after the Italians occupied Eritrea. The Italians also controlled Somalia as they too tried to impose a colonial influence over parts of Africa. Disagreements over translations of the treaty resulted in the Italians claiming Ethiopia an Italian Protectorate. War broke out in 1895 and lasted until the Ethiopians

were victorious at the Battle of Adwa and the two parties signed the Treaty of Addis Ababa in 1896 granting
Ethiopia sovereignty.

In Britain, after 20 years of lobbying, Parliament finally
passed an act to abolish the slave trade in 1807. The main driv-
ers for this included William Wilberforce MP, and Olaudah
Equiano an activist. In reality this just meant that British
people could no longer be involved in movement of slaves, but
the ownership of slaves continued to exist.

In America in 1808 Congress enacted a law against the
importation of slaves but it was only enforced during the
American Civil War in 1861.

In 1821 the American Colonization Society, an organisation set up to help freed African American slaves return
to Africa, founded a colony in West Africa, renaming it
Liberia in 1824. Freed slaves returned to the colony and it
became an independent nation in 1847.

Between 1820 and 1880 the Royal Navy diligently tried to
patrol the seas and prevent the slave trade.

In 1833 British Parliament passed an emancipation act
that paved the way for the ending of unpaid labour by 1838
in the Caribbean, when 800,000 slaves were freed.

This was also the century that saw the rapid decline of the
Ottoman Empire. It lost Greece which revolted in 1830,
becoming an independent nation, and in 1878 Romania,
Serbia and Bulgaria followed suit.

In 1818, The Ottoman Empire, which felt threatened

by the rapid growth of the First Saudi State besieged its Capital Diriyah and destroyed it.

The Al Saud family regained control of their State and moved their capital to Riyad and formed the Second Saudi State. However in 1865 they were again overpowered by the Ottomans and fled to Kuwait until 1902 when they returned and retook Riyad [114](see 1902).

In 1819 modern Singapore was established. The British wanted to establish a port in the region and a Lieutenant Stamford Raffles was sent to see the area. He negotiated a treaty with the local rulers and established Singapore as a trading station.

In 1820 a Russian expedition became the first to officially sight the continent of Antarctica. The expedition was led by two explorers, Bellingshausen and Lazarev.

In London between 1820 and the 1840s Trafalgar Square was built and named in honour of Lord Nelson's famous victory at the Cape of Trafalgar against Napoleon's fleet. Nelson's column at 56 metres high dominates the square.

In 1823 the internal combustion engine was patented for the first time by Samuel Brown in England. The combustion engine had had previous versions (with a Swiss Engineer Francois Isaac de Rivaz building one in 1806), but Brown's was the first to be patented for industrial use.[115]

This was further developed in 1870 by Gottlieb Daimler and his partner Wilhelm Maybach along with Nikolaus Otto. Daimler and Maybach were instrumental in further developments of the engine over the next decades, as was another engineer Karl Benz who later placed his engines in the first automobiles in production.

In 1893 Rudolph Diesel patented his diesel engine.

In 1825 George Stephenson further developed the steam engine, adapting it for use in train locomotives, transforming the railways across Britain and then the rest of the world.

In 1829 the then-home secretary of Britain's government, who later went on to become prime minister, Robert Peel, formed the London Metropolitan Police. These police officers came to be nicknamed "Bobbys", a nickname derived from the name Robert.

In 1831 Michael Faraday, an English scientist, discovered that electricity could be created by moving magnets inside copper wire. This meant that electricity could be generated and conducted. [116]

Faraday's discovery had come about after an Italian scientist, Alessandro Volta (after whom the volt is named) had discovered how to generate electricity through a voltaic pile (using salt water, zinc and copper). This set great minds thinking and before Faraday, in 1802, a British chemist Sir Humphry Davy used Volta's works to produce an electric arc lamp. Further developments by British scientists Warren de la Rue and then Joseph Swan in lightbulbs of varying types finally led to the first patent of a commercially successful lightbulb in 1870 by Thomas Edison who perfected the filament in his design and then teamed up with Swan to manufacture lightbulbs en-masse.[117]

Then in 1883, Eddison built the world's first power station in Holborn, London. A coal-powered steam engine drove a generator to generate electricity for the surrounding buildings. Edison also went on to build the Pearl Street Power Station in New York.

Edison also teamed up with another great investor Nikola Tesla in 1884 but the two parted ways. Tesla went on to invent AC, alternating current, which allowed high voltage electricity to be conducted with little maintenance over long distances, thus making the use of electricity more commercially viable.

In Spain the Spanish Inquisition was finally abolished in 1834 by the Queen Regent. Its influence after the 15th and 16th century had diminished in the 1700s and had been supressed and reinstated a few times in the 1800s before its final abolishment.

In the 1800s in China the Qing Dynasty encountered far more problems than in the peaceful, stable 1700s. The previous century's increase in standards of living had also increased the population from 300 million to 400 million which was most acute in the eastern side of China with increased population densities in the urban areas. Food shortages resulted in famines, and taxation and corruption both rose.

In 1850 a rebellion broke out, the Taiping Rebellion in Guanxi, led by a self-proclaimed Christian prophet Hong Xiuquan and the members of his group called the God Worshipping Society. The rebellion took 14 years to quell with many millions of lives lost in the process.

At the same time, pressure increased from beyond their borders. China's increased prosperity had garnered interest from abroad, and foreign powers, Britain chief among them, tried to secure access to ports through trading rights with China. Missionaries also flocked to China intent on spreading Christianity.

By 1838 the illegal importation of opium into China reached approximately 40,000 chests annually and the Chinese authorities tried desperately to curb the smuggling, and use, of the drug which was having severe consequences inside the country socially and economically. [118]

The British had started to import opium trade into China in 1773, initially for medicinal purposes, but as tobacco smoking became more popular in China so did opium use. The British East India company imported the opium from Bengal, India at considerable profit, financing the British purchases of tea, silk and porcelain. Eventually the Chinese Emperor banned its importation and the Opium Wars ensured, with Britain trying to protect its economic interests. These Opium Wars were two separate armed conflicts between Britain and China.

> The first Opium War, from 1839 to 1842 was won by the British and resulted in Hong Kong being ceded to the British, along with increased trading privileges.

> In the second Opium War, from 1856–1860 the French aligned with the British against the Chinese who again lost to the Western countries. The Chinese were then forced to legalise opium, and the opium trade increased into the next century, until its eventual decline from 1906 (see 1906).

After the Chinese Emperor Xianfeng's death in 1861, the Empress Dowager Cixi took control in a palace coup. Cixi was originally a concubine of the Emperor, who became close friends with the Empress Cian, the chief consort. Cixi then gave birth to the Emperor's only son in 1856 and when Xianfeng died, this son became Emperor Tongzhi. However, as he was only six at the time, eight regents were to rule China until the young Emperor came of age.

Cixi and Cian teamed up with 2 of Xianfeng's brothers to engineer a coup and throw out the regents. Cixi then governed until the young Emperor came of age, stepped down when he did, and then re-governed again after he died of smallpox only two years after taking over from her.

Cixi then adopted her three-year-old nephew to be the new emperor, but again only when he came of age. Prior to this however, she took China to war against the French.

The French had designs on Vietnam and by 1880 controlled its southern provinces. They then started to move north, clashing with the Chinese who had their own influence on Vietnam. The Sino-French war occurred from 1883 until a Peace Treaty was signed in 1885. Although militarily the war was a stalemate, France did take control of the northern Vietnam region.

Cixi finally ceded power to the new Emperor Guangxu in 1889.

Between 1894 and 1895, under Emperor Guangxu, China and Japan went to war, the First Sino-Japanese War, over Korea, as they both wanted greater influence over the country for trade. Japan won the war fairly quickly which emphasised their strength, and China's weakness, at the time. The Chinese signed a peace treaty which included handing over Taiwan to Japan.

Japan occupied Taiwan through until 1945, but they had wanted to take Taiwan since the 16th century.[119] Prior to the 16th century Taiwan had been home to various tribes until the Han Chinese arrived in the 15th century. The Spaniards and Dutch had influence in Taiwan during the 17th and 18th centuries as they traded there, which resulted in them both trying to colonise the island in the 17th century; the Dutch in the South and the Spaniards in the North. However, both were ejected by the Chinese Ming who had retreated there from the Qing in mainland China. The Qing however eventually took over and in 1885 they named Taiwan as a Chinese province until the Japanese took over in 1895.

In 1898 tensions between the Emperor Guangxu and Cixi boiled over and he was eventually arrested over a plot to assassinate her. Cixi again took over the reins of power until her death in 1908.

All in all, under Cixi, China built a navy, opened up to the outside Western world, reorganised the country's finances, banned foot binding, and allowed marriage between Han and Manchu.

Also in China the Boxer Rebellion started in November 1899, but as this mainly occurred in 1900 and 1901, see next century for details.

In England the Victorian Era began as Queen Victoria took to the throne in 1837. She ruled until her death in 1901, a period of unprecedented economic and industrial growth throughout the United Kingdom and the expansion of the British Empire.

In 1839 classical cell theory was proposed by Theodor Schwann. Following the discovery of the cell by Robert Hooke (see 1665), Schwann's theory had three proposed parts:

i. All organisms are comprised of cells
ii. Cells are the basic units of life
iii. Cells come from pre-existing cells that have multiplied

In 1840 in New Zealand the British established their first governor to curtail lawlessness in the new territory and to prevent the French from establishing it as a French colony. The Treaty of Waitangi was then signed with the local chiefs who then gave themselves the term Māori – which means ordinary – to differentiate themselves from the foreigners. Various land related conflicts between the foreigners and the Māori lead to war on the North Island, whilst in the South economic development continued. Railways were built and the agricultural sector grew strongly. The North Island conflict lasted 20 years but only resulted in further land being confiscated by the British as they established the new country.

In 1893 New Zealand was the first country in the world to give women the right to vote.

Pyotr Ilyich Tchaikovsky, one of Russia's most famous composers, was born in 1840. He composed *Swan Lake* and *The Nutcracker*.

In 1845 the Irish Potato Famine, or the Great Hunger, began as the Phytophthora fungus ruined over half of the national crop over the next seven years. As Ireland was severely dependent on potatoes as a food source, the famine resulted in over a million deaths before it ended in 1852.

In 1848 Switzerland evolved into a Federal State.[120] Its previous evolution had been in 1291 (see 1200–1300) when its three founding cantons had decided to support each other militarily. In the intervening period five separate wars were fought internally and then in 1798 French Revolutionary troops invaded. In 1815 the European powers agreed at the Congress of Vienna that Switzerland could become neutral. A slow internal civil war followed which put an end to conflict between Catholics and Protestants in which the Protestants triumphed and the new Federal State was created.

In 1848 *The Communist Manifesto* was published in London, written by German born socialist Karl Marx, and assisted by Friedrich Engels. The *Manifesto* set out the main beliefs of the Communist Party. Amidst the backdrop of major economic reforms in Europe, as people moved from rural areas to urban areas for work, Marx observed that most workers lived in poverty as the ruling class lived in wealth. Marx and Engels did not feel this was sustainable and the *Manifesto* argued that in the end capitalism would fail and be replaced by socialism and then its more extreme version, communism, as workers (the proletariat) would revolt against the power held by the ruling class (the bourgeoise).

In England as the British Empire grew, Queen Victoria's husband, Prince Albert, organised the world's first World Fair in 1851, called the Great Exhibition, as a means to grow international trade and bring countries together. Crystal Palace, the world's largest glass greenhouse was purpose built to hold the exhibition and over 6 million people attended 13,000 exhibits.

In 1848 Morse Code was developed in Germany as the electric telegraph replaced the optical telegraph during this 19th century. Telegraphy is the long-distance transmission of messages. This was initially conducted optically, via flags and other visual signals sent from tower to tower, and conveyed by sight and interpretation, but then electronically, as messages were able to be sent down telegraph wires, speeding up the process. It was named after Samuel Morse, the American inventor and painter who devised the system.

In 1851 King Frederick Wilhelm IV of Prussia, a German state, appointed Otto von Bismarck as the Prussian representative to the German Confederation. Then in 1862 he became prime minister. Bismarck's ambition was to unify the disparate German states with Prussia at its centre.[121] He started by capturing two states from Denmark and then went to war with France in the Franco-Prussian War in order to create unity among German states. He won the war as well as the support of the southern German states and in 1871 a German Empire was created.

Von Bismarck was appointed Chancellor of the new German state and he set out to lessen the influence of the Catholic Church and introduced socialist policies including pensions and health insurance.

In 1888 the new German Emperor Wilhelm II took power and he and Bismarck soon began to disagree on both foreign and local policies. These disagreements continued until 1890 when Bismarck resigned.

Germany then entered a period of colonial expansion (see the paragraphs on European powers vying for power and control of Africa earlier in this chapter).

In 1858 the Crimean War broke out. This was an interesting war in that whilst most wars were fought over either territory or religious differences, the Crimean War was fought over both.

Prior to the war, Russia, Britain and France were all competing for influence over the Middle East, especially Turkey. At the same time, Catholic France and Orthodox Russia were vying for control over religious sites in the Holy Land including Bethlehem, which was controlled by Turkish Ottoman. Rioting broke out and some Orthodox monks were killed by French Catholic monks, and the Russian Tsar Nicolas I blamed the Turks. When the dispute was not resolved, Nicholas went to war against what he called "the sick man of Europe", Turkey. Britain and France, concerned that their trade routes and influence in Turkey, and the region, would be under threat from any Russian imperial expansion, declared war on Russia in March 1854.

The British and French plan was a full assault on Crimea to take the port of Sevastapol.

After an initial victory for the British and French at the Battle of Alma the Russians counterattacked at the Battle of Balaklava and although repulsed, inflicted serious damage on the British and French, especially in the famed Charge of the Light Brigade. In this battle the Earl of Cardigan led over 600 Cavalrymen up one of the two valleys near the port of Balaklava, but they were bombarded from both sides and almost wiped out altogether, with the remnants of the brigade saved only by a simultaneous charge of the French cavalry. Alfred, Lord Tennyson, immortalised the suicidal charge of the Light Brigade in his poem, "The Charge of The Light Brigade".

Balaklava also became famous later for the knitted head-wear worn by soldiers there, covering their whole head and face, save for eye and mouth holes.

Following Balaklava, Sevastapol was then put under an 11-month siege by the Allied forces, with the city defended by the Russians until it eventually fell. With the Russians losing this war they sued for peace. Back in Britain and France the war was very unpopular, so Britain and France quickly agreed to this, and in 1856 the Treaty of Paris was signed, ending the war.

The war was the first war to use modern military technologies, including explosive shells, with devastating effect. It was also one of the first wars in which news was quickly communicated via telegraphy back to Britain and France, where it was disseminated to the public by the increasingly popular newspapers.

It was also during the Crimean War that Florence Nightingale sprang to fame whilst serving as a manager and trainer of nurses. In the war she organised the nursing of the wounded soldiers and put in place new standards for their hygiene and hospitalisation.

Her famed night rounds checking on the wounded soldiers led to her becoming known as "The Lady with the Lamp".

One of the world's most iconic newspapers, *The Telegraph*, was founded in 1855 as *The Daily Telegraph and Courier*, and by 1876 boasted the largest circulation in the world.[122]

In 1856 Englishman Henry Bessemer developed an effective way to introduce air into molten iron. With further refining of the methods by another Englishman Robert Mushet, and then Welshman, Sydney Thomas, eventually iron ore from anywhere in the world could be refined into steel, and steel production costs decreased dramatically. As a result the world steel industry boomed.

This led to the birth of the steel industry which created internationally known business magnates Charles Schwab and Andrew Carnegie.

After the unity of the Mughal Empire in India in the 17th, and early 18th, century, the latter part of that 18th century saw the decline of that empire as Britain established its power base there via the British East India Company.

In 1857 trouble brewed when an Indian sepoy (soldier) employed by the East India Company rebelled and attacked British officers. He was executed which led to disquiet among the other Indian sepoys. Hearing they would be subjected to mistreatment at the hands of the British (it was believed they would be forced to bite down on rifle cartridges greased with pig and cow lard which their Hindu religion forbade them to consume), they refused the cartridges, which was viewed as subordination by the British. [123] Punishments were meted out until May 1857 when the sepoys mutinied. This became known as the Sepoy Mutiny of 1857 as the sepoys managed to march to, and seize, Delhi. The mutiny was eventually put down by the British in 1859.

The result of this mutiny was that Britain abolished the East India Company in favour of direct rule, and passed the Government of India Act of 1858, with India then presided over by a Secretary of State for India with control of the actual country handled by viceroys on the ground in India.

From 1858 through to 1909 the Government of India was increasingly centralised, and private clubs and military cantonments became a way of life for the British. Land revenue, the opium trade and salt taxes all added to the income received by the British and a country-wide rail network was established which also led to coalmining and coal production, to fuel the steam engines. Tea and coffee plantations were also established, mainly in Assam.

In 1885 however, the first meeting of the Indian National Congress was held. This was a broad-based Indian political party opposed to Britain's control of India, and sought Indian independence.

Gradually the British Empire in the region expanded northwards up as far as Afghanistan.

There, alarmed at Russian influence in the region, the British prime minister, Benjamin Disraeli, urged intervention and in 1878 Britain invaded in what was the Second Anglo-Afghan War. The first had been from 1839–1842 when Britain first invaded and then withdrew from Afghanistan. During the First Anglo-Afghan War a title of prince was bestowed on an influential leader called the Aga Khan who had supported the British in that war. There were other princes in the region but what set the Aga Khan apart was the fact that he was the leader of a specific sect of Islam and was seen by the British as a politically important ally. The Second Ango-Afghan War ended with the Treaty of Gandamak in 1879. The British troops withdrew in 1881 and Afghanistan agreed to pass its foreign policy through India, which was under British control.

Also during this period, Britain conquered Burma and in 1886 Upper Burma was annexed to Britain.

In 1858 the French came to Vietnam and through a combination of trade and missionary activity slowly dominated the country which became a semi-French colony in the 1880s when France incorporated it into Indochina.

In 1859, Big Ben, the bell inside the Clock Tower in the new Palace of Westminster in London, was completed. When operational the clock was the largest and most accurate four-faced clock in the world and stood 96 metres high. After a fire had mostly destroyed the Palace of Westminster in London in 1834, Charles Barry designed the new palace, which incorporated the new clock tower which itself was designed by Augustus Pugin.

Also in 1859, Charles Darwin published *On the Origin of Species, or the Preservation of Favoured Races in the Struggle for Life*. Darwin had first tried to study medicine but then decided on the clergy, but after qualifying he followed his real interests, zoology and botany, and took up a position on HMS *Beagle* which set sail for South America in 1831. It took almost 30 years of collecting specimens and developing theories before he felt he was ready to publish.[124] Darwin was aware that the book went against religious thought at the time. His new theory centred on evolution by natural selection rather than on design by a higher being. By the time he died in 1882, although his theories were still controversial, he was respected enough to be given an honorary doctorate by Cambridge University and be buried in Westminster Abbey.

In 1861 in Russia, serfdom, the system by which peasants were legally tied to the land on which they lived, and therefore worked for nobility, was abolished.

Serfdom differed from slavery in that the noble who owned the land did not own the serf. However, the serf was bound to the land on which he lived and therefore could not move and had to look for work on that land. The system dated back to 1649 but eventually Tsar Alexander II abolished it. The defeat in the Crimean War had convinced the new Tsar that reforms were needed if Russia was to become a strong nation again and he abolished serfdom with the words "It is better to begin to destroy serfdom from above than to wait until that time when it begins to destroy itself from below."[125]

In 1881, Tsar Alexander II was assassinated by a member of the People's Will movement, whose aim was to overthrow the monarchy. Following the assassination some groups claimed foreign influence in his assassination and this sparked a wave of anti-Jewish riots, resulting in the rape and murder of a number of Jews, the larger scale emigration of Jews from Russia, and the early Zionist movement to create a homeland for Jewish people. This anti-Jewish movement was known as pogroms, a Russian word meaning to wreak havoc, or to devastate.

Russian problems continued in 1891–1892 as up to 400,000 people died of famine.

In the late 1800s people began boiling milk to improve quality and lessen milk-borne illnesses which included typhoid and scarlet fever. In 1864 however Louis Pasteur perfected the process of heating liquids to just below boiling point for a long enough period to remove the unwanted pathogens. This was Pasteurisation. Pasteur actually developed the process for wine, but it was adopted in milk production by the late 1800s.

In 1868 a coup in Spain turned into a Revolution and deposed the Spanish Queen Isabella II, leading to a new constitution in 1869.

> Previously, in 1807 Napoleonic France had invaded Spain. In 1808 a Spanish uprising led to the War of Spain or War of Independence and lasted six years. The Spanish wanted the French out. A constitution was adopted in 1812, and Ferdinand VII declared the legitimate King of Spain. Isabella II succeeded her father Ferdinand VII and became queen but against a background of desire within Spain for a more equal society and a free market economy. And so it was that the coup/revolution occurred in 1868.
>
> In 1873 the First Republic was proclaimed by Spain's National Assembly but was dissolved two years later and the monarchy restored, with Isabella II's son Alfonso XII placed on the throne. When the new King died, his wife Maria Christina took over leading to a period of internal political stability from 1885–1902.

In 1883 the last Quagga, a subspecies of the plains zebra, died at Amsterdam Zoo. The Quagga had previously been hunted to the edge of extinction. With the death of the Quagga in Amsterdam, the species was rendered extinct.[126]

In Paris, some years prior to the Exposition Universelle (an international exhibition that was to be held in in 1889, a date that marked the 100 years since the French Revolution) a competition for a new iconic building was launched.

The competition was won by Gustave Eiffel and in January 1887 construction of the Eiffel Tower began, with the tower completed in March 1889.

In 1889 Japan adopted its first written constitution, the Meiji Constitution. This was a step towards the creation of the modern Japanese state. Meiji was the emperor at the time and the new constitution established Japan as a constitutional monarchy with a parliament with an elected lower house.

Prior to the Meiji Constitution Japan did not have a written constitution and the emperor held all power, governing through a legal system. Over time however the emperor's powers had been side-lined and in effect he ruled mainly as a symbolic figure.

The new Meiji Constitution was based on Britain's and Germany's and aimed to establish Japan as a modern and civilised state.

In 1894 one of London's most iconic landmarks, Tower Bridge, was completed.

Needing to build a bridge downstream from London Bridge, but without disrupting essential river traffic, in 1876 a competition was launched by a new Special Bridge Committee for the design of the new crossing. In 1884 Sir Horace Jones, working with John Wolfe Barry, won the competition with his design that allowed the bridge to open for shipping traffic.

By the time it was complete in 1894 it was the largest bascule bridge ever completed (bascule meaning seesaw in French).[127]

In 1895 Wilhelm Conrad Rontgen invented the x-ray, a form of radiation used mainly in medical radiography to view the internal sides of an object or body.

In 1896 the first Modern Olympic games were held in Athens, Greece. The Ancient Olympic games had occurred from 77C BCE–CE 393 but were then discontinued. In 1894 Baron Pierre de Coubertin proposed their revival and the Modern Olympics started again in 1896, running every four years thereafter.[128]

In 1898, war between the United States and Spain broke out, the Spanish-American War.

> For the preceding years Cuba had fought for independence from Spain. The United States wanted to rid their whole area of European colonial influence, hence their sympathies lay with the Cubans, and when an American warship was sunk in Havana harbour mysteriously, America decided to intervene in the fighting between Cuba and Spain. Victory for the US resulted in Cuba's independence, and Spain ceded its rights to Guam and Puerto Rico over to the US, which was also then granted the rights to purchase the Philippines from Spain, which it did in 1899.

Chapter 9. The Twentieth Century

CE 1900–1999

CE 1900–1938

Indian Nationalism, Mahatma Gandhi and Growing Resistance to the British Raj, The Boxer Rebellion, Mao Zedong and the Chinese Civil War, Union of South Africa Formed, Southern and Northern Rhodesia Become Colonies Under British Rule, British and Indian settlers Arrive in Kenya, Belgian Congo Established, Continued French Colonisation of North and West Africa, Britain Recognises Egypt as an Independent State, Panama Canal Opened, Kingdom of Saudi Arabia Established, Russo-Japanese War, Albert Einstein and The Theory of Relativity, The Mexican Revolution, Scott and Amundsen's Race to the South Pole, Sinking of the Titanic, The First and Second Balkan Wars, Assassination of Franz Ferdinand and World War One, Marie Curie, End of the Ottoman Empire, The Russian Revolution, Rasputin, Lenin, Trotsky, Stalin, The USSR, Switzerland Becomes a Federal State, The 1918 Influenza Pandemic / Spanish Flu, The League of Nations, The Irish Independence War and The Irish Civil War, The Rif or Moroccan War, Spanish Civil War, Prohibition, Hollywood, Mount Etna, Vatican City Becomes a Sovereign State, The Great Depression, First Football World Cup, Communist Party Formed in Vietnam, New Zealand Offers State Housing and Pensions, Al Capone, Second Italo-Ethiopian War, Emperor Haile Selassie, Weimar Republic in Germany, Adolf Hitler named Chancellor of Germany, Third Reich Established, Germany Invades Poland

In India many Indian businesses started supporting the Indian National Congress financially as they resisted British taxes imposed on them. Between 1858 and 1909, after the Indian Sepoy Mutiny, the British rule over India, also known as the British Raj (in Hindi language Raj means to rule), had become increasingly centralised, and private clubs and military cantonments became a way of life for the British. [129]

165

Further resistance to the pace of development grew as periodic famines occurred. With the expansion of the railways throughout the country, many rural Indian farmers had moved from subsistence farming of grain and food products to the commercial production of cotton and other raw material exports required for the world economy. In the good years this reaped rewards, but in the poor years rural areas were left short of food products. Added to this, by 1921, the population of India had reached over 300 million.

Thus, the seeds of nationalism were sown as discontent grew and support rose for the Indian National Congress and the Muslim League, which had been formed in 1906. Terrorism in Bengal increased dramatically between 1910 and 1912 and Britain moved its capital in India from Calcutta to Delhi.

In 1914 WWI overtook all other events with extensive support provided to Britain by India. The National Congress assumed that its support of Britain in its hour of need would be repaid after the war with political concessions. After the war an economic and political depression hit India as the British returned to life as normal, much to the dismay of the Indians who expected change. Over one million Indian soldiers who returned found themselves no longer treated as deserving soldiers but again as inferior workers.

In 1919 the Rowlatt Acts imposed repressive and autocratic rules on India and a young Barrister, Mahatma Gandhi, who had recently returned from South Africa, and was seen as a rising leader of the Congress Party, called on peaceful disobedience against the Acts. Friction flared up in various areas and in 1919 over 10,000 people gathered in a square /

garden in Jallianwala Bagh. With gatherings banned by the Acts, the British fired into the crowd, causing stampedes. Over 400 people were killed in what became known as the Jallianwala Bagh Massacre.

By now Gandhi was revered as both a spiritual and political leader and support for his philosophy of peaceful disobedience grew into mass boycotts of British-made goods.

Gandhi also tried to create bonds between the Indian Hindus and Muslims, but this was not successful. From 1920 to the start of WWII increasingly violent conflicts occurred between Indian Hindus and Indian Muslims, as well as the rising movement towards Indian Independence.

In 1922 Gandhi was arrested and sentenced to six years in jail and Motilal Nehru rose through the ranks of the Indian National Congress Party. Gandhi was released after two years and continued to mobilise the population, including against the unpopular Salt Tax in 1930. Also in the 1930s, Motilal Nehru's son, Jawaharlal Nehru, joined Gandhi as a prominent leader of the Congress.

During the years preceding WWII, the Muslim League also grew in strength and so it was that by the time WWII occurred India was at a three-way splitting point between Britain and the Indian Hindus and Muslims.

Although it started in November 1899, it was during 1900 and 1901 that the Boxer Rebellion in China occurred. An organisation known as the Society of the Righteous and Harmonious Fists[130] led the uprising, known as Boxers by Westerners due to their fighting skills. Many of the rebels originated from poor areas such as Shandong province and they were upset with the numerous economic and land concessions the Chinese had given to the Westerners and Japanese after the previous century's Opium Wars and Sino-Japanese War. By 1900 the uprising had spread to Beijing, leading Empress Cixi to declare war on foreigners. All Western and Japanese foreigners were under siege in their Beijing quarters and the foreign country powers combined to send a 20,000-strong military force to their aid.

In September 1901 the Boxer Protocol was signed which brought an end to the rebellion and China had to pay millions in compensation and were banned from importing arms for two years. All this severely weakened the Qing Dynasty which had been in place since 1644.

In 1911 the Wuchang Uprising began as various groups rose up against Qing rule. Led by Sun Yat-sen, a revolutionary alliance was formed and eventually this came to be known as the Xinhai Revolution. Sun Yat-sen set up a provisional government in Nanjing under the Nationalist Party. One of the Qing Generals, Yuan Shikai, joined up with Sun Yat-sen and this forced the young Qing Emperor Puyi to abdicate his throne.

This was 1912 and the Qing Dynasty came to an end, to be replaced by the Republic of China. Whilst Sun Yat-sen had been elected president of the party in 1911, he had agreed with Yuan that if he overthrew the Emperor, Yuan could become leader. In 1913 Yuan was elected leader of the Republic of China, but soon adopted dictatorial tendencies and did away with many Republican institutions Sun Yat-sen had established. In 1915 Yuan declared himself Emperor but died in 1916 and China descended into areas ruled by warlords. Sun Yat-sen tried to set up a government but lacked a military to support him, and in this environ- ment numerous demonstrations occurred including the May Fourth Movement (a demonstration against Western influences replacing Chinese customs).

Various intellectuals involved in the May Fourth Movement were then involved in the setting up of the new CCP, Chinese Communist Party, with Mao Zedong one of the founding members.

In 1927 the Shanghai Massacre occurred as the new Nationalist Party leader Chiang Kai-shek ordered the execu- tion of Communist Party members and sought to take control away from various warlords. Meanwhile, the Communists had set up the Communist Red Army and from 1927–1937 the Ten Year Chinese Civil War took place between the Nationalist Party (Kuomintang or KMT) and CCP.

This is viewed as the first phase of the Chinese Civil War, with the second phase occurring after WWII, from 1946– 1949 (see 1945–1999). This first phase of the war saw the two parties not only vying for power of China but also saw internal struggles inside the CCP as Mao Zedong fought for its control. In the mid-1930s Mao took control of the party and then in 1939 the hostilities between the CCP and the KMT were put on hold as China faced the Japanese invasion of WWII and the Second Sino-Japanese War.

In Africa, further colonial developments were occurring at pace:

In 1900 the Second Boer War was in full force having erupted in 1899 as the British sought to bring the two Boer Republics of Transvaal and Orange Free State under their control in a united South Africa. The Boers were originally Dutch settlers but were now South African born and considered South Africa their only home.

After initial successes for the Boers, the British sent out more reinforcements under Lord Kitchener and pushed the Boers back. The Boers, under commanders including Jan Smuts, began counter-attacking through guerrilla warfare, resulting in the British employing a scorched earth policy including herding captured Boers into concentration camps, with a reported 20,000 dying in these camps.

The war ended in 1902 with the Treaty of Vereeniging and, whilst the British had won, they then offered, and granted, limited self-governance to the Afrikaners in 1906 and 1907 and formed the Union of South Africa in 1910.

In 1912 the South African National Congress was formed which later changed into the African National Congress (ANC) as Black Africans sought more representation. The White-run government of the Union of South Africa passed laws in 1913 and 1936 banning Black South Africans from owning land. Over the next four decades the foundations for racial segregation were set as the union's economy grew strongly on the back of mining (gold and diamonds) and agriculture, interrupted only by South Africa's support of Britain in both WWI and WWII.

Meanwhile, north of South Africa, Rhodesia continued to be governed by the British South Africa Company, belonging to Cecil John Rhodes. Rhodes died in 1902 and in 1922 the White settlers of Rhodesia voted to become a colony governed by the British Empire rather than part of the Union of South Africa, and in 1923 the colony of Southern Rhodesia was formed (present-day Zimbabwe).

Further north, Northern Rhodesia (present-day Zambia) moved from being a protectorate governed by the British South Africa Company into also being governed by the British government in 1924.

In Kenya the British-built railway was complete by 1901 and the British arrived in greater numbers settling on the agricultural land.

Indians also arrived in large numbers in the cities and formed a middle class.

In 1921 the East Africa Association was formed to represent local Kenyans' rights, which became the Kikuyu Central Association in 1924.[131]

In the Congo Free State the regime that had been put in place by King Leopold and his investors was so brutal that pressure was exerted on the Belgian King by Britain, and in 1908 he had to abolish the Congo as his personal possession and hand it over to the Belgian government. The Belgian Congo was born in 1908.

In this pre-WWI period, Germany also played a prominent role in colonial Africa having annexed or taken control of South-West Africa (Namibia), Cameroon, Togo, Tanganyika (Tanzania), Rwanda and Burundi. They developed a ruthless reputation in dealing with any uprisings, especially with the Herero uprising in South-West Africa where 60,000 people were killed[132], and the Maji Maji Rebellion in Tanganyika. Colonial administrative structures were set up with a Governor heading up each country and Germany was still in the process of setting up these structures when WW1 occurred. The loss of WWI by Germany resulted in Germany forfeiting all of its colonies to Britain, Belgium and France.

By 1900 in French Africa, Algiers had been incorporated into France as French Algeria, and France had established the French protectorate of Tunisia and followed this up by establishing another protectorate, Morocco, in 1912. By the early 20th century, in looking to broaden and increase her economic interests, France also held large areas in the west of Africa including Benin, Burkino Faso, Guinea, Ivory Coast, Mali, Niger and Senegal.

In America in 1902 the US Congress approved the purchase of the assets belonging to the failed French attempt to build the Panama Canal.

Panama was, at the time, part of Columbia who refused to ratify the sale. The US backed Panama and their rebels to fight successfully for independence from Columbia, which it gained in 1903. Over 375 million dollars later, the canal was completed and opened in 1914, with an estimated 25,000 lives lost over the 30 years it had taken, including the failed French attempt from 1881 and 1889. Interestingly, Gustave Eiffel, the designer of the Eiffel Tower, had been called in to consult on the lock system during the French attempt. The Panama Canal is over 80 kilometres long and saves ships from having to travel over 15,000km south around the dangerous Cape Horn, the southernmost point of South America.[133]

Also in 1902, Abdulaziz, the heir to the Al Saud family who had retreated to Kuwait after the Ottomans had taken control of Riyadh in 1865, returned with a small force of just 40 followers and took control of the garrison that protected Riyadh, and so re-established the Saudi State and marked the beginning the modern Saudi State.

> In 1932 it was officially named the Kingdom of Saudi Arabia. The House of Saud is the term given to the Royal family who established and rule this kingdom.

Between 1904 and 1905 Russia and Japan fought a brutal territorial war, the Russo-Japanese War. Japan decisively won the war which was seen as a precursor to WWI as major world powers flexed their muscles and tried to position themselves, fighting over key ports and territory.

In 1905 Albert Einstein had four papers published in a highly respected Physics journal, one of which outlined his Special Theory of Relativity. He followed this up in 1916 with his paper on the General Theory of Relativity. This theory outlined the inadequacies of Newton's theory of mechanics and redefined gravity as being a warping of space rather than just a force that attracts one object to a larger mass.[134] [135] [136]

> Born in Germany in 1879, Einstein trained as a teacher of Physics and Mathematics in Switzerland and then gained his doctorate before moving to Prague to become professor of Theoretical Physics. He returned to Germany from 1914 to 1933, and then renounced his citizenship upon disagreeing with the political direction in which Germany was moving, and emigrated to America.

From 1910 through until 1917 (officially), but with continued fighting until the 1920s, Mexico experienced a revolution during which power changed hands numerous times. The revolution started under President Diaz Mori who tried to implement infrastructural reforms but at the expense of the rural class who had their land taken away, with much of it allocated to foreign interests. As the country revolted against these injustices Diaz was overthrown, and the next president, Francesco Madero, was quickly replaced when he didn't implement the promised land reforms. After another president (Huerta) also failed to unite the country, eventually President Carranza came to power in 1914 and in 1917 the Constitution of Mexico was signed.

> Personalities that emerged from the war included Pancho Villa, Pascual Orozco and Emiliano Zapata who were all revolutionary army leaders who fought against the political establishment.

In 1911 Norwegian Roald Amundsen became the first person to reach the South Pole, beating Robert Falcon Scott of Britain. Scott and his team of five all died on the return journey having eventually reached the Pole just a month after Amundsen.

> There was some controversy concerning the "race to the pole" in that Scott was not even aware that Amundsen was also trying to reach the South Pole. Amundsen had originally intended to be the first person to reach the North Pole, but on hearing that Americans Cook and Peary had already done so in 1909, he instead set sail for the South Pole.[137]

> All of Scott's team perished during the return journey including Captain Lawrence Oates whose last words before exiting

his tent to die in a blizzard were: "I am just going outside and may be some time", and Scott himself whose last camp was just 11 miles from the depot containing fuel and food.

In 1912 the Titanic sunk after striking an iceberg in the North Atlantic on her first ever voyage, en route from Southampton to New York. More than 1500 died including Captain Edward Smith, of a total crew and passenger list of 2,224.

Whilst the previous century saw the decline of the Ottoman Empire, this century saw its end. In 1912 the First Balkan War began when Greece and Serbia declared war on the Ottomans. Earlier the Austrian-Hungarian Empire had annexed Bosnia and Herzegovina which antagonised both Serbia and Russia who felt threatened by their independence. Bulgaria also then pushed for independence and – encouraged by the Russians – Greece, Serbia, Bulgaria and Montenegro formed an alliance taking control of Ottoman territories. The Ottoman Turks were driven back, no longer holding territory in South-East Europe. The major European powers convened a congress in London to try and bring back control to the region and reset national boundaries. A very short-lived month of peace returned to the area in 1913 when an agreement split Macedonia between the four countries. This was, however, done at Bulgaria's ire who felt cheated, and a month after the war ended Bulgaria turned on Greece and Serbia starting the Second Balkan War. Bulgaria was defeated and Bulgaria lost more of the Macedonian territory it had just been granted. Tensions continued to simmer, with Austria-Hungary wary of Russian Serbian Slavic influence, a concern shared by the Germans.[138]

The whole of Europe was now in a state of tension.

WWI

In the 19th century Franz Joseph had created the Austro-Hungarian Empire and was King of Hungary and Emperor of Austria simultaneously. When his own son Archduke Rudolf committed suicide in 1889, and his brother Archduke Charles Louis died in 1896, Joseph's nephew Franz Ferdinand became the next in line to succeed the Austro-Hungarian throne.

Whilst Frans Joseph was still alive he held the throne, but Ferdinand's powers grew in both foreign affairs and the military and in 1913 he became Inspector General of the army. In June 1914, accompanied by his wife Sophie, he arrived in Bosnia Herzegovina to inspect the army amidst the turbulent times of the Balkan Wars where Serbia wanted to take control of Bosnia.

Whilst travelling in a motorcade through Sarajevo, Bosnia, a Serbian nationalist, Nedjelko Cabrinov, attempted to murder the couple by throwing a grenade at the car. It missed but injured some of Ferdinand's officers. After continuing to complete their official business that day, Ferdinand and his wife then insisted on visiting the injured officers in hospital. On the way to the hospital their motorcade driver accidentally took them back via the same route where the morning's assassination attempt had occurred, the area where the Serbian nationalists were predominant. There, a 19-year-old, Gavrilo Princip, a compatriot of Cabrinov, saw his opportunity and stepped forward and shot both Ferdinand and Sophie. Sophie died on the way to the hospital and Ferdinand died at the hospital. Cabrinov and Princip were both jailed and both died in prison of tuberculosis, Cabrinov in 1916 and Princip in 1918.[139]

Anti-Serbian rioting broke out throughout the Austro-Hungarian Empire and in July 1914 Austria-Hungary declared war on Serbia. Austria-Hungary's allies were Germany and Italy, whilst Serbia's allies were Russia, France and Britain. Russia stepped forward to defend Serbia, Germany declared war on Russia, France declared war on Germany, who invaded Belgium, and Britain declared war on Germany.

World War I had started.

In the West, having invaded Belgium, Germany then attacked France too. In the south, Austria-Hungary fought Serbia whilst in the east, Germany were attacked by the Russians. One of the first major battles was the battle of the Marne in the West. After they invaded Belgium, Germany advanced to within 30 miles of Paris before meeting the combined forces of the French and British Expeditionary Force. These Allied forces held back the Germans preventing any early victory on the Western Front.

On this Western Front, the remainder of this war became a brutal fight along a long line of trenches, from the French–Belgian border across to the French–Swiss border and in 1916 a decisive battle occurred on the banks of the Somme River in northern France. In the Battle of the Somme over 3 million men fought and one million died, one of the deadliest battles in human history. The battle ended with the British and French significantly pushing the Germans back into their territory.

Over to the East, much of the war occurred against the Turkish Ottomans. In 1915 the British and French attacked a strategically important strait in Turkey called the Dardanelles but did not succeed in taking the strait. They re-attacked it later, combined with a ground invasion of Gallipoli. A fierce resistance was put up by the Turks and the Allied campaign, strongly supported by Australian and New Zealand (ANZAC) troops, again failed. There were approximately half a million casualties on both sides and Winston Churchill had to resign his position within the admiralty.[140]

During 1916 and 1917 the war was dominated by the trench warfare so well known now as being the way in which WWI was conducted. Millions of lives were lost on both sides as a result and the war entered a stalemate until, in 1917, America was pulled in as a result of attacks on American warships in the Atlantic, and the 1917 Russian Revolution caused Russia to pull out of the war.

By the time 1918 arrived the troops of Germany and Austria-Hungary were heavily demoralised, and mutinies were occurring, until on 11 November 1918 Germany agreed to sign an armistice. The war, in which 65 million men had fought, was finally over. Austria-Hungary was broken up into various countries and in the Treaty of Versailles Germany had heavy economic penalties, and restrictions on developing their military, levied upon it. From these extremely harsh penalties on Germany grew the seeds of resentment that eventually partially caused the rise of the Nazi Party.

It was during WWI that Marie Curie devoted much of her work and time to alleviate the suffering of wounded through the use of radium. A brilliant scientist, Marie had replaced her husband, after his death (he died when he fell under a horse drawn carriage), as Professor of General Physics at the

Sorbonne in Paris, the first woman to do so. Marie and her husband managed to isolate polonium and radium, going on to then discover radium's therapeutic qualities. During her life Marie won the Nobel prize twice, once shared with her husband for Physics, and once for Chemistry.

The Ottomans had entered WWI on the side of Germany and Austria-Hungary, and so they were also defeated in 1918 with any final territories divided between Britain, France, Greece and Russia. In 1922 the title of Ottoman Sultan was done away with, and the Ottoman Empire was officially ended, 600 years after its formation.

In 1923 Turkey was declared a republic and went through a period of rapid westernisation through until 1938.

In 1917, and whilst war was raging across Europe, the Russian Revolution occurred.

Public protests started in Petrograd in 1917 (St Petersburg had been renamed Petrograd in 1914 to make it sound less German due to Russia and Germany being on opposing sides during WWI). These protests led to the abdication of Tsar Nicholas II. These events had not occurred in isolation, however.

Earlier in the century from 1905 to 1907, in a country weakened after the Russo-Japanese War, with a people much poorer than those in neighbouring Europe, a failed revolution had occurred. In 1905 troops shot and killed 1000 peaceful demonstrators at the Winter Palace in St Petersburg, and sailors mutinied on a Russian battleship which then led to further demonstrations at the port of Odessa which were again brought under control by a strong response from the army. With public opinion moving against him the Tsar issued a manifesto promising increased civil rights, decreased power for the monarchy and the establishment of a parliament, the Duma.

WWI did not serve Russia well as she was militarily weaker than Germany and whilst Tsar Nicholas II was away at war his wife Tsarina Alexandra began firing many officials on the advice of her adviser Grigori Rasputin.[141] Rasputin was a self-proclaimed holy man who had become so after a religious experience at a monastery. A colourful character, Rasputin became a society figure in St Petersburg with his reputation as a mystic and a prophet. He met and befriended the Tsar and his wife and acted as a healer to their haemophiliac son Alexei.

Interestingly Aspirin had been recently discovered and was likely being prescribed by doctors to the Tsar's son Alexei as it was not known then that Aspirin was also a blood thinner. When Rasputin took over the role of healer of Alexei, he refused to let the boy take any normal medicine. By taking Alexei off Aspirin, Rasputin unknowingly took away the drug that may have been exacerbating Alexei's condition, leading the Tsar and his wife to believe Rasputin really did have healing powers.

Rasputin also became famous for his numerous affairs, to the knowledge and acceptance of his wife to whom he remained married (they had three daughters) and whom he continued to support.

All in all, Rasputin soon became a divisive figure within Russian society with many nobles increasingly agitated at his influence. His reputation also had a detrimental effect on the reputation of the monarchy among the general public.

In 1916, hoping to reinstate the reputation of the monarchy and his own family's influence over the Tsar, Prince Felix Yussupov invited Rasputin to dinner. Yussupov later claimed that he poisoned cookies with cyanide which apparently had no effect on Rasputin, who he then shot. This too did not kill him immediately and so the Prince and his conspirators had to finish off the "Mad Monk", as he was known, by drowning him. However, one of Rasputin's daughters disputed this story and claimed her father did not like sweet food so would not have eaten the cyanide-laced cakes, and his autopsy revealed he was probably just shot in the head at close range.[142]

With the stage set for a revolution in 1917, the Petrograd demonstrators took to the streets leading to the Tsar's abdication, and a provisional government was put in place. This was known as the February Revolution. However, this new government continued with Russia's involvement in WWI, a very unpopular decision with the public. Food riots occurred as food shortages occurred until later in 1917, a second revolution occurred.

The Bolshevik Party, led by Vladimir Lenin, launched a coup against the new provisional government in what became known as the October Revolution. Lenin's Bolsheviks (Bolshevik meaning "One of the Majority") were members of the Russian Social-Democratic Workers Party who were opposed to the fact that the new provisional government were still members of the bourgeois ruling class.

Lenin's party took over and the world's first communist state came into existence, with the capital moved to
Moscow, and Russia then withdrew from WWI.

However, a Russian civil war then occurred with Lenin's
Red Army pitted against the White Army representing the
monarchists and capitalists.

In 1918 the Tsars and his family, the Romanovs, were
moved to Yekaterinburg, where they were executed. The
monarchy was dead. Lenin survived an assassination
attempt in 1918, and a series of mass uprisings and arrests
followed, known as the Red Terror. The Civil War continued until December 1922 when the new state, the Soviet
Union, was formed.

In 1922 a treaty between Russia, Ukraine, Belarus, and
what today are known as Georgia, Armenia and Azerbaijan
created the USSR, the Union of Soviet Socialist Republics.
It was controlled by the Communist Party and Lenin
remained as leader of the party, and Joseph Stalin was
appointed the General Secretary.

Lenin died in 1924 and Stalin took over as party leader
succeeding his main rival, Leon Trotsky.

Trotsky had been one of the key figures in the revolution.
As a Marxist, Trotsky had been arrested for revolutionary
activities in 1898, exiled to Siberia, and then escaped to
London where he became friends with Lenin. He helped
organise the 1905 Revolution where he was again arrested
and sent to Siberia, before again escaping. After the 1917
Revolution, Trotsky returned to Russia and became part
of the Bolsheviks. After Stalin came to power, Trotsky

became a strong critic of Stalin and again went into exile and was eventually assassinated in 1940 in Mexico by a member of one of the USSR's interior ministries.

Over the next ten years Stalin aimed to modernise the new Soviet Union into an industrialised nation. He did this through force, with heavy government control of the economy which initiated a collective agriculture scheme. Any dissent was harshly dealt with, and millions died or were sent to forced labour camps, the Gulags. This was known as The Great Purge. Famines were common as collective agriculture did not work efficiently, and millions more died across the USSR from hunger.[143]

In the UK in 1918 women won the right to vote. This was passed through the Representation of the People Act 1918 which allowed women over the age of 30, with other qualifying classifications such as property ownership, the right to vote. This had followed the Suffragette Movement in the UK which had been formed by Emmeline Pankhurst. The activities of the Suffragettes included various protests. The most famous of these protests occurred in 1923 when Emily Davison tried to attach a flag to the King's horse in the Epsom Derby. The horse ran over Davison and four days later she died of her injuries. The press at the time reported she had thrown herself under the King's horse in protest, but later analysis led to the conclusion that she was not trying to kill herself but rather stage a publicity protest.

In 1918 Switzerland moved towards proportional representation. It had become a federal state in 1848 (see 1800–1900) and human rights and the rule of law were established. However, Switzerland had a majority system whereby the winner had to win more than all the opposition together (i.e.

50.01%), so when a winner came to power they would wield a strong majority of more than 50%, but that could also mean that 49% of the electorate remained without their views being represented. In 1918 Switzerland voted to move to a representative system, whereby each group of voters is represented proportionally in government.

Also in 1918, the 1918 Influenza pandemic broke out, often incorrectly referred to as the Spanish Flu. Censorship after WWI caused there to be a distinct lack of reporting across most of Europe, but in Spain, which had largely remained out of WWI, it was strongly reported, leading many to believe it originated there. The flu spread quickly across Europe which was just coming to the end of WWI and over the next two years it is estimated that the flu caused between 20 and 50 million deaths.

In 1919, in the aftermath of WWI, and after the bilateral agreements and armistices had been signed that had ended the war, the Treaty of Versailles was signed, at the Palace of Versailles, by the Allied Powers, namely France, Britain, the US and Italy and Germany, although over 32 countries signed the actual Treaty.[144]

Included in the Treaty was the Covenant of the League of Nations. This Covenant laid out the conditions for joining the League of Nations, the appointment of a Secretary-General, the establishment of its secretariat in Geneva and the budget allocated to it, as well as its remit, which included disarmament, and social and political objectives for member nations. The idea was to promote cooperation and communication between the member nations and to move away from force (war) as a means for member nations to realise objectives.

The League of Nations officially started in January 1920 with 41 original member nations meeting in Geneva.[145]

In 1919 in Egypt (which the British, worried about their investments including the Suez Canal, had invaded and occupied since 1882), anti-British riots broke out leading to Britain recognising Egypt as an independent state in 1922. However, Britain remained heavily involved, controlling the communications and legal systems and granting the King of Egypt, Fuad, and then his son, Farouk, only limited powers.

Between 1919 and 1921 the Irish fought the Irish War of Independence. In 1918 the Irish Sinn Fein party had won the election and gone on to declare an Irish Republic. Ireland had been ruled by London since the union with Ireland in 1801 when the United Kingdom of Great Britain and Ireland had been formed. In 1916 a pro-independence Easter Rising had been quashed by British forces, leading to two years of tensions and riots until Sinn Fein won the 1918 general election. However, in the north of the country, in Ulster, the vote had gone against Sinn Fein as the people there were mostly pro-British.

After the election the war between the British state and the Irish Republican Army started. The war peaked in 1920 and on Bloody Sunday 14 Irish civilians were killed at a football match in Dublin's Croke Park after the earlier killing of British intelligence officers.

In July 1921 a truce was negotiated between the British and the Irish Republican forces with Michael Collins leading the Irish delegation to create a new Irish free state, but agreeing to dissolve the previously established Irish Republic. In this Anglo-Irish treaty, most of Ireland became part of this Irish free state but the northeast pro-British counties remained within the United Kingdom as Northern Ireland.

Fighting, however, continued in the north of the country between northern Protestant pro-British Loyalists and the southern Irish Catholic Republicans and from 1922–1923 the country was at civil war. The main point of disagreement was whether or not the country should accept the Anglo-Irish Treaty that Michael Collins had agreed with the British. The pro-Irish wanted Ireland to be a totally free republic not just have an Irish free state.

In 1923 the Party who were for the Anglo-Irish Treaty, known as Cumman na nGaedheal won an election and by March 1924 the war was ended.[146]

However, the legacy of these two wars was a highly polarised country, British northern and Irish southern.

In 1921 the Rif War, or Moroccan War, between Spain and Morocco, occurred. Having lost her colonial possessions during the previous century, Spain was keen to try and re-establish herself as a colonial power, in part due to her need to increase resources when faced with an ever-increasing population.

In 1912 in a French Spanish Treaty, Spain was granted a protectorate along the Moroccan Mediterranean coast. However, the area granted them was a mountainous area inhabited by various Berber peoples known as the Rif who were strongly opposed to being governed by Spain.

From 1921–1926 the Rif War, or Moroccan War, broke out. The war began with a calamitous defeat of the Spanish by the Rif when up to 10,000 Spanish were massacred at Annual and Spain lost much of her new territory, as well as some lands she already held.

in 1923, with the problems associated with the Moroccan War, an ever-increasing population, and further political problems causing outbreaks of social unrest, General Primo de Rivera staged a coup d'etat and Spain came under military control. The General then tried to put in place a single-party state and negotiate with the trade unions but failed, and following the financial depression of the 1930s, he was forced to resign. In 1930 a military uprising in favour of a republic took place and in 1931 the Second Republic was formed and the King, Alfonso XIII, went into exile.

A new constitution was formed, also in 1931, and over the next two years, democratic, decentralised reforms took place. However, a swing back to the right then occurred and by 1936 the military again staged an uprising. The military rebels were the Nationalists and the Government in place were the Republicans.

In 1936 the Spanish Civil War started. Francisco Franco, head of the Nationalist rebels, took control of the army in Morocco and Nationalist troops controlled vast swathes of the country including Andalusia, Toledo, San Sebastien and Navarre, whilst the Republican strongholds included Madrid, Catalonia, Valencia and Bilbao. The Republicans then moved the cabinet to Valencia, and the Nationalists appointed Franco head of government and commander of the army.

In 1937 the war intensified, and international help arrived for both sides. By 1939 the Nationalists had taken control of the remaining Republican strongholds and Republicans went into exile. Franco's dictatorship was established, and during WWII, whilst supposedly neutral, Spain became isolated from the outside world.

From 1920 -1933 the Prohibition Era started in the US with the banning of the sale and transport of alcohol. This led to the illegal underground production and sale of alcohol known as bootlegging in illegal drinking clubs known as speakeasies. Support for the law fell as illegal activities and gang-related crimes increased and in 1933 the amendment was repealed.

During the 1920s Blues and Jazz became popular in Western societies, especially the United States, where Country Music also started becoming popular. Hollywood developed as the centre for film making in America, and in 1927 the first full-length feature film with sound, *The Jazz Singer* was released and in 1929 the Academy Awards began. The story goes that in 1931 the Academy Awards librarian claimed the Academy Awards statuette looked like her uncle Oscar, and the name took off and the statues have been called Oscars to the present day.

In 1928 Mount Etna, the Sicilian volcano, erupted in one of her most famous and largest eruptions, destroying the village of Mascali. Etna is one of the most active volcanoes in the world, even today, but few eruptions were as large as this 1928 one.

In 1929 the Vatican City was established as its own sovereign state. Popes had previously controlled territories known as Papal States but land disputes arose in 1870 with the Italian government taking control of all land. In 1929 the Lateran Treaties were signed between Pope Pius XI and the Italian Prime Minister Benito Mussolini that granted sovereign status to the Vatican City. It is the world's smallest sovereign state at just over 100 acres and is home to the Pope and approximately 700 citizens, including the Swiss Guard, the Pope's security detail since 1506.

From 1929, and throughout the 1930s, The Great Depression occurred in the US and spread to Europe. In the US, the depression included a stock market crash and bank panics as bank account holders lined up to withdraw cash.

Prior to 1929, from 1920, the US economy had expanded rapidly, doubling in size, hence the term the Roaring Twenties. Wall Street, the home of the US stock market, had seen incredible sums invested into it, from seasoned investors through to all members of the public, causing a speculative bubble that peaked in August 1929.

However, by this stage the economy had started to slow down, unemployment had risen, and stock valuations were too high. By October 1929, a stock sell-off started on Thursday 24 October, Black Thursday, through to the following Tuesday, Black Tuesday. The crash was well and truly on, and as the stock market woes spread to businesses and manufacturing, unemployment rose further, and earnings fell. Inevitably consumers began missing credit payments and home and goods repossessions rose.

Over the next four years consumer runs on banks occurred and thousands of banks closed. FD Roosevelt, who had won the 1932 election and took over office from the incumbent Herbert Hoover, tried to restore confidence through evening radio broadcasts known as fireside chats and made his famous "there is nothing to fear but fear itself" speech. Additionally, during his tenure, the Securities and

Exchange Commission (SEC) and the Federal Deposit Insurance Corporation were created, along with the "New Deal" infrastructure projects and the Social Security Act providing, for the first time, Americans with unemployment, retirement and disability benefits.[147]

Whilst growth did then occur from 1934 to 1937, economic contractions then occurred again, and the continued effects of the depression were felt in both the US and Europe through to the end of the decade.

In 1930 the first ever Football World Cup was held. Prior to this football was played at the Olympics but as football became professional, it no longer fit with the Olympic ethos, and in 1928 the governing body, FIFA, decided it would host a standalone event, the World Cup.

The first event was held in Uruguay in 1930 and was won by Uruguay, with 13 nations taking part. It has been held every four years to this day, with the exception of 1942 and 1946 due to WWII.

In 1930 in Vietnam, the Communist Party of Vietnam was formed, headed by President Ho Chi Minh who rebelled against the French colonialists with different factions finding support coming from different countries, all with their own designs on the region. The country remained a semi-feudal colony, but the new Communist Party resisted colonial control and in 1945 successfully seized power and the Democratic Republic of Vietnam was formed.

New Zealand in the 20th century, became the first country in the world to offer state pensions and then, in the 1930s, state housing to its workers.

In 1931 Al Capone, at age 33, was convicted of tax evasion and sentenced to 11 years in Federal Prison. He was released eight years later and died of a heart attack in 1947.

Also known as Scarface, his full name was Alphonse Gabriel Capone. Capone was a businessman and gangster who gained fame during Prohibition as boss of the Chicago Outfit that he co-founded. The Outfit, or Chicago Mafia, was an organised crime syndicate run by Capone and Johnny Torrio (the other co-founder) that fought for control of the illegal distribution of alcohol, and was also involved in other activities including prostitution, loan-sharking, gambling and extortion. Capone's Outfit forced venues to buy alcohol from them, and if they did not, they were bombed. Hundreds of people died in these bombings and similar numbers of gangsters were murdered. Unable to convict him of these illegal activities, the authorities eventually jailed Capone on the tax evasion charges.

Ethiopia enjoyed relative stability after the First Italo-Ethiopian War of 1895–1896 through until 1935 when the Second Italo-Ethiopian War broke out, known in Ethiopia as the Italian Invasion. Italy moved into Ethiopia from neighbouring Eritrea which Italy already controlled.

Benito Mussolini, Italy's Prime Minister, was pushing towards expanding his colonial empire as the other European nations were already doing.

The invasion forced the Ethiopian Emperor Haile Selassie into exile and by 1936 Italy claimed Ethiopia as a colonial possession and united Ethiopia (also called Abyssinia) with Italian Somaliland and Eritrea.

The defeat of Ethiopia and the exile of Haile Selassie is considered a step towards WWII as the League of Nations was seen as incapable of acting against the wishes of individual states such as Italy. The League of Nations had condemned Italy's act of aggression but were ignored and Selassie in exile spoke out against the invasion at the League of Nations, but nothing came of this either.

In January 1933 Adolf Hitler was named Chancellor of Germany after his Nazi Party had become the largest party in parliament in 1932. This all occurred after continued discontent in Germany after WWI.

It was not just Haile Selassie who was unhappy with the League of Nations. Germany was left furious by what they felt were the extremely harsh terms imposed on it after WWI. Further, Germany felt that the reasons for WWI had not been resolved and that the Western powers had been imposing their beliefs and territorial ambitions on others.

The Treaty of Versailles not only side-lined these concerns, but they placed full blame for the war on Germany itself. Prominent economist John Maynard Keynes predicted the German economy would collapse if it was forced to pay off the near USD$33 billion levied on it in the treaty.[148]

After WWI, Germany experienced immediate political change. Kaiser Wilhelm II abdicated in 1918 and in 1919 a coalition was formed in Weimar – and the new government became known as the Weimar Republic. It was this government that signed for and agreed to the conditions imposed on it by the League of Nations.

Under the treaty conditions, besides the payment Germany had to make, Germany was forced to demilitarise, limit the size of her navy, and was disallowed an air force. With the huge financial burdens imposed, Germany found itself unable to create revenues through generating coal and iron ore, and it defaulted on its debts. France and Belgium then breached the League of Nations by occupying part of Germany in order to take coal and iron ore in lieu of payments due. German industrial strikes followed, and the economy began to collapse.

In response the Weimar Republic printed more money and between 1921 and 1923 hyperinflation occurred, with the German Mark falling from 320 Marks to the US Dollar in 1922 to a rate of 4,210,500,000,000 to the US Dollar during 1923. [149] In August 1923 the Mark was replaced by the Retenmark.

The League of Nations then asked a US banker Charles Dawes to help reconstruct the payment plan the Weimar Republic had to pay. Dawes received the Nobel Peace prize for the plan he put together which did stabilise the German economy for a while, but with the Great Depression this stability was short lived. American investment flowing into Germany dried up and Germany saw the return of increased failed businesses and unemployment. [150]

The German public were now tired and distrustful of their current leadership and turned to more extremist leaders, and so in 1932 the Nazi (the Nationalist Socialist German Workers) Party won the most votes of any party in the German Reichstag (Parliament), and in the coalition that was then formed, the President of Germany elected Hitler to be Chancellor.

Hitler, born in Austria, had served Germany in WWI. In 1919 he joined the German Workers Party – which later became the Nazi Party – and became its leader in 1921. In 1923 he staged a failed coup to take control of government in a Munich Beer Hall, and was sentenced to jail where he wrote *Mein Kampf* (My Struggle). He was released from jail early in 1924 and from then until he gained power, he attacked the Treaty of Versailles and grew his support base, based on antisemitism, anticommunism and German Nationalism.

Once in power, Hitler and the Nazi Party lost no time in pushing through laws to suppress communism and civil rights, and pass laws without having to first seek approval from the president or government. In 1934, when the President of Germany died, Hitler merged the offices of President and Chancellor into one office and in a subsequent referendum was confirmed as sole leader of Germany: the Fuhrer. In short, he soon established a dictatorship under the Nazi State, officially called the Third Reich. This Third Reich implied that the German State was the successor to the Roman Empire (that ruled the area until 1806), and the German Empire which had ruled until its defeat in WWI. In the short term this Third Reich enjoyed success as it stabilised the economy and increased employment through its large-scale government spending on the military and public works.

Hitler then embarked on a systematic campaign at home against Jews, who he blamed for Germany's economic woes, as well as Romany groups and foreigners in general. Jews bore the brunt of this with Jewish businesses and Synagogues burned and shut down. People, mainly Jews, but also Romany groups, foreigners and disabled people, were rounded up and sent to concentration camps.

Hitler simultaneously developed an increasingly aggressive foreign policy, first seizing Austria and then part of Czechoslovakia and then signed a non-aggression pact with the Soviet Union and, on 01 September 1939, invaded Poland.

CE 1939–1945, WWII
Poland Invaded. Churchill Became Prime Minister of Britain, Blitzkrieg, Dunkirk, Mussolini, The Battle of Britain, The Blitz, The North Africa Campaign, Pearl Harbour, Guadalcanal, The Battle of Midway, The Battle of the Bulge, Hitler's Suicide, Potsdam Conference, Iwo Jima, Okinawa, The Atomic Bombing of Hiroshima and Nagasaki, The Bretton Woods Agreement, The IMF and World Bank Formed

World War II started two days later, on 03 September 1939, when Britain and France, who had previously guaranteed to support Poland, declared war on Germany.

The Soviet Union then joined the attack on Poland and invaded from the East, and Poland soon fell. The Soviet Union took the East of Poland and Germany the West, and the Soviet Union then also took control of Estonia, Latvia and Lithuania before warring with and defeating Finland in the Russo-Finish War.[151]

In April and May 1940 Germany embarked on blitzkrieg – rapid invasions – of Norway, Denmark, Belgium and the Netherlands before then invading France.

In May 1940 Winston Churchill was voted in as Prime Minister of Britain, replacing Neville Chamberlain whose policy of appeasement with Germany, prior to Germany's invasion of Poland, had not worked.

France fell in six weeks and by late May the Allied troops (Britain and her Allies who opposed Germany) retreated to France's west coast where the British launched the famous rescue in which over 300,000 of the British Expeditionary Force, along with French and Belgian and other Allied soldiers, were rescued from the beach at Dunkirk by over 800 different vessels. France was now split into two, the Vichy government controlled by Germany and the Free France government in exile in London led by Charles de Gaulle.

Hitler and Italy's fascist leader, Benito Mussolini, then agreed an alliance between the two nations. In the Far East, Japan, who saw an opportunity to become the dominant force in Asia, then signed an Axis agreement with Germany and Italy. These three powers became known as the Axis whilst Britain and those who supported her were known as the Allies. At this stage the Allies were Britain, Free France, Belgium, Poland, Norway, Holland, Greece, Yugoslavia and members or ex members of the British Empire including India, Canada, South Africa, Australia, New Zealand and the two Rhodesias, North and South (present day Zambia and Zimbabwe). As the war progressed the Allies grew to include the USA, China and the Soviet Union.

In Europe, with France now fallen, Germany's attention was now on Britain, and Britain was the sole country left able to fight the Germans, who were intent on forcing Britain into signing a peace treaty. The war took to the sea and skies. At sea, the Battle of the Atlantic saw the Royal Navy fighting the German U Boats (submarines), and in the air, the Royal Air Force with their Hurricanes and Spitfires protected Britain from the aerial bombardment, known as the Blitz, of the German Luftwaffe and their Messerschmitts.

Interestingly the idea that carrots aid night vision came about due to a counter-intelligence campaign run by the British to hide the fact that they had developed a new radar system capable of tracking German aircraft at night. To disguise the radar system, the British spread the rumour that their troops were able to spot the aircraft as they were eating extra carrots which increased night vision.

Britain did not capitulate and eventually their air superiority won through, and the Germans were unable to continue with the Blitz. The Battle of Britain was Germany's first defeat in the war and lead to Churchill's famous speech, "Never in the field of human conflict was so much owed by so many to so few".

In Eastern Europe: Hungary, Romania and Bulgaria had joined the Axis powers and Germany invaded Greece and Yugoslavia. Hitler then broke his non-aggression pact with the Soviet Union and in June 1941 Germany, in Operation Barbarossa, invaded the Soviet Union. The Soviet Union, now fully dragged into the war, became one of the major Allies.

In March 1941 America agreed the Lend Lease programme. This was a law that enabled the US to provide supplies to Britain and her Allies, specifically France,

Russia and China, and was considered imperative to the safety of America. Over the course of the war this, through food aid, fuel and military supplies, amounted to USD$50 billion.

In the Far East, Japan were at war with China in the Second Sino-Japanese War. Japan had been present in Manchuria (North-East China) since 1931 following the Russo-Japanese War. They saw Manchuria as a source of the raw materials they needed for their industrial growth. In 1937 fighting broke out between the Japanese and Chinese outside Beijing which soon spread as far south as Shanghai in the three-month Battle of Shanghai and Battle of Nanjing, in which the Japanese conquered. The Battle for Nanjing was notable for the brutal massacre that occurred during the fighting.

Japan then realised that, with Europe and the powers there at war, the only country capable of preventing their ambitions of becoming the predominant power in Asia was the United States. In December 1941 Japan launched a surprise attack on the US Navy in Pearl Harbour, Hawaii, where they hoped to destroy the Navy's power. The following day the US Congress agreed to declare war on Japan and the USA was now also brought into the war as another one of the major Allies.

The Battles of Guadalcanal and Midway ensued. In Guadalcanal in the Solomon Islands in the Pacific, the Japanese tried to establish an airbase and were attacked and defeated by the Allies. In the Battle of Midway, the Japanese Navy and Air Force were defeated by the Americans who were defending their base at Midway island in the North Pacific. The Japanese hoped to take the island and weaken the US presence in the region, but the opposite happened with the Japanese defeated and weakened.

In Africa, WWII was called the North Africa campaign, and started when British troops in Egypt crossed into Libya to fight and defeat the Italians there. The campaign in Africa was headed by Montgomery for the Allies and Rommel for the Germans and came to a head in the Battle of El Alamein in 1942 where the Allies defeated Rommel's army in Tunisia.

1942 proved decisive. The Allies invaded Italy and Mussolini was defeated in July. The fighting against the Germans continued for the remainder of the war but the tide there had turned. In the East in the Battle of Stalingrad, where 2 million people died, the Germans were defeated by the brutality of the weather and resistance of the Soviets and in 1944 the Germans also failed in their almost three-year siege of Leningrad (St Petersburg).

On 06 June 1944, the British, American and Canadian Allies landed in Normandy and began the European invasion. Hitler then concentrated solely on Western Europe and tried to fight off the Allied invasion. This allowed the Soviets in the East to take control of Poland, Hungary, Czechoslovakia and Romania. As the Allies progressed, the running battles with the Germans peaked with the Battle of the Bulge in the Ardennes in Belgium, fought over six brutal winter weeks mainly between the Americans and the Germans. The Allied line against the Germans formed a Bulge – and hence the name of the Battle. The Germans failed in their aim to divide the Allies and a coordinated aerial bombing campaign of Germany followed as the Allies also advanced into Germany.

In May, Soviet forces broke through to Berlin, followed by the other Allies, and on 08 May Germany surrendered. Earlier, on 30 April, Hitler, who had married his long-term girlfriend Eva Braun on 29 April, had committed suicide by first taking cyanide and then shooting himself in the head. Eva Braun also committed suicide by cyanide and prior to the dual suicide Hitler had the cyanide used on his dog Blondi to test how effective it was. Blondi also died.

The Allied Leaders of Winston Churchill (Britain), Harry S. Truman (the US) and Joseph Stalin (the Soviet Union) then met at Potsdam near Berlin. Truman had only been in power for three months as Franklin D. Roosevelt, the previous President, had died whilst in office. At the Potsdam Conference these leaders agreed how Germany would be divided up and administered by the Allies.

In the Far East, however, the war continued, and the US suffered heavy casualties in two huge battles on the islands of Iwo Jima and Okinawa, both near Japan in the Pacific. Fears of larger losses that could be incurred with a land invasion of Japan led Truman to authorise the use of two new nuclear bombs in an operation named the Manhattan Project. From 1939 the US had been researching the significance of nuclear fission in weaponry and those involved had included Albert Einstein. By 1945 over USD$2 billion had been spent on research and in July 1945 the first ever atomic bomb was tested near Albuquerque, New Mexico. The explosion was codenamed "Trinity" and where it landed was christened "Ground Zero", a term that was first used then and has since become the chosen term for the site of a bombing or such event. The explosion was a devastating success.

On 26 July at the Potsdam Conference and after Germany had already surrendered, the three Allied leaders of Truman, Churchill and Stalin issued Japan with an ultimatum, surrender or be destroyed. With no surrender forthcoming two atomic bombs were sent to the Pacific, Fat Man and Little Boy. On the morning of 06 August 1945, the pilot of the plane selected to fly the first bomb, Little Boy, Colonel Tibbets, requested his plane be named Enola Gay, his mother's name, and this was painted on the plane's nose. Hiroshima, the city that housed the head of Japan's second army was the target and Little Boy was dropped at 08.15 am, detonating in the air about 500m above Hiroshima. The temperature immediately after detonation at Hiroshima was 7000 degrees centigrade and 70,000 people were instantly killed and the resultant mushroom cloud reached over 10km into the atmosphere.

After two days with no surrender from Japan, the Soviet Union declared war on Japan and invaded Manchuria and Sakhalin Island. On 09 August, America launched a plane with a second atomic bomb on board; this time it was Fat Man. The original target was a city called Kokura but haze did not allow for a clear view of the city, so Nagasaki was chosen as a target instead and bombed at 11am. 40,000 people were killed instantly this time. The following day Emperor Hirohito let it be known that he thought Japan should surrender and the Japanese government surrendered, accepting the terms of the Potsdam Conference.

With Japan and Germany now both surrendered, the terms of the surrender were agreed and finalised and on 02 September 1945 WWII was officially over.

Some of the major contributors to the war in terms of officials involved included: [152]

Field Marshall Bernard Law Montgomery, a British general, who outwitted Rommel in North Africa and was also involved later in West Europe.

Charles de Gaulle a French officer who was appointed Under Secretary for War during WWII. When Germany invaded, he was exiled to London where he led Free France who declared themselves the legitimate French government. In 1944 he became the head of the Provisional Government of the French Republic.

General George S. Patton, an aggressive American general heavily involved in the war in West Europe.

Marshall Georgy Zhukov, general of the Red Army, involved in both the Battle of Stalingrad and the Siege of Leningrad.

Field Marshall Erwin Rommel, a supremely respected German general, who achieved fame in North Africa. He later was involved in a plan to assassinate Hitler, which failed, and Rommel committed suicide.

General Douglas MacArthur, one of the most important Generals in the War in the East against Japan.

Field Marshall Erich von Manstein, and General Heinz Guderian were two of the pre-eminent generals leading Hitler's plans for the invasion of France and the Blitzkrieg respectively.

It is estimated that 60 million people died in WWII of whom 45 million were civilians and 15 million in battle, with some of the countries sustaining the heaviest casualties being:[153]

Soviet Union	24 million deaths
China	20 million
Germany	8 million
Dutch East Indies	4 million
Japan	3 million
India	2 million
Britain	450,000
USA	420,000

It is thought up to 2.7 million people were killed in concentration / extermination camps alone, with the main 3, all in Poland, being:

Auschwitz-Birkenau	1.1 million deaths
Treblinka	800,000 deaths
Belzec	600,000 deaths

Altogether it is estimated that 6 million Jews were killed in the war, in the Holocaust, Germany's deliberate and targeted extermination of the Jews who Hitler blamed for the economic troubles that Germany had experienced prior to the war.

In 1944, whilst the war was grinding its way to an end in Europe and the Far East, in Bretton Woods, New Hampshire, in the USA, the United Nations Monetary and Financial Conference was held in July.

The result was the Bretton Woods Agreement and System in which it was agreed that Gold would be the basis for the US Dollar, and that other country's currencies would be pegged to, and measured against, the US Dollar. The reason was to create stability and prevent trading devaluing currencies in order to promote international trade and promote post-war restructuring of economies.[154]

In addition to the Agreement and System, the International Monetary Fund (IMF) and the World Bank were also formed. The aim of the IMF was to oversee world monetary systems and ensure stability whilst the World Bank was set up to provide assistance to countries that most required it.[155]

CE 1945–1999

Nuremberg Trials, Himmler, Goering, Goebbels, Atlee Replaces Churchill as British Prime Minister, Taiwan Returns to Chinese Administration After Japan Withdraws, The Cold War Starts, USSR Invents its own Atomic Bomb, India Gains Independence From Britain, Partition occurs as Pakistan Formed and Separates From India, Gandhi Assassinated, The State of Israeli Formed, The First Israeli-Arab War Occurs, Apartheid Starts in South Africa as the National Party Comes To Power, Marshall Plan for Europe, NATO formed, Germany Splits into 2, People's Republic of China Formed under Mao Zedong's Communist Party, Chinese Nationalist Party Imposes Martial Law in Taiwan, Spain renews Relationship with the UN, Korean War, Macau Officially Becomes a Portuguese Overseas Province, Stalin Dies, Khrushchev Gifts Crimea to Ukraine, Mau Mau Uprising, Federation of Rhodesia and Nyasaland, Coronation of Queen Elizabeth II, The Cuban Revolution, Fidel Castro and

Che Guevara, Vietnam Split into 2, The Warsaw Pact,
Morocco and Tunisia Gain Independence, The 1956 Suez
Canal Crisis, Ghanaian Independence, Treaty of Rome
Establishes the European Economic Community and the
European Atomic Energy Community, The European
Union formed, The Space Race Starts, Yuri Gagarin
Becomes First Man in Space, France's Fifth Republic,
The Great Leap Forward in China, Independence of
Singapore, Castro Takes Power in Cuba, The Sharpeville
Massacre in South Africa, 17 African Countries Gain
Independence, The Pill, Berlin Wall Built, India Retakes
Goa, Malaysia Formed, Kenyan Independence, Vietnam
War, Tanzania and Zanzibar Act of Union, Malawian
and Zambia Independence, Rhodesian UDI and Civil
War, China's Cultural Revolution, Gang of Four, Che
Guevara, The Six Day War, Nicolae Ceausescu, Martin
Luther King Jr, The Al-Fateh Revolution and Gaddafi, Franco
Dies, Moon Landing and Neil Armstrong, Woodstock,
Bangladesh formed, Idi Amin, Raid on Entebbe Hijacking,
Yom Kippur War, 1973 Oil Crisis, Golda Meir, Watergate
and Deepthroat, Nixon Resignation, Carnation Revolution
in Portugal, Mozambique and Angolan Independence,
Pol Pot and Cambodia, Chairman Mao Dies, Elvis Presley
Dies, Space Invaders, Ayatollah Khomeini and the Iranian
Islamic Revolution, The Soviet Afghan War, Zimbabwean
Independence and the End of Rhodesia, Margaret Thatcher,
Iranian Embassy Siege London, John Lennon Murdered,
Anwar Sadat Assassinated, AIDS, Live Aid, NASA Space
Shuttle Disaster, Democratisation of Taiwan Begun,
Armenian Earthquake, End of Iran-Iraq War, Lockerbie Air
Disaster, Tiananmen Square Protests, Berlin Wall Torn Down,
Nelson Mandela Freed, End of Apartheid, Hubble Telescope,
Gulf War, Mikhail Gorbachev, Collapse of USSR, Boris Yeltsin,
Ukraine Independence, Crimea Becomes an Autonomous

Region, The Yugoslav Wars, Kosovo War, Bosnian War, EU Single Market Formed, Rwandan Civil War and Genocide, Mother Teresa Dies, Hong Kong returns to China, Lady Diana Dies, Macau Returns to China, The Y2K Bug

In 1945, the main Allies of Britain, America, France and the USSR agreed to set up a joint trial, called the International Military Tribunal, in Nuremberg, Germany to try some of the remaining leaders and institutions of Nazi Germany for war crimes, and to gather evidence of the atrocities committed.

Three of Germany's main Nazi leaders, Hitler, Goebbels and Himmler, had already committed suicide. Heinrich Himmler had been head of the SS (Schutzstaffel) which was a crack Intelligence unit and an elite guard of the Nazi regime, and was the main architect of the Holocaust and the setting up of concentration camps, whilst Joseph Goebbels was very close to Hitler and in charge of propaganda for the Nazi Party, and strongly antisemite.

The Nuremberg Trials then centred on the other architects of the German side of the war, the Holocaust and other atrocities committed. Over the course of the next 4 years, over 190 defendants were tried and over 160 convicted. More than thirty five of the guilty were sentenced to death and 2, Hermann Goering and Robert Ley, also committed suicide. Many of those sentenced to jail were sent to the Spandau prison in Berlin.

In Britain, in 1945, the Conservatives were voted out of power and Clement Atlee the Labour leader replaced Churchill as Prime Minister. During the war the country had been governed by a coalition with Churchill at the helm. However, prior to the war the Conservatives had been blamed for high unemployment and immediately after the war the Labour government produced a manifesto on how they would rebuild Britain, establish a National Health Service, reduce unemployment and set up a social security system. Whilst Churchill himself was extremely popular, it was the Labour manifesto that won the day as people voted Labour into power to help rebuild Britain.

Taiwan had been occupied by Japan since Japan had won the first Sino-Japanese War, but in 1945 it was returned to China following the Japanese surrender. The island was adminis-tered by the Chinese Nationalist Party (KMT) who were the ruling part of the Republic of China. However, there was no legal transfer of the sovereignty of the island.

In 1947 the Cold War started. Following the destruction of WWII much of Europe needed rebuilding. The USA and USSR had different views on how this should occur. The USA believed in capitalism and free markets; the USSR was building a network of countries who believed in commu-nism. Whilst the ideology of communism was well merited and resulted in low unemployment and a more equal society, it involved state-run economies which were inefficient and resulted in shortages and lack of production. In the US capi-talist model, production increased rapidly and new advances were made in all areas of the economy, which also led to wide differences in wealth between members of their societies.

The Cold War was based on an idea put forward by US dip-lomat George Kenan in a famous 1947 "Long Telegram" that stated that in order to understand Stalin and the USSR one had to understand they would never "agree to disagree" and would always be pushing for the other countries to adopt their communist way of life. As such, the best means of combatting this was to adopt a policy of "containment" and, over a long-term strategy, slowly and patiently support countries and peoples who wanted a free way of life away from Stalin's USSR policy of subjugation. (It was George Orwell in an essay who first coined the term Cold War.)[156]

In 1947 India achieved independence from Britain. Prior to WWII India had been at a three-way splitting point between Britain and the Indian Hindus and Muslims, but differences had been put on hold in support of the British war effort. When war did break out, the British unilaterally declared that India too was at war with Germany, a decision that inflamed tensions as neither Nehru nor Gandhi were consulted on the matter.

During the war, whilst Indians served the British war effort and millions died fighting for the Allies, the divisions between the Hindu Congress Party and the British Raj grew wider. The Muslim League, the third party in India, led by Mohammed Ali Jinnah, supported Britain more openly as they moved further from the Congress Party, demanding the set-up of a separate state called Pakistan in the country's Muslim north-western and north-eastern provinces. The name Pakistan was derived from the Persian for "Land of the Pure". Hindu opposition for the war continued resulting in Nehru, Gandhi and thousands of Congress members being jailed by the British during the war. With America joining the war, India became a major base for the Allies against the Japanese, and manufacturing and other industries grew strongly in support of the war effort.

After the war, however, with the new Labour government in power in Britain, the new Prime Minister Clement Atlee's main concern was how to withdraw Britain from

India with as many assets as possible; as India, with its resistance to Britain and its internal Hindu Muslim conflict, was now seen as a liability.

In December 1945 and January 1946, general and then provincial elections were held in India. The Congress won a majority in the general election, but the Muslim League won all the seats reserved for Muslim parties, leaving Britain unable to hand over power exclusively to one party which would have been a simpler and preferred path for them. Adding to complications for the British were Sikh demands for their own independent nation.

During 1947 civil war broke out as various Indian factions, mainly Nehru's Congress against Jinnah's Muslim League, fought for their territories and rights and Lord Mountbatten was sent out as viceroy to try and find a solution as to how to transfer power. Mountbatten immediately opted for a "partitioned" India, something that Gandhi was so against he suggested rather that Jinnah be given the opportunity to govern a united India, but Nehru refused this option. In July 1947 Britain passed the Indian Independence Act ordering that India and Pakistan be partitioned into separate states by 15 August. This came to become known as Partition. In less than a month, as the two countries scrabbled to define borders, over one million people died as the largest mass movement of people in history occurred when people relocated to the new state that they wanted to live in.[157]

On 15 August 1947 the two new countries were formed and the British control of India, the Raj, came to an end.

As the mainly Muslim states had been situated in both the

north-west of India and the north-east of India, when independence occurred and the new country of Pakistan was born, it had two distinct parts to it: West and East Pakistan, with India in between. Located between them in India was Kashmir which remained neutral but with a Hindu leader and a mainly Muslim population. Civil unrest broke out in Kashmir in 1947 as different factions fought to either join Pakistan or India and in 1949 a ceasefire was agreed with a Line of Control (LOC) imposed which separated the Pakistan-controlled section of Kashmir from the India-controlled section. This supposedly temporary situation exists to this day.

As Pakistan was born and millions of people were displaced from their homes and had to find new homes in the two different countries, religious intolerance took its hold and violence frequently occurred. Gandhi, who had been against Partition, undertook a number of hunger strikes to protest the violence and urge the people to stop fighting. Whilst millions supported him, a more fanatical Hindu element saw this as too much support for the Muslims, and in 1949 one fanatical Hindu nationalist assassinated Gandhi, shooting him three times.

In 1948 the State of Israel was created.

In the first century, when Rome had conquered the region, they renamed the area Palestine (which means the land of the Philistines, who were the people from that area at the time) and relocated many of the Jewish population, but not all. Over the next 2000 years Jews still regarded the area surrounding Jerusalem as their homeland.

After WWI the League of Nations gave control of Palestine

to the British government who signed the Balfour declaration which was an agreement to provide Jews with a homeland in Palestine. By the time WWII occurred there were already over half a million Jewish people living in Palestine. The Jews were therefore pressing for a homeland in the area whilst Palestinian Arabian Nationalism was also on the rise with Arabs against an Israeli homeland, fearing they would be sidelined.

In 1947 with Britain no longer willing to govern the area, the United Nations formulated a committee which recommended the partition of the area into two separate states: one Jewish and one Arab. Whilst the Israeli nation supported the idea, the Palestinians rejected it on the grounds that whilst they had a larger population they should be provided a greater share of the land and so the dispute centred around what territories each should be provided.

In February 1948 Israel was officially established as a new independent state but a second state for Palestine was not established and conflict broke out. The1948–1949 War of Independence / Arab-Israeli War occurred as Palestinians tried to prevent the establishment of Israel, but the Israeli Defence Force managed to end the war and Israel was established.

The Palestine Liberation Organisation (PLO) was formed in 1964 with the aim to unify Arab nations and create a state of Palestine (for more on the PLO and the Palestine-Israeli conflict see Yasser Arafat death in 2004).

In 1948 South Africa, where a union had been formed in 1910 after the Boer War and racial segregation had been implemented, the National Party came to power.

> The National Party then undertook a policy of Apartheid, which was a legal system of political, economic, and social segregation of the races.

In 1948 President Truman of the USA signed the Economic Recovery Plan for post-war Europe. The plan was to help Europe rebuild itself and its economies, both for the good of all (including the USA), as well as to avoid the same political extremism that had led to WWII due to the economic hardships that Germany had experienced.

> This Economic Recovery Plan came to be known as the Marshall Plan after the US Secretary of State George Marshall who had proposed the plan in 1947 in a speech at Harvard University.

It was also in 1948 that the Communist Party, backed by the Soviets, overthrew the government in Czechoslovakia. With the Cold War underway and Western Germany becoming more and more part of the democratic West, Berlin, isolated inside Eastern Germany but supposedly still also the capital of Western Germany, was blockaded by the Soviets resulting in the Berlin Airlift, with supplies flown in by the Western nations to support Berlin's citizens.

> It was thus, during this period of escalating tensions of the Cold War, and whilst the Marshall Plan was being implemented, that the Western Union was created, later to become the Western European Union, an agreement for military coordination between Western European democracies,

which laid the groundwork for the formation of NATO, the North Atlantic Treaty Organisation, which was signed in April 1949 and brought America into the agreement.

There were 12 original founding members of NATO, these being: the USA, the UK, France, Belgium, the Netherlands, Denmark, Italy, Portugal, Luxembourg, Norway, Iceland and Canada, and the basis of the agreement was that these states would all defend each other, and if one was attacked, it be taken as if each had been attacked.[158]

In 1949 Germany split into two, East and West.

Following the Potsdam Conference, Germany had been split into four areas, controlled by Britain, France, USSR and the USA, and lost a large portion of its territory to Poland and the USSR.

Berlin, the capital, was entirely surrounded by the USSR-controlled section. The USSR-controlled section also held much of Germany's agricultural land and an agreement was put in place that this section was to provide agricultural pro-duce and foodstuff to the rest of Germany. Failure to agree compensation with the USSR for its losses during the war led to disagreements and the agreement to supply foodstuff never materialised. As the Cold War developed, Germany evolved into two distinct regions, the East and the West. Concerned that extreme economic hardships could lead to political extremism, the Western-controlled areas implemented reforms, followed the Marshall Plan, and introduced a new stable currency, the Deutsche Mark. This further angered the Soviets and in 1949 the Western section drafted a con-stitution for a new government (political parties had already formed in both west and east regions) and in May 1949 the

Federal Republic of Germany was formed, to be known as West Germany. This led the East to form their own constitution and in October 1949 the German Democratic Republic was formed, known from then on as East Germany.

In was also in 1949, in August, that the Soviet Union matched what the USA had managed in WWII and exploded their first atomic bomb, in a test site in Kazakhstan. The bomb was code named "First Lightning" and was equal in strength to "Trinity" the bomb the Americans had first tested back in 1945. This led to the beginning of the Arms Race as both the USA and USSR poured billions into the development of new weapons and technologies that could both attack and defend.

In 1949 the People's Republic of China was formed. Following the 1912 overthrow of the Qing Dynasty by Sun Yat-sen the Republic of China had been formed, only to then enter a bitter internal struggle with the Chinese Communist Party (CCP) of China in the Chinese Civil War. Mao Zedong's Communist Party won the civil war and on 01 October 1949, Mao, in a ceremony at Tiananmen Square, Beijing, proclaimed the founding of the People's Republic of China. Mao was its first leader from 1949 until 1976.

Having lost the Civil War the Republic of China Nationalist Party (Kuomintang, or KMT) retreated to Taiwan and the leader of the KMT, Chiang Kai-shek, used the military under martial law to take control of the island which the KMT then ruled for 40 years through until the1980s when democratic reforms occurred.

In 1950 Spain, which had become isolated from the outside world due to its Franco-led dictatorship, renewed its relationship with the UN, taking its seat there in 1955. Its territory in Morocco became independent in 1955 and student riots erupted in 1956. Massive inflation followed and an International Monetary Fund led stabilisation plan was implemented in 1959 followed by a First Development Plan in 1963 and then a Second Development Plan in 1968, all of which led to a recovery in Spain's economy over the following years.

In 1950 the Korean War started. Japan had annexed the Korean Peninsula in 1910 prior to which it had existed as an independent dynasty for 500 years.

When Japan surrendered at the end of WWII the Korean Peninsular split into 2, the US-controlled South and Soviet-controlled North. With the advent of the Cold War in 1947, 2 separate governments and capitals formed; Seoul in the South and Pyongyang in the North. A Soviet-and-Chinese-trained Korean leader, Kim Il-Sung, took command of the North and in 1950, with the go-ahead from Stalin and with Soviet aid, invaded the South, hoping to unite the country under his leadership. The South, led by Syngman Rhee and backed by the UN, and specifically the US, responded and the two Koreas were at war.

An armistice was signed in 1953 and a demilitarised zone (DMZ) was established to separate the two countries. Although an Armistice was signed, no peace treaty ever was, meaning technically the two countries are still at war.[159]

In 1951 Macau officially became a Portuguese overseas province. The first Portuguese ship to land in Macau had done so in 1513 and by 1553 it had become a Portuguese territory and their main Asian trading port.

Libya became independent in 1951, the first African country to do so. Prior to that it had been under British and Free French occupation during WWII and an Italian colony from 1912–1947. It declared itself an independent nation as the United Kingdom of Libya under King Idris.

In 1953 Joseph Stalin suffered a stroke and died. He had been in power since 1924 and had industrialised the USSR and led it through WWII, but he had led by force, initiating Gulags and the Great Purge (see 1930s). It is estimated as many as 20 million Soviets died as a result of his dictatorial regime, including those from hunger as a result of his failed Command agricultural schemes.

> Nikita Khrushchev took over from Stalin and in 1954 gave Crimea to the Soviet Republic of Ukraine in celebration of 300 years of unity between Russia and Ukraine. Crimea had been part of Russia for the previous 200 years since the second Russian-Turkish war (see 1787–1791) which resulted in Turkey officially recognising Crimea as Russian.

In 1952 the Mau Mau Rebellion broke out in Kenya. Resentment against colonial rule had been simmering since WWI and in 1945 Jomo Kenyatta of the Kenya African Union began pushing for political rights. The Mau Mau was a militant group comprised of mainly Kikuyu fighters who attacked colonial farms. The British declared a state of emergency and heavily responded, with the state of emergency in place until 1960.

The Federation of Rhodesia and Nyasaland was formed in 1953, led by Sir Roy Welensky and Sir Godfrey Huggins. Prior to this, Southern Rhodesia and Northern Rhodesia (present-day Zimbabwe and Zambia) moved from being a protectorate, governed by the British South Africa Company, into being directly governed by the British government in 1924. Nyasaland (Malawi) had been a British Protectorate since 1907 and had been known as British Central Africa prior to this.

The Federation came about as more European (mainly British) settlers arrived in the region after WWII. In Southern Rhodesia this was due to the increase in secondary industries and manufacturing, and in Northern Rhodesia it was due to the boom in copper mining in the copper-belt. The settlers wanted to amalgamate the countries to counterbalance the minority populations they represented in the region, but the Black nationalists in each country were against it, seeking independence.

In 1959 this came to a head in Nyasaland with various outbreaks of social unrest which led to a state of emergency and the British to believe that it was time to transfer power to the Black majority, however it was only in 1964 that independence came to Zambia and Malawi (see 1964).[160]

Queen Elizabeth II of Britain was coronated Queen in 1953 following the death of her father King George VI in 1952 whilst Elizabeth was on holiday in Kenya. The coronation made her Queen of the United Kingdom, Canada, Australia, New Zealand, Pakistan and South Africa.

In 1953 the Cuban Revolution started, lasting until 01 January 1959 when President Batista fled the island. The Revolution was started and led by Fidel Castro who trained as a military lawyer. He was supported in the rebellion by his brother Raul and by Che Guevara, an Argentinian Marxist, who later went on to help revolutions in Congo and Bolivia too. The revolution was started when Castro and his brother

Raul attacked military barracks in revolt against the military dictatorship in place under Batista who had come to power in a coup in 1952.

In 1954 an accord split Vietnam into 2, a communist North and a pro-French then pro-American South Vietnam.

The Warsaw Pact was signed in 1955 and was an immediate response to Western Germany joining NATO, also in 1955. The original members of the Warsaw Pact were the Soviet Union, East Germany, Albania, Czechoslovakia, Bulgaria, Hungary, Poland and Romania, and, like NATO, it was also a military alliance between these states, who agreed to defend each other.[161]

The Warsaw Pact and NATO thus became the opposite military divisions of the Cold War, as the Eastern Bloc, defended by the Warsaw Pact, and the Western Bloc, defended by NATO, began to form, each growing over time and taking on more member states.

Also in 1954, war broke out in Algeria. In 1830 the French had invaded Algiers and had incorporated it into France as French Algeria by 1948, but by 1954, following WWII, the Algerians wanted their independence.

Both European and Muslim Algerians had fought for France in the war and in 1954 the FLN (National Liberation Front) was formed, calling for the restoration of the Algerian State. Disquiet and disturbances grew into full-scale war with serious repercussions in France. French forces in Algeria resisted the independence movement with force but this created further resentments in Algeria and turned the French population in France against the war which resulted in a change in government in France.

By 1960 the UN had passed a resolution recognising Algeria's right to independence, Charles de Gaulle opened negotiations with the FLN, and by 1962 Algeria received its independence and in the ensuing chaos it was estimated 1,000,000 European Algerians (Pied-noirs) returned to France.

In 1956 Morocco gained independence from France. Independence had been brewing since the end of WWII. From 1912 it had been a French protectorate but after the war, the Sultan of Morocco, Mohammed Ben Youssef, aligned himself with the independence party Isiqlal. The Moroccan National Front was formed and during 1952–1953 demonstrations against French rule increased. The French resisted and the Sultan was forced into exile to Madagascar, but the demonstrations then increased further, as did international pressure on France. In 1955 Morocco was granted independence and the Sultan returned.

A similar situation unfolded in neighbouring Tunisia. There, the French government tried to create a system of joint sovereignty, but the Tunisians resisted, and independence demonstrations and French crackdowns followed, until in 1955, just weeks after Morocco, Tunisia too was granted independence. [162]

In 1956 the Suez Crisis occurred as Arab nationalist Gamel Abdel Nasser became President of Egypt and nationalised the Suez Canal company which was predominantly owned by British and French companies. Israel, backed by Britain and France, then invaded the Sinai Peninsula, but the invasion was condemned internationally, and the Israelis withdrew to be replaced by a UN-led force. The Suez was reopened but remained under Egyptian control. The British Prime Minister at the time, Anthony Eden, resigned in part due to the British government's role in the crisis.

Ghana, colonised by Britain in 1874 and renamed the Gold Coast, attained its independence in 1957, the first British colony in sub-Saharan Africa to do so.

In 1949 Kwame Nkrumah formed the Convention People's Party (CPP) and began a period of non-cooperation with the British-led government for which he was jailed for one year. His CPP won the 1951 elections and he was released from jail to lead the government business and became Prime Minister in 1952. In 1957 Ghana was formed as a result of Gold Coast and British Togoland being merged into one new independent state.

The Treaties of Rome were signed in 1957 which were the agreements to establish the European Economic Community (EEC) and the European Atomic Energy Community.

In 1949 a Council for Europe had been established to promote democracy and safeguard human rights following WWI and WWII, and in 1951 the European Coal and Steel Community came into being as six European member states agreed to run their coal and steel industries under a single management plan.

There were six original members of the EEC, and the two treaties signed came into effect in 1958. The six original members wore Belgium, France, Germany, Italy, Luxembourg, and the Netherlands and in 1968 they became a customs union as they removed customs duties from goods imported into their individual countries from other EEC member states.[163]

In 1957 the USSR was the first ever country to launch a space satellite, Sputnik 1, which they followed up a month later with Sputnik 2, with Laika, a dog, on board the spacecraft.

In 1958 the USA established NASA, the National Aeronautics and Space Administration, and the Space Race began as part of the Cold War, as both the USSR and USA sought to gain dominance in technology, space and the associated propaganda for their respective way of life. Whilst Laika unfortunately died in orbit, in 1960 the USSR sent up two other dogs, Belka and Strelka, into space, and brought both successfully home alive. A year later, in 1961, the USA sent up Ham, a chimpanzee, and also successfully returned him alive.

In 1961, with Yuri Gagarin aboard Vostok I, the USSR achieved the remarkable feat of sending the first ever man into space. Gagarin made a single orbit around Earth and returned successfully.

1958 saw the collapse the of French Fourth Republic and the start of the Fifth Republic.

After the French Revolution France had become a republic with the First Republic being from 1792–1804, from the Revolution until Napoleon took control in a coup. Napoleon created an Empire, not a republic, which lasted until the Second Republic from 1848–1852, after Napoleon was defeated. After the Second Republic the Second Empire formed under Louis Bonaparte which lasted until 1870 when the Third Republic was formed which collapsed under the German invasion of WWII in 1940.

France's Fourth Republic from 1946-1958 helped rebuild France with the aid of the Marshall Plan until the Algerian War caused huge internal conflict and divisions.

When the Independence War broke out in Algeria (see 1952) this caused the French government to respond but the manner of the response caused alarm among the French military and the Pied-noirs (European Algerians). These two groups felt that the French government was acting incompetently in their handling of the Algerian War and, worried that for the sake of political expediency the government would pull out of Algeria in a manner that would not benefit France, a coup was in the offing against this government.

In 1958 former Algerian Governor General Jacques Soustelle returned to France to help organise the coup. Right wing elements in Algeria took power and enormous pressure was put on the government, with the rebels wanting Charles de Gaulle to take control. The French Fourth Republic collapsed, and de Gaulle stepped in to preside over a transitional government and the creation of a new constitution, France's present-day constitution.[164]

The Great Leap Forward, Chairman Mao of China's attempt to industrialise the nation's agricultural output, ran from 1958 until 1962.

The campaign was based around the plan to enforce farmers to farm on larger collective farms rather than small private plots, with inputs and outputs controlled by the state.

Simultaneously, as part of this industrialisation process, the state also organised enforced increases in industrial steel production through the mass building of numerous steel furnaces in both urban areas and on the collective farms.

Both schemes failed. Industrialisation of the steel industry failed to achieve any growth and the quality of steel produced was extremely poor. Meanwhile central planning of resources failed to allocate resources to where they were needed and not only did agricultural activity plummet, but millions of young males, who historically farmed on private plots, were moved into urban areas and needed to therefore buy rather than produce food. The agricultural strain on society was enormous and an estimated 30–40 million Chinese died of starvation before the campaign was abandoned.[165]

In 1959 Singapore, which had been established as a trading port by the British in 1819, achieved independence.

It had been attacked by the Japanese in WWII who occupied the state from 1942–1945. After the Japanese surrender, the island was handed to the British Military Administration and became a British Crown Colony in 1946. By 1959 calls for independence led to the country's first elections, which were won by Lee Kuan Yew of the People's Action Party.

On 01 January 1959, President Batista of Cuba fled the country as Fidel Castro's revolution came to a victorious end, and Castro became the new president of Cuba. Castro established the Communist Party of Cuba and under this party and Castro's regime, Cuba became a communist country, companies were nationalised, and Cuba became a strong supporter and friend of the USSR.

The effect of this was far reaching with Cuba supporting Marxist / Communist rebellions elsewhere, most notably in Congo and Bolivia where Che Guevara, the Argentine Marxist who had left Argentina to help Castro with his rebellion, moved on to try and spread Marxism elsewhere in the world.

In 1960 in Sharpeville, South Africa, demonstrations broke out against the restriction of movement of blacks.

In 1955 the Freedom Charter had been adopted by the Congress Alliance, an alliance of various South African races, and in 1958 the Pan African congress was formed, a breakaway division from the African National Congress.

In 1960 both the PAC and ANC planned demonstrations against restrictions on movement imposed under the Apartheid Laws of the National Party and in March the demonstrations occurred in Sharpeville. After using tear gas to try and disperse the demonstrators who were marching on the police station, the police opened fire on the demonstration resulting in the death of 69 people, of whom almost half were children.

In the remainder of Africa in 1960, independence was sweeping across the continent as 17 countries became independent in the 12-month period. This independence movement was based on a number of factors including the recent gain of independence by India, as well as the promises made by Britain and France for the support provided them during WWII.

In February 1960 Harold Macmillan, the British Prime Minister, made a famous "Winds of Change" speech to the South African parliament detailing that Britain would no longer stand in the way of those countries that sought independence.

The Belgian Congo was ruled by Belgium from 1908–1960 after taking over control from a private consortium of investors including King Leopold II. In 1958 Patrick Lumumba launched the Congo National Movement, and riots supporting independence broke out in 1959, leading to full independence in June 1960. It became the Democratic Republic of Congo (DRC) in 1964 before being renamed Zaire in 1971 and reverting to DRC again in 1997.

Cameroon, Togo, Madagascar, Somalia, Benin, Niger, Burkina Faso, Ivory Coast, Chad, Central African Republic, the Republic of Congo, Gabon, Senegal, Mali, Nigeria, and Mauritania all became new independent states during the remainder of 1960.

In 1960 "The Pill", the first oral contraceptive was approved by the FDA (Food and Drug Administration) in America and within two years over 1 million women were using it in America, and it soon spread around the world. In America it was only legalised for married women in 1965 and for unmarried women in 1972.

By 1961, after NATO and the WARSAW PACT were signed in 1955, the divisions between East and West Germany increased, it was estimated that over 2.5 million people, many aged under 30, had crossed out of the East.

This caused a problem for the East German leadership and in 1961 their Council of Ministers announced that they would install border controls and by the end of the year the initial temporary barriers with barbed wire were replaced by concrete walls and guard stations. The Berlin Wall was built, and virtually overnight streets and neighbourhoods became separated from each other.

In 1961 India invaded Goa and it once again became Indian territory. It had been the capital of Portugal's Asian Empire since 1510 when Afonso de Albuquerque captured the city from the Muslim King Yusuf Adil Khan, but after India became independent in 1947 Portugal had come under increasing pressure to cede the area back to India. By 1961 India's patience had run out and they retook the territory by force.

In 1961 and 1962 The US President, John Fitzgerald Kennedy (JFK), was involved in two major Cuban-related crises. The first was the Bay of Pigs Invasion and the second was the Cuban Missile Crisis.

The Bay of Pigs Invasion was a failed (it was later called a fiasco) attempt to remove Castro from office, by the invasion of Cuba by 1400 Cuban exiles, supported by the USA and in particular the CIA. As the invasion became strategically outmanoeuvred, which caught the public's attention, JFK withdrew support, the invasion failed and a rift developed between the CIA who had supported the operation, and JFK.

In 1962, the Cuban Missile Crisis, a confrontation that brought the world to the brink of nuclear war, broke out.

Nikita Krushchev, the Soviet Premier, supported Cuba's Socialist approach and provided Cuba with nuclear self-defence missiles. These had the capability of reaching mainland USA and America objected strongly. JFK launched a naval blockade around the island preventing any more missiles arriving on the island after the first initial consignment had arrived. Tensions rose high as both the USA and the Soviet Union negotiated and eventually the Soviets agreed to remove the missiles and not send any more and the USA agreed to never invade Cuba.

Marilyn Monroe died in 1962.

One of the great superstars of modern Hollywood, Monroe represented the revolution of women and their sexual freedom that had been brought about by the Pill and was one of the top billed actresses of the previous decade.

Her death was ruled to be a suicide by overdose. She had suffered depression and drug use at various points in her life and career and whilst some reports suggested an accidental overdose, the coroner ruled it a suicide.

In 1963 modern day Malaysia, which was amalgamated with Singapore, was formed.

Up until 1511 the area was the Sultanate of Malacca until it was conquered by Portugal who ruled it through to 1641 when the Dutch took control and in 1824 the British took over the whole territory through to Singapore.

Like Singapore, Japan invaded and held Malaysia during WWII after which it reverted to the British who, under pressure to allow for independence, granted autonomy to the Malay rulers in a Federation of Malaya in 1948 under British protection. This was not the sought-after full independence that Malays wanted, and counter-insurgency disturbances occurred through until 1957 when Malaya became an independent member of the Commonwealth.

Plans for the full establishment of an independent state were set for 1963, with this state incorporating both Singapore and the island of Borneo.

Tensions existed for two years between the rulers of Singapore and Malaysia who had different economic opinions and in 1965 Singapore split away to then exist as its own independent nation.[166]

With the wave of independence sweeping across Africa it was inevitable that Kenya, where Jomo Kenyatta's Kenya African Union had been began pushing for political rights since WWII, and the Mau Mau had attacked colonial farms, would also eventually gain independence. In 1963 the Kenya African National Union (KANU) won an election and in 1964 Jomo Kenyatta became its first independent president.

In 1963 in America the President John. F. Kennedy (John Fitzgerald Kennedy, JFK) was assassinated. Part of a political dynasty, JFK's brother was killed in WWII while JFK himself had been seriously injured and awarded for bravery.

In 1960 Kennedy took office and in 1963 began campaigning for a second term. Part of this campaign included a tour of Texas and in November 1963, whilst he and his wife Jacqueline rode an open limousine through Dallas, an assassin shot him twice, once in the neck and the other in the head. Lee Harvey Oswald, a Dallas citizen, was accused of the murder but Oswald, whilst in custody, was then killed by Jack Ruby. A commission decided later that Oswald had acted alone but conspiracies still abound that the assassination was either part of a plot to remove Kennedy by the CIA or that it was orchestrated by the criminal underworld, which Ruby was part of, who were angered by the Kennedy government's crackdown on crime.

In 1964 war broke out in Vietnam. Officially the war started in 1955 after an accord in 1954 had split Vietnam into two, a communist North and a pro-French then pro-American South Vietnam. The North wanted reunification but the South, controlled by the West, managed to prevent this until the 1960s when the National Liberation Front for the South was formed. The North and their Vietnamese allies in the South, opposed to the American foreign influence, were known as the Vietcong.

The Vietnam War then broke out as America sent its armed forces, to prevent the spread of communism and promote capitalism, to the country and region.

The Vietnam War ran from through until 1975. The Paris Peace Accord was signed in 1973 but the end of the war itself, and America's troop withdrawal, only occurred in 1975.

Over 2 million people died in the conflict, including 58,000 Americans.

In 1976 the country was renamed the Socialist Republic of Vietnam and in 1977 Vietnam became a member of the United Nations.

In Tanzania in 1964 Julius Nyerere, President of Tanzania, signed an act of union agreement with Abeid Karume, president of Zanzibar, to bring the two nations together as the United Republic of Tanzania.

Nyerere was the former leader of the Tanganyika African National Union, and had become President of Tanzania in 1961 when it became independent from Britain, which had acquired the right to govern the country from Germany after WWI.

In 1964 both Malawi and Zambia gained their independence from Britain.

Malawi was governed by Hastings Banda who went on to form a one-party state and governed until 1993 when a referendum there resulted in multi-party elections and the emergence of a multi-party state in Malawi.

In Zambia it was Kenneth Kaunda who took control after winning their elections. He also initiated a one-party state, and, following the lead of Julius Nyerere in Tanzania, adopted a socialist approach to government with a planned rather than laissez-faire economy. In 1990 riots broke out in dissent of Kaunda's rule and in 1991 reforms were introduced and multi-party elections were held in which Kaunda lost and Frederick Chiluba won.

In November 1965 Rhodesia declared itself unilaterally independent from Britain. This became known as the Rhodesian UDI (Unilateral Declaration of Independence) and it was only the second country to ever do so after Thomas Jefferson wrote the USA's Declaration of Independence in 1776.

After the failed Federation of Northern Rhodesia (Zambia), Southern Rhodesia (Zimbabwe) and Nyasaland (Malawi), whilst Malawi and Zambia gained their independence in 1964, a stalemate between Britain and Southern Rhodesia ensued. The White self-governing government of Ian Smith resisted Black majority rule which the British government supported. The first ever sanctions imposed by the UN were then imposed on Rhodesia which fell into civil war until April 1980 as the Black nationalists fought for control of the country against the Smith-led Rhodesia.

In 1966, in China, Chairman Mao, after his failed Great Leap Forward of 1958–1962, embarked on the Cultural Revolution.

The aim of this was to introduce his personal philosophy of communism as a replacement for capitalism or traditional Chinese culture. Mao's Little Red Book gained fame as a number of his personal sayings were compiled and published and distributed and the Red Guard was formed as youths who supported Mao formed rebel groups against capitalism and in support of Mao's Chinese communism. The Red Guard Youth led violent rallies, and schools were often shut and books burned. The violence led to chaos and in turn more violence. Over 1 million people died as a result of this violence, often in large-scale massacres. Mao declared the Revolution over in 1969 but in reality the chaos continued until 1976 when Mao died.

It was also during the Cultural Revolution that the Gang of Four rose to prominence. Led by Mao's last wife, the Gang were responsible for the worst of the chaos and violence that marked the Revolution and in 1976, after Mao's death, they were arrested, leading to life imprisonment for them all.

In 1967 Che Guevara, the famed Argentinian Marxist who had joined Castro's Cuban revolution and gone on to become an MP there before moving abroad to help organise other revolutions, was captured and killed in Bolivia.

Prior to Bolivia, Guevara had also been trying to support and promote Marxism in the Congo. In Bolivia his campaign was unsuccessful as he was unable to get full support from the Bolivian Communist Party whose army was better organised than expected. Guevara failed to get support from the local Bolivians and many of them informed on his movements. The Bolivian Special Forces tracked him and surrounded him, before wounding him in battle and capturing him. Soon after he was executed by the Army. Apparently Guevara, prior to the execution, proclaimed they were only killing a man, but not his ideas.

In 1967, from 05–10 June, the Six Day War occurred as Egyptian President Nasser who had closed the Straits of Tiran in the 1956 Suez Crisis (meaning Israeli shipping was blockaded), again announced the closure of these same Straits.

Egypt then joined with Jordan and Syria and mobilised forces on the Israeli border. In a series of pre-emptive airstrikes catching the Egyptian Airforce by surprise, Israel first destroyed the Egyptian Airforce and then moved across ground, taking the Gaza strip and Sinai Peninsula before then taking further territory in the West Bank and Golan Heights.

At the end of the war the Israelis and Egyptians were stationed at either side of the Suez Canal and in the resulting standoff it did not re-open. It remained closed for eight further years (see 1973 Oil Crisis and Yom Kippur War).

In 1967 Nicolae Ceausescu came to power in Romania. He had risen within the communist system after the USSR had had troops stationed in the country following WWII, and the country became a totalitarian regime under the Communist Party. Ceausescu imposed economic policies which failed catastrophically over the following two decades.

When the Soviet Union began to collapse in 1989, Ceausescu sent out the army to quell demonstrations in his own country with many killed or injured. Further demonstrations occurred and Nicolae and his wife Elena had to flee by helicopter. They were later captured, tried for various crimes – including genocide – and sentenced to death. The means of death was firing squad and the couple were executed on Christmas day 1989.

Martin Luther King Jr was assassinated in 1968.

King, born into a Christian minister's family, and a Baptist minister himself, had been a leader in the American Civil Rights movement since 1955. He was inspired by Gandhi's non-violence protests. His most famous speech was given in 1963 in a March on Washington. The speech became known as the "I have a dream" speech with its most famous line being:

"I have a dream that one day this nation will rise up and live out the true meaning of its creed: 'We hold these truths to be self-evident, that all men are created equal'."

In 1968, however, in Memphis where King was supporting a Black Labour movement, he was shot dead by James Earl Ray, a career criminal.

In 1969, in Libya, Colonel Muammar Gaddafi led a coup against the Libyan King Idris I and Libya became a republic. This came to become known as the Al-Fateh Revolution but Libya soon became a dictatorship with political dissent banned by 1973.

In Spain, in 1969, Parliament appointed Don Juan Carlos de Borbon, the Count of Barcelona, as successor to Franco.

> In 1970 a preferential trade agreement was signed with the European Common Market and in 1975, when Franco had a number of heart attacks and died, Don Carlos took over. The new king immediately legalised political parties and in 1977 elections were held and Spain returned to a democracy.

In 1969, aboard Apollo 11, Neil Armstrong and then Edwin Buzz Aldrin reached, landed and walked on the Moon. They were the first humans to ever do so. Their colleague Michael Collins who was also on board Apollo 11 orbited the Moon whilst awaiting them.

A month after the Moon Landing, in August 1969, the Woodstock Music and Art Fair occurred, forever after to be known simply as Woodstock.

> On a farm just south of the town of Woodstock in New York State, the event took place over three days with an expected 150,000 attendees. The number swelled to over 400,000 and the event went on to define the hippie 1960s movement and generation. This was a time when many young Americans began to protest against the Vietnam War and instead embraced the movement of "Peace and Music" which was how the event was promoted.[167]

Woodstock is now considered one of the most important rock concerts ever held.

In 1971 Bangladesh was formed.

Following the 1947 "Partition", Pakistan had been created as a separate country from India. However, Pakistan was geographically split into two separate areas, East and West Pakistan, with India between them. East Pakistan then campaigned for its own independence from Pakistan as a whole, which included the Western part. India supported this cause, which resulted in a short military confrontation between India and Pakistan known as the Indo-Pakistani War. This was a short two-week war which resulted in Pakistan's surrender and the creation of Bangladesh which means "Land of the Bengalis", as prior to Partition it was East Bengal, an area within Pakistan.

Idi Amin seized power in Uganda in 1971 in a coup whilst serving under Milton Obote and immediately started to put in place a police state.

Elections were abolished, parliament dissolved, and the secret police spread throughout society ensuring fear was spread and power consolidated. In 1972 he expelled all Asians from the country, and an estimated 35,000 were forced to flee.

In 1972 a hijacking of an Air France airliner from Tel Aviv to Athens to Paris was forced down in Entebbe, Uganda. The hijackers were Palestinian militants who demanded the release of Palestinian prisoners held in Israel. Non-Israeli prisoners were released and over 100 mainly Israeli hostages and Air France crew held captive. In a daring raid, immortalised in the movie *Raid on Entebbe*, the Israeli defence forces flew to Entebbe and all but 4 of the hostages were rescued, with three killed in the raid. The last hostage, Dora Bloch, was taken to hospital in Uganda and dragged from her hospital bed and executed. Amin had supported the hijackers and was angry that the raid had occurred. The killing of Bloch confirmed for many the theory that Amin suffered from syphilis and was becoming insane.

Estimates on the number killed under Amin's regime range from 80,000 to 500,000 but in 1979, after raiding neighbouring Tanzania, Tanzania invaded and Amin fled, initially to Libya and eventually to Saudi Arabia where he died in 2003. As a Muslim his rule brought disrepute to Islam and it was presumed the Saudis allowed him into Saudi Arabia to silence him and prevent further harm being brought to the religion.

In 1971 Richard Nixon became the first ever American President to visit China whilst serving his presidency. This marked the beginning of the opening up of China to world trade.

President Nixon then visited Crimea in 1974 as he promoted world trade and endeavoured to create ties with the Soviet Union and encourage the Soviets to trade with the USA. This was perhaps the beginning to the opening up of the Soviet Union during the long Cold War.

In 1973 the European Union member states grew to nine as Denmark, Ireland and the United Kingdom joined the original six member states of the EEC (see 1949) which were Belgium, France, Germany, Italy, Luxembourg and the Netherlands.

The Yom Kippur War, named after the Holy Day on which the War started, occurred in 1973.

As a result of the Six Day War in 1967, Israel had taken the Sinai Peninsula, which resulted in the Suez Canal remaining closed in a standoff, with the Egyptian Army on one side and the Israelis the other. Then in 1973 Anwar Sadat, the Egyptian President, along with his Syrian counterpart, Hafez Al-Assad, attacked Israel.

President Nixon of America backed Israel and supplied them with weapons, whilst the Soviets backed Egypt and Syria. The war lasted three weeks until the UN negotiated a peace treaty. However Saudi Arabia and other Arab oil-producing countries decided to punish those who supported Israel by decreasing oil output. Nixon increased his support for Israel which in turn led OPEC, the Organisation of Petroleum Exporting Countries, to cease oil exports to the USA and Western Europe.

This was the 1973 Oil Crisis when fuel prices soared from $2 to $11 per barrel due to the lack of supply. The crisis ended in 1974 when one of the US advisers, Henry Kissinger, met the Saudi king and brokered an end to the embargo on oil exports and set up a tour of Egypt, Israel and Saudi Arabia by President Nixon which helped rebuild relationships between the three countries.[168]

Golda Meir, Israel's first female Prime Minister, who served as its PM from 1969–1974 was in charge during the Yom Kippur War and the public's unhappiness with the fact that Israel had been caught unaware in the invasion by Egypt and Syria resulted in her resignation in 1974.

In 1974, as a result of the Watergate Scandal, US President Nixon resigned.

In 1972 five men were arrested for breaking into the Democratic Party offices in the Watergate office complex. They had previously broken in to take photographs of Democratic documents and tap into the phones but as the initial phone taps did not work, in June 1972 the men broke in again and were arrested doing so.

President Nixon and his staff denied any knowledge of the incident and Nixon won the presidency for a second term in November 1972. However, two reporters for the *Washington Post*, Bob Woodward and Carl Bernstein, via an anonymous source known as "Deepthroat", reported that Nixon was involved, probably mainly in the cover-up and in authorising payments made to the arrested five to retain their silence. Investigators demanded Nixon hand over tapes of all the discussions he held in the Oval Office, and when he refused, the Supreme Court ordered he do so. Nixon resigned rather than be impeached. He was the first US President to ever resign from office.

30 years later "Deepthroat" was revealed to be the deputy director of the FBI, Marc Felt, Snr.

Portugal in 1974 experienced the Carnation Revolution. Portugal had been a republic since 1910 when the monarchy ended, but after a coup in 1926, had been a dictatorship under Antonio de Oliveira Salazar. Discontent led to civil war until the 1974 Carnation Revolution which saw young captains in the army form the Armed Forces Movement and create democratic reforms and elections. Portugal became a democracy, and all its colonies became independent.

These colonies included East Timor, Angola, Mozambique, Cape Verde, Sao Tome and Principe, whilst Macau, which had become a Portuguese overseas province in 1951, was granted more administrative autonomy.

In 1975 the Khmer Rouge took power in Cambodia, led by Pol Pot.

Pot, who had studied in Paris, had joined the Khmer Rouge in the 1950s when it was an underground movement. Once in power they tried to reset Cambodia as a rural communist society with everyone in the country working in agricultural communes and all private ownership of money or property banned. Religion was not allowed either and over the following years tens of thousands died from starvation and violence at the hands of the tyrannical government.

In 1979, after the Khmer Rouge had started to raid them, Vietnam invaded and overthrew the Khmer Rouge. Pot escaped to Thailand until he was arrested in 1997, sentenced to life under house arrest but died in 1998.

In 1976 Chairman Mao, who had led China since forming the People's Republic of China in 1949, died. This ended the Cultural Revolution, his violent reform programme, and ushered in a new more open era under Den Xiaoping and the opening up of China to global interaction and trade.

Elvis Presley, the King of Rock and Roll, died in 1977.

He had released numerous successful albums, sold 500 million records worldwide, and become a Hollywood star, but years of prescription drug abuse led to his heart attack and death at age 42.

Space Invaders, the highest grossing video game of all time, at the time, was launched in 1978 and is considered to be one of the most influential video games of all time as it ushered in the era of digital gaming, which started as video arcade games.

In 1979 the Iranian revolution, or Islamic Revolution of Iran, resulted in the toppling of the pro-Western Shah of Iran's government, and an Islamic government was instead put in place under the Ayatollah Khomeini.

In November 1979 militants in Tehran invaded the US Embassy there and held over 50 US Diplomats and Citizens hostage for over a year until 1981 when the Algiers Accords were signed which resulted in the freeing of the hostages and America agreeing not to intervene in Iranian politics. This became known as the Iran Hostage Crisis.

From 1979 to 1989 the Soviet Afghan war occurred, a war fought mainly within Afghanistan's borders, as the Mujahideen, backed by the US, Pakistan, China, Iran, Saudi Arabia and the UK, fought against Soviet occupation of Afghanistan.

Leonid Brezhnev, the leader of the Soviet Union, ordered the Soviet Army to invade after the Soviets felt that Afghanistan, traditionally an ally, was about to switch allegiances. Afghanistan at the time was going through its own revolution, embracing land reforms, trying to modernise, open up, and move away from traditional power structures. As many as 1,000,000 Afghans died in the conflict, until 1987 when the Soviet Union went through its own reforms under Mikhail Gorbachev who ordered the beginning of the troop withdrawal.

By 1989 all Soviet troops had left Afghanistan.

In 1979, following a decade-long civil war, Rhodesia changed its name to Zimbabwe-Rhodesia. The White government led by Ian Smith reached an accord with Bishop Abel Muzorewa to establish a biracial democracy, and Muzorewa became Prime Minister.

However, Zimbabwe was not yet fully independent and the two main leaders fighting for African Nationalism and majority rule during the civil war were Robert Mugabe of the Zimbabwe African National Union (ZANU) and Joshua Nkomo of the Zimbabwe African Patriotic Union (ZAPU). Talks were held by all parties in London at Lancaster House and on 21 December 1979 agreements were reached and the civil war was officially over.

In February 1980 elections were held which were won by Robert Mugabe's ZANU and Zimbabwe-Rhodesia became Zimbabwe, an independent country on 18 April 1980.

In May 1979, Margaret Thatcher became Britain's first female Prime Minister. She had held the position of Leader of the Opposition (as leader of the Conservative Party) since 1975, and the Conservatives went on to win the general election in 1979. She went on to become Britain's longest serving Prime Minister of the 20th Century serving as PM through until 1990.

For six days, from 30 April – 05 May 1980, the Iranian Embassy in London was held under siege as six Iranian Arabs protested for the independence of Khuzestan Province, a province in Iran. Embassy staff including diplomats were held hostage. Negotiations ensued and five of those kidnapped were released but over 20 remained, and on the sixth day one hostage was killed and his body thrown out of the embassy window. The British SAS launched a dramatic rescue mission and abseiled in, killed five gunmen and arrested the sixth who was later tried and convicted. Nineteen hostages were rescued but one was killed during the operation.

In December 1980 John Lennon was shot dead outside his New York apartment by a fan who was said to dislike the hypocrisy of Lennon's rich lifestyle, which did not fit with what he felt Lennon said he stood for. John Lennon was co-founder, co-lead vocalist and co-lead songwriter for the Beatles, one of the biggest and most influential bands of all time.

In October 1981 Anwar Sadat (Muhammad Anwar el-Sadat) the President of Egypt was assassinated. He had brought about multi-party politics to Egypt and had led them in the Yom Kippur War, before entering into a peace treaty with Israel which won him and the Israeli Prime Minister (Menachem Begin) the Nobel Peace prize. He was shot dead during a parade in Cairo by those who were opposed to the peace treaty with Israel as they felt it had weakened efforts to bring about a separate Palestinian state.

In 1982, AIDS became an officially named and recognised disease after the first cases were recorded in 1981. AIDS is Acquired Immune Deficiency Syndrome and by 2000 became the fourth largest killer of humans worldwide.[169]

In 1982 a short 2-month war, the Falklands Conflict, occurred between Great Britain and Argentina after Argentina invaded the British Falklands Islands and South Georgia, claiming them to be their own. After the British responded with force and after almost 1000 lives were lost, Argentina surrendered, and the islands reverted to Britain.

In 1983 The US invaded Grenada, a Caribbean Island nation. The reason given was to protect US citizens after the assassination of Grenada's Prime Minister, but the more likely reason was that the US opposed the incoming left wing communist Military Council and fears that they would support revolutions in South America. After the invasion a Governor General was installed until new elections were held in 1984.

Live Aid, the concert held across two main venues in London and Philadelphia, occurred in 1985. At the same time concerts were held in Australia, Canada, USSR, Japan, West Germany, Austria, Norway and Yugoslavia and over 1.5 billion people around the world watched them on TV. The event was organised by Bob Geldof and Midge Ure to raise funds for the famine disaster in Ethiopia.

In April 1986 the worst accident in nuclear power station history happened in Ukraine at the Chernobyl Power Station. In a failed experiment to see if the nuclear reactor (where atoms are split to release energy) could still be cooled if the plant lost power, the resultant power surges as the reactor could not be cooled led to explosions that exposed the nuclear core, and radioactive material escaped into the atmosphere. The Soviets first denied that anything had happened and the nearby town outside Chernobyl was not evacuated for 36 hours. Swedish monitors, however, detected the abnormally high radiation levels in the atmosphere and the Soviets had to admit the accident.

Firefighters dumped enormous quantities of sand onto the site to contain the fires. 335,000 people were then evacuated from the area and an exclusion zone of over 20km was established around the nuclear plant. Whilst official figures state only 28 people died in the accident, other reports state up to 6,000 children developed thyroid issues and cancers in later years, however these figures are disputed.

In 2016 a massive steel containment structure sealed off the area, and it is estimated that the immediate plant area will not be habitable for 20,000 years.[170]

In 1986 the NASA Space Shuttle Challenger disintegrated on launch instantly killing the seven astronauts on board.

In Taiwan in 1986 the Democratic Progressive Party was formed. Chiang Kai-shek, who was leader of the Chinese Nationalist Party (KMT) that had retreated to Taiwan after losing the Chinese Civil War to Mao Zedong's Communist party in 1949, had ruled Taiwan under military martial law until his death in 1975. The new leader of the KMT, Chiang Ching-kuo did not threaten the new party and in the following year, martial law in Taiwan was abandoned and the beginning of the democratisation of Taiwan began.

An earthquake in Armenia in 1988 killed between 30,000 and 60,000 people with another 130,000 injured. The quake measured 6.8 surface wave magnitude and Mikhail Gorbachev, despite Cold War tensions, requested and allowed foreign assistance into the affected areas.

In 1988 the eight-year-long Iran-Iraq war came to an end. Iraq had invaded Iran in 1980. Iran under Ayatollah Khomeini was mainly a Shia Muslim state and, although Iraq under Saddam Hussein had a mainly Sunni government, the population of Iraq was heavily Shia and Saddam Hussein's government was fearful that Iran would encourage the Iraqi Shias to rise up against their government.

Prior to the 1980 Islamic revolution, Iran had held a close relationship with the West and the USA. With Khomeini taking power in Iran, he took a more hard-line approach to the West and Iraq saw this as an opportunity to replace Iran as the most powerful state in the region.

The war was a long arduous one and eventually a ceasefire was brokered by the United Nations Security Council in 1988.

In Scotland, in December 1988, the Lockerbie Air Disaster happened. A Pan Am Boeing 747 with 259 passengers and crew was blown up in mid-air by an onboard bomb whilst en route from London to New York, crashing over the town of Lockerbie, killing an additional 11 people on the ground. It is the deadliest terrorism act and aviation disaster to occur on British soil.

In mainland China in 1989, in Beijing, the June Fourth Incident occurred, an event that became known worldwide as the Tiananmen Square Protest.

What started as student protests, precipitated by the death of a pro-reform leader of the Chinese Communist Party, and concerns among students as to their future once they graduated, soon led to a full confrontation against the People's Liberation Army as the government declared martial law. In the government crackdown against the protests, it is estimated that between 200 (official figures) and over 1000 (unofficial figures) deaths occurred, mainly students, shot by the army.

Tiananmen Square is in central Beijing and, although it is thought that no actual deaths occurred there, the place became synonymous with the protests due to an unknown protestor, a man who stood in front of the army tanks and refused to move. The man became known worldwide as Tank Man and the photograph of his stand off against the tank became one of the most famous photographs of the 20th century.

28 years after it was built, the Berlin Wall was torn down in 1989.

Having been built in 1961 as the Cold War took hold and East Germany tried to stop Germans from crossing out of the East, the wall separating East and West Germany fell, as communist rule collapsed.

Whilst the wall had separated the nations, West Germany had tried to create a better relationship through a policy known as "Ostpolitik" (Eastern Policy) from 1969. In 1987 the new US President, Ronald Reagan, visited the Brandenburg Gate in Berlin and made a now famous speech in which he implored the new Soviet Leader (Mikhail Gorbachev) to "Tear down this wall" with the speech broadcast into both West and East Germany. Also in 1987, the East German leader Erich Honecker made an official visit to the West and by 1989 many neighbouring Soviet countries had relaxed travel restrictions for their citizens to travel to Western Europe. Protests against communism in East Germany spread until eventually communist rule collapsed and the people of Berlin physically dismantled the wall amid historic scenes as the two nations once again reunited.

In 1990 the two counties were officially unified as a Federal Republic.

In South Africa in 1990, after 27 years in jail, Nelson Mandela was released.

Following the Sharpeville massacres in 1960 (see 1960) Mandela, who was then deputy president of the ANC (African National Congress), decided to shift ANC policy from that of non-violent resistance to one in which they formed a paramilitary branch known as Umkhonto we Sizwe. Mandela was arrested in 1961 and then again in 1962 where he was initially convicted for five years, before facing trial again in 1964 at the Rivonia Trials where he was sentenced to life imprisonment for sabotage.

He spent 18 years in jail at Robben Island and was then moved to house arrest on the mainland. In 1989, however, political isolation and increased protests led the new leader of the governing National Party, F.W. de Klerk, to start relaxing the Apartheid controls. He lifted the ban on the ANC, and then in 1990 released Mandela from jail.

Mandela then led the ANC into negotiations with the National Party to end Apartheid, which occurred in 1993, and then finally in 1994 national elections were held and the ANC won, resulting in Mandela becoming the new president of South Africa.[171]

The Hubble Telescope was launched into space in 1990 and still remains in operation as one of the strongest and largest space telescopes. It was named after Edwin Hubble, a renowned American astronomer.

The Gulf War broke out in 1990.

Iraq invaded Kuwait in August 1990, angered that Kuwait consistently exceeded the OPEC quota on the amount of oil they should export. Kuwait was extremely oil rich and by exporting more than their quota they were helping to lower the oil price. Iraq, on the other hand, had an $80 billion debt following their eight-year war with Iran and needed a high oil price. Iraq also thought that countries like Kuwait had a debt to them for standing up to Iran, feeling that Iran may have invaded Kuwait had Iraq not gone to war with Iran.

However, the Iraqi invasion of Kuwait was met with a swift and unified response from the West that it, the invasion, was unacceptable. America, along with support from 34 other Western and Arab countries, quickly put together an invasion force to free Kuwait, and Operation Desert Storm was launched in January 1991 with six weeks of airstrikes followed by a ground invasion.

Iraq collapsed swiftly and on 26 February Kuwait City was liberated. The war was officially over by the end of April 1991. [172]

The USSR collapsed in 1991 after having been formed in 1922 out of a treaty joining Russia and a number of her neighbouring countries. As a result, the Cold War, which had begun in 1947 following WWII, ended.

The leader of the USSR, Mikhail Gorbachev, who had come to power in 1985 and realised the depth of their economic woes, decided reform was necessary in order to reinvigorate the country. His reforms took shape in two ways.

The first was Glasnost, meaning "openness", which pro-moted a more transparent government and more freedom of speech throughout the country, whilst the second was Perestroika, which meant "restructuring", and involved the restructuring of the economy through privatisation and other strategies aimed at increasing efficiencies.

With these two reforms underway, people began to pro-test freely on the streets against government, especially as the restructuring took time and led to a worsening of the situation before the efficiencies began. Countries surrounding Russia that were part of the USSR began to rebel and push for independence, and in August 1991 there was an attempted coup against Gorbachev as some government members were against his reforms. The sol-diers were ordered onto the streets to quell the protests, but the soldiers refused to fire upon their own people and the coup failed.

Without a hard-line military to enforce rule, the protests and calls for independence increased and in December 1991 the Soviet Union was dissolved, Gorbachev resigned and the USSR separated into the 15 independent states of: Russia, Armenia, Azerbaijan, Belarus, Estonia, Georgia, Kazakhstan, Kyrgyzstan, Latvia, Lithuania, Moldova, Tajikistan, Turkmenistan, Ukraine and Uzbekistan.

Boris Yeltsin became the first president of the new state of Russia.

Ukraine, which had only existed as a separate state briefly from 1917 to 1922 before being absorbed into the USSR, was independent again. Prior to 1917 it had existed in various forms including Kievan Rus from the 9th century and then divided up between Russia and Poland in the 17th century before becoming part of Russia in 1708.

> Just prior to the collapse of the USSR, however, Crimea, which had been gifted to Ukraine in 1954 by the Soviet Premier Khrushchev (see Joseph Stalin 1953), was given the status of Autonomous Region by the Ukrainian government. This resulted in Crimea becoming a separate republic within Ukraine.

1991 saw the beginning of the Yugoslav Wars which were a series of wars that ran through until 2001. Yugoslavia had been formed in 1918 following WWI, after the breakup of the Ottoman Empire, to which it had previously belonged. It was initially called the Kingdom of Serbs, Croats and Slovenes, but renamed Yugoslavia in 1929.

> The Yugoslav Wars were a series of independence wars that resulted in the breakup of Yugoslavia into six republics that became the six new countries of Serbia, Bosnia and Herzegovina, Montenegro, Macedonia, Slovenia, and Croatia. The wars, which included the Bosnian War, the Kosovo War, and the Croatian and Slovenian Independence Wars, became the deadliest since WWII, with 140,000 deaths recorded including the Bosnian Genocide, and mass wartime rape.

> The Kosovo War from 1998–1999 was one of these Yugoslav Wars and was fought between Kosovo's Serbian and Albanian communities until peace was brokered in 1999 and Kosovo became a self-administered area within Serbia. In 2008 Kosovo broke away from Serbia to become a partially recognised country in its own right.

The European Union formed the single market in 1993, whereby the members of the EU agreed four freedoms, these being: freedom of movement of people, goods, money, and services.

By 1995, Austria, Sweden and Finland joined the EU expanding the membership to 14, with the whole of Western Europe being members.

Beginning in 1994, the Rwandan Genocide lasted only 100 days but, during that short time, over 1,000,000 Tutsi and Hutu were killed.[173]

In 1964, Rwanda gained its independence from Belgium which had taken over the country from Germany (Germany had previously ruled Rwanda but lost all of its colonies as a result of losing WWI). In the new independent Rwanda, mainly ethnic Hutus were left in positions of political power and over the following decades resentment grew as Hutus discriminated against the Tutsis. In 1990, Tutsi rebels (the Rwandan Patriotic Front, RPF) out of Uganda rebelled against the Hutu-led Rwandan government resulting in civil war. The government launched a campaign denigrating Tutsis as traitors. Then in 1994, the Hutu Rwandan President Habyarimana's plane was shot down and this sparked the mass killings/genocide of Tutsis by Hutus. Over the next three months 800,000 Tutsis and 200,000 Hutus were murdered. By July 1994, RPF had pushed the Rwandan government out of power, and the civil war, and genocide, ended.

Mother Teresa died in 1997. She was a Catholic nun born in what is now Macedonia, who lived most of her adult life in India having decided as a teenager that she would devote her life to God and become a Christian missionary. She founded a religious order called "The Missionaries of Charity" that grew to have over 4000 nuns within it, and was active around the world managing homes with people who needed caring for, many of whom had terminal illnesses. She won the Nobel Peace Prize in 1979 and was canonised as a Saint by the Catholic Church in 2016 as Saint Teresa of Calcutta.

> The above Mother Teresa should not be confused with another Mother Teresa of England, who was the founder of the Franciscan Servants of Jesus and Mary (FJSM), a ministry that served those who needed help throughout England, based out of Posbury, Devon. Having started training as a nurse, Mother Teresa experienced a religious conversion in 1909 and the FJSM was founded in 1926 and this, English, Mother Teresa, died in 1979. [174]

At midnight on 01 July 1997, after over 150 years, Hong Kong was returned to China by Britain.

> China had ceded the island to the British in 1841 after having lost the First Opium War (see 1841) which had ended with China signing the Treaty of Nanking in 1842. Initially the Island City was ceded for 50 years but, as trade flourished there under British rule, in 1898 Britain leased further territory and China and Britian agreed to another 99 years, extending the agreement until 1997. In 1984 agreement was reached in the Sino British declaration as to how Hong Kong would be returned to China with the date agreed as 01 July 1997, with China agreeing to pre-serve Hong Kong's capitalist system thereafter.

> The handover ceremony cemented the peaceful transfer of power and so began China's policy of One Country – Two Systems.

Lady Diana died on 31 August 1997. She had been involved in a car crash in the Pont de l'Alma tunnel in Paris and was just 36 years old. Also in the vehicle with her were Dodi Fayed (her partner), Henri Paul (the chauffer), both of whom also died, and Trevor Rees-Jones, (her bodyguard) and the only survivor of the crash. Diana had been married to Prince Charles, now King Charles, of Britain but divorced in 1996.

Macau was also returned to China in 1999, in this case from the Portuguese under an agreement reached previously in which China agreed to provide autonomy to Macau for a further 50 years after China took control, therefore until 2049.

At the turn of the century the Y2K problem, also known as the Millennium Bug, captured the world's attention. Many computer programs were only able to identify a year by its final two digits, meaning 1900 and 2000 would be represented in the same way, raising huge concerns about possible loss of data when computers' clocks changed automatically from 1999 to 2000. In the end any problems were either dealt with, or did not occur, as few issues actually occurred.

Chapter 10. Today's World

CE 2000 – Present Day

CE 2000–Today

Y2k Bug, Netherlands Approves Same Sex Marriage, The 9-11 Attacks, Anthrax Attacks, War on Terror and the Afghanistan War, China joins WTO, Euro Currency Launched, Trial of Slobodan Milosevic, Bali Bombings, Sierra Leone Civil War, Iraq War and Toppling of Saddam Hussein, Madrid Train Bombings, Beslan School Siege, Yasser Arafat Death, 2004 Boxing Day Tsunami, 2005 London Bombings, Angela Merkel Germany's First Female Chancellor, Global Financial Crisis, Sichuan Earthquake, President Obama, European Sovereign Debt Crisis, Michael Jackson Death, Moscow Metro Bombings, Burj Khalifa, SA Football World Cup, Julia Gillard, WikiLeaks, Julian Assange, Arab Spring, Syrian Civil War, Burmese Parliament Convenes, Fukushima Nuclear Disaster, Osama Bin Laden Dies, Russia Joins WTO, Norway Attacks, Kim Jong-il Dies, Hugo Chavez Dies, Nelson Mandela Dies, Ukraine's Maidan Revolution, Annexure by Russia of Crimea, Malaysian Airlines MH370 Disappears, Malaysia Airline Flight 17 Shot Down, US–Cuba Relations Thaw, Charlie Hebdo Shooting, 2015 Paris Terrorist Attacks, Myanmar General Election, European Migrant Crisis, Brexit Vote, Donald Trump Elected US President, Fidel Castro Dies, Barcelona Terror Attacks, Catalonia Declares Independence, China Revoke Presidential Term Limits, Cambridge Analytica, Donald Trump Impeached, Hong Kong Protests, Julian Assange Arrested, First COVID-19 Case, Britain Leaves EU, COVID-19 Declared a Pandemic, Hong Kong Security Law Enacted, US Capitol Riots, Trump's Second Impeachment, Perseverance and Zhurong Rovers land on Mars, Myanmar Coup, Rohingya Genocide, War In Afghanistan Ends, James Webb Telescope Launched, Russia Invades Ukraine, US Supreme Court overturn Abortion Law, Shinzo Abe Assassinated, Queen Elizabeth II Dies, Turkey-Syria Earthquake, Webb Telescope Information Questions How the Universe was Formed

In December 2000 the Netherlands became the first country in the world to legalise same sex marriage after its government passed legislation allowing members of the same sex to marry, divorce and adopt children.

On 11 September 2001, the 9/11 attacks occurred.

19 terrorists from the Al-Qaeda network hijacked four aeroplanes over US soil and carried out four suicide attacks.

Two of the planes were flown into the twin towers of the World Trade Centre in New York; one was flown into the Pentagon, the US head office for their department of defence; and the fourth crashed into a field in Pennsylvania after the passengers fought against the hijackers in an effort to prevent a fourth suicide attack, possibly on The White House.

Almost 3000 people died in the four attacks, mostly when the twin tower buildings both collapsed due to the enormous heat generated by the fires from the plane crashes.

In October 2001, just one month after the 9-11 attacks, a series of anthrax attacks occurred.

Anthrax (a deadly bacteria) was posted through the US postal services to some Senators and Media offices, killing five people who came into contact with it. Some of the letters accompanying the anthrax contained death threats and phrases including "Death to America" and "Death To Israel". Although the FBI eventually concluded that the attacks were carried out by a single person, naming Dr Bruce Ivins as the culprit, Dr Ivins committed suicide in 2008, and a 2011 report by the US Governmental Accountability Office found the FBI investigation was flawed, leaving doubts as to the accuracy of the FBI's conclusion.

In the immediate aftermath of the 9/11 attacks, the term "War on Terror" was first used in America to describe their view that they were now at war with any form of terrorism.

Intelligence reports after the attacks ascertained that the terrorists were financed and trained by the Osama Bin Laden "Al-Qaeda" terrorist organisation. Just prior to the 9/11 attacks the Lion of Panjshir, Ahmad Shah Massoud, who was an anti-terrorism expert and leader of the Northern Alliance (an anti-Taliban coalition), was assassinated by Al-Qaeda and this gave Bin Laden the confidence that after the 9/11 attacks he would be able to evade US troops, as he would be protected by the Taliban.[175]

The War on Terror thus started in 2001 with the war against Afghanistan, when the US led an invasion into Afghanistan where it had determined Bin Laden was hiding. By November the Taliban was in retreat and by December 2001, Bin Laden had escaped into Pakistan after a battle in the caves of Tora Brava between Taliban and US-backed Afghan fighters.

By the end of 2001 Hamid Karzai was installed as interim head of Afghanistan and in 2002 was picked to lead the new Afghan government as restructuring of the country began.

Separately in 2001, after over a decade of negotiations, China became a member of the WTO (World Trade Organisation), leading to a massive increase in exports from China resulting in it becoming the largest exporting nation on Earth by 2009.

In 2002 the Euro became legal currency in 12 of the member countries of the European Union. Britain and Denmark, which were members of the EU, did not adopt the currency.

In February 2002 the trial at the Hague began against Slobodan Milosevic for crimes against humanity during the Yugoslav Wars (see 1991 Yugoslav Wars), and specifically relating to Kosovo and the genocide in Bosnia. Critics felt the timing of the tribunal was aimed at justifying NATO's involvement in the wars and Milosevic defended himself at the tribunal. He died during the trial (see 2006).

In October 2002 over 200 people were killed and another 200 injured in three consecutive bomb blasts in Bali, Indonesia. Many of the victims were tourists, with half those killed being Australian or English. A voice recording, supposedly that of Osama Bin Laden, stated the bombings were in retaliation for those who supported America in the War on Terror.

Also in 2002, the decade-long Sierra Leone Civil War came to an end. Charles Taylor in Liberia had supported the Revolutionary United Front (RUF) who attempted to overthrow the sitting government in Sierra Leone. With strong British support for a United Nations force, the Sierra Leone government eventually defeated the RUF, ending the Civil War.

In February 2003 the NASA Space Shuttle Columbia disintegrated on re-entry to Earth killing all seven astronauts on board. This was the second such disaster to have happened to NASA (see 1986 Space Shuttle Challenger disaster).

Also in February 2003, Colin Powell, the US Secretary of State, declared to the UN Security Council that Saddam Hussein, the Iraqi president, was trying to build nuclear weapons and in March 2003 the Iraq War began with an invasion of Iraq by a coalition led by the US, but including Australia and Britain.

George W Bush was quoted as stating the aim of the war was "to disarm Iraq of weapons of mass destruction", which were never found, and therefore the justification for the war remains disputed to this day. Within two months, by the end of April, the coalition troops reached Baghdad and the image of the statue of Saddam Hussein being toppled became one of the most memorable images of the 21st century.

Whilst the initial invasion and removal of Saddam Hussein was a success, the war was not and ran on in a prolonged and protracted manner until 2011, during which time no weapons of mass destruction were found.

In December 2003, Saddam Hussein was found in hiding and captured. The new Iraqi interim government began a trial against him for crimes against humanity during his terms in power (for verdict see 2006).

In 2004, in March, ten bombs exploded on four trains near the city centre of Madrid killing 190 people and leaving over 1800 injured.

Initially the government blamed a Basque separatist group called ETA, (Euskadi Ta Askatasuna meaning Basque Homeland and Liberty) that campaigned for Basque to become an independent state from Spain, for the bombings.

However, with elections just three days after the bombings, within two days of the event, the police investigation led to the fact that Al-Qaeda were probably to blame as the

Spanish government had shown strong support for the US-led coalition's War on Terror and the invasion of Iraq.

With most of the Spanish population against the support for the Iraqi invasion, the Spanish government lost the elections to the Spanish Socialist Workers' Party who had been against the invasion.

In 2007 Islamic fundamentalists, not ETA, were convicted of the bombings.

In 2004 the total member countries of the EU climbed to 25 as ten new countries joined, including former Eastern European countries, meaning European divisions created after WWII were finally ended.

The Beslan School Siege occurred in 2004 in Beslan, North Ossetia, a Russian autonomous region.

In the siege, terrorists held over 1,100 people hostage, including more than 750 children, as they made demands for the withdrawal of all Russian troops from Chechnya which they wanted to be independent from Russia.

On the third day of the siege, and whilst negotiations were still underway, an explosion triggered shooting and a fire started on the roof of the school gymnasium where the hostages were being held. The roof collapsed, killing many hostages, and some tried to escape. Shooting then broke out between the security forces and the terrorists and the security forces then stormed the school.

By the end of the battle that ensued, and the end of the siege, more than 300 people had died, of which over 180 were children. It is considered the deadliest school shooting in history.

Yasser Arafat, leader of the Palestine Liberation Organisation (the PLO), died at age 75 in France.

Arafat had been opposed to the 1948 creation of the Israeli State and in the 1950s had founded a political party, Fatah, which sought the removal of the Israeli state and the formation of a Palestinian state instead.

He joined the PLO in 1967 and whilst he had initially been opposed to the state of Israel, by the 1990s he had accepted it and supported the idea of a two-state solution to the Israeli–Palestinian conflict, an Israeli state and a Palestinian state. In 1994 he won the Nobel Peace prize for his efforts (along with Israeli Prime Ministers Yitzhak Rabin and Shimon Peres).

To this day the two-state solution has not materialised due to disputes over the respective territories.

In 2004, in Afghanistan, a new constitution was adopted and Hamad Karzai became the first democratically elected president of the country. Shortly afterwards Bin Laden released a taped video message saying Al-Qaeda wanted to restore freedom to the country.

On Boxing Day, 26 December, 2004, a massive tsunami hit 14 Indian Ocean countries including Thailand, Indonesia, India, and Sri Lanka.

The cause of the tsunami was a 9.1 magnitude undersea earthquake off the coast of Sumatra, Indonesia, along the fault line of the Burma and India tectonic plates. The earthquake was the largest ever recorded and the resulting tsunami created waves as high as 30 metres. Over 225,000 people died as a result of the tsunami, one of the deadliest natural disasters in history.

In July 2005, in London, four suicide bombers set off three bombs on the London Underground and one on a double decker bus. Fifty-two people died in the bombings.

In November 2005, Germany's first ever female Chancellor, Angela Merkel, took office. Having studied Physics, she earned her doctorate in 1978 and entered politics in 1989 after the fall of the Berlin Wall. She served as Chancellor until 2021.[176]

In 2006, three years after his capture, Saddam Hussein's trial came to an end. He was found guilty of crimes against humanity, mainly relating to the deaths of Shia Iraqis in 1982. He was sentenced to death and hanged in 2006.

In 2006 the union of Serbia and Montenegro that had formed after the breakup of the former Yugoslavia (see 1991 Yugoslav Wars) broke up, and Montenegro took its independence creating the two separate states of Serbia and Montenegro. In 2008 Kosovo declared itself independent from Serbia, forming another state.

Beginning in 2007 and running through 2008, the Global Financial Crisis was the worst worldwide financial crisis since the Great Depression (see 1929). Excessive and aggressive lending within the real estate market, and derivatives linked to these investments, led to too much money being secured by property prices. Once these "mortgage-backed securities" fell in value the huge investments held by various banks lost immense value leading to a banking crisis.

With concerns arising that if too many banks went bankrupt, a run on banks became a real possibility as queues started forming outside some banks as the worried public tried to withdraw savings. Governments around the world handed out massive bailouts to banks to ensure they remained liquid and prevent a collapse in the global banking system. In the US, Bear Sterns had to bail out two of its hedge funds with $20 billion secured against these debt obligations; New Century, a real estate investment trust, filed for Chapter 11 bankruptcy protection; in Europe, BNP Paribas froze two of its hedge funds; in the UK, Northern Rock had to receive help from the Bank of England to prevent a run on the bank and was fully nationalised in 2008; in September 2008 Lehman Brothers, one of the world's largest investment banks, went bankrupt; later in 2008, the US Congress passed a $700 billion bailout fund to purchase mortgage-backed securities from banks; and in November Iceland had to apply for a loan from the International Monetary Fund to bail out its banks.[177]

Quantitative Easing (injections of credit into the financial system carried on by central banks around the world through purchasing government bonds) continued in the following few years as the worldwide crisis slowly eased and economies gradually recovered.

In China, in 2008, over 60,000 were killed and millions left homeless after an earthquake measuring 7.9 / 8.0 occurred near Chengdu, Sichuan Province.

In November 2008, Barack Obama was elected as the first African American President of the United States.

In 2009 the European Debt Crisis began when it became apparent that Greece would default on debt repayments due. Over the next few years the debt crisis spread through to Portugal, Ireland, Italy and Spain who had to be bailed out by the European Central Bank which feared the collapse of the Euro as a currency.

In 2009 Michael Jackson died suddenly aged just 50. His death was due to cardiac arrest caused by over-use of sedatives and anaesthetics. His album *Thriller* is the best-selling album of all time, and in the 1980s he had nine number one singles.

The first Bitcoin wallet, software that stores information pertaining to who owns the underlying blockchain technology, was released by Satoshi Nakamoto in 2009 and blockchain technology was born. This is a decentralised ledger recording all transactions of crypto currencies, meaning no one person or entity can control the underlying currency.

In 2010 Russian Suicide bombers attacked metro trains in Moscow leaving 40 dead and 100 injured. The bombings were perpetrated by Islamic groups fighting for independence of some of the Russian states in the north Caucus region of Russia.

In Dubai in 2010 the world's tallest building was officially opened, and signified Dubai's speedy rise to modernity as the city sought to establish itself as a worldwide trading centre. The Burj Khalifa remains to this day the world's tallest building at 828 metres high.

South Africa became the first African nation to ever host the FIFA Football World Cup in 2010

Also in 2010, Australia elected their first ever female Prime Minister when Julia Gillard took office.

In Portugal, in 2010, NATO members agreed and signed a resolution to hand over power in Afghanistan to Afghan troops. Over the past four years an increase in militant activity in the country had destabilised the democratic country, which had had coalition troops provide security and train the Afghan army.

In 2010 WikiLeaks, which had been launched in 2006 in order to leak documents to the public, rose to international prominence when it published leaks provided by Chelsea Manning, a US Army intelligence analyst (Chelsea Manning had been born Bradley Manning but identified as a woman and in 2013 requested to be known as Chelsea Manning thereafter). The documents included:

Collateral Murder – a video showing US helicopters shooting at civilians in Iraq's Baghdad, which also killed two Reuters journalists.

Cablegate – that revealed classified cables that had been sent from over 250 US consulates and embassies and diplomatic missions to the US State Department. Western media outlets simultaneously published some of the documents.[178] Some of the key points leaked included:

The US had instructed its diplomats to spy on people working at the United Nations
That Arab nations had called for airstrikes against

Iran's nuclear facilities
That China was losing patience with the North Korean leader Kim Jong-Il.

The release also led to Julian Assange being wanted in the US over various charges including spying. In 2010 he was accused of rape in Sweden after a trip there and Sweden issued an arrest warrant. Assange, who was in London when the warrant was issued, turned himself into the British police, claiming sex was consensual, and fought extradition to Sweden as he feared they would extradite him to the US.

Losing his appeal in the UK, Assange took up refugee status in the Ecuadorian Embassy in London where he claimed and was granted asylum and lived for seven years [179] (see 2019 for what happened next to Julian Assange).

In December 2010, protesting against police harassment in Tunisia, a young vegetable trader set himself alight. Whilst he, Mohamed Bouazizi, died in January 2011, by then his single act of protest had spread around the country as people rose up to protest the cost of living and the authoritarian government led by Zine al-Abidine Ben Ali. Ali, who had been in power for 23 years, was forced to flee, becoming the first Arab leader to ever be removed by popular protest.[180]

The protests caught on across the Arab world leading to what became known as the Arab Spring.

In Egypt, where the protests moved to next, Hosni Mubarak, who had been in power for 30 years, was forced out and resigned after a month of protests in February 2011.

In Bahrain protests also occurred but were dealt with rigorously by the police.

Yemen, which had been ruled by Saleh for 33 years, also descended into chaos as protests spread and Saleh handed power to his deputy.

In Libya, what started as an Arab Spring uprising degenerated into civil war as Muammar Gaddafi tried to violently quell protests against his rule.

The country fell into civil war, and, after having ruled the country as a dictator for 42 years, Gaddafi was captured and killed. The country remains split, ruled by Eastern and Western factions.

In Syria, as with Libya, the Arab Spring uprising became a full-blown civil war in its own right.

President Bashar al-Assad used brutal force to quell protests, and blamed the West as the war became entrenched.

Bashar was supported by Iran and Russia in his fight to retain power and control of the country, and to date over 400,000 have been killed and over 10 million have lost their homes.

It was in Syria that ISIS first came to prominence. Initially known as ISIL, the Islamic State of Iraq and the Levant (the East), ISIS stands for the Islamic State of Iraq and Syria and used social media to recruit fighters to its causes of retaining power in Syria and fighting Western beliefs.

ISIS was responsible for a number of executions of military as well as civilian captives including journalists and aid workers.

In January 2011, the Burmese parliament met for the first time in 20 years, signifying the end of military rule. A year earlier, in 2010, democratic leader Aung San Suu Kyi had been released having served 15 out of 21 years under house arrest.

In 2011 Burma allowed peaceful protests within the country and in 2012 Suu Kyi won a seat in Parliament.

In 2011 a huge earthquake off the coast of Japan caused a tsunami that swept over Honshu island killing almost 20,000 people and flooding the reactors of the Fukushima nuclear power plant. Authorities had already shut down the nuclear reactors after detecting the earthquake and before the tsunami hit their defences, switching on diesel generators to keep the core cool. The tsunami, however, overwhelmed the generators and, before power could be restored, over the next 3 days the reactors overheated, and radiation leaked into the atmosphere.

Whilst the event was labelled a nuclear disaster, no one died in the incident and by 2021 a UN report detailed that there had also been few reports of adverse reactions or illnesses among people in the surrounding areas.

In 2011, Osama Bin Laden was found and killed by US troops in Pakistan. In June 2011 President Obama announced a troop withdrawal from the country, and in December 2011 a ceremony in Baghdad declared the end of the mission to Iraq.

After 18 years of negotiations Russia became part of the World Trade Organisation in 2011

The Norway attacks occurred in 2011 when 77 people were killed by far-right activist Anders Behring Breivik, who first detonated a car bomb in Oslo, then opened fire on participants at a political youth group just outside the city. Breivik was caught, tried and convicted.

In December 2011, North Korea's supreme leader and dictator Kim Jong-il died, and his son Kim Jong-un assumed power. Jong-il had taken over from his father Kim Il-sung in 1994 and his father had ruled since the country was established in 1948. This means to date, since 1948, North Korea has only had three leaders.

Venezuela's president Hugo Chavez died of cancer in 2013. He had used high oil profits to fund socialist policies in the country but eventually the country hit economic woes under his policies.

Also in 2013, Nelson Mandela died at age 95. He had been South Africa's first democratically elected and first Black president (see 1994)

In 2014 protests broke out across Ukraine against the decision taken by President Victor Yanukovych not to sign an Association Agreement with the European Union. [181] The largest protest occurred in the Maidan Nezalezhnosti (Independence Square) in Kiev and so these demonstrations became known as the EuroMaidan Revolution.

By refusing to sign the Association Agreement with the European Union, Yanukovych was manoeuvring Ukraine away from its pro-European path, and towards the path favoured by Russia (Yanukovych was pro-Russia), and an alternative treaty which was the Eurasian Customs Union.

Over 100 people died in the protests, but the protestors won, Yanukovych had to flee the country, and the pro-Russian government collapsed.

Having lost its influence over Ukraine, Russia then occupied Crimea and annexed the Crimean Peninsula.

Prior to this, in 1954, when Nikita Khrushchev took over from Stalin he had given Crimea to the Soviet Republic of Ukraine in celebration of 300 years of unity between Russia and Ukraine. Crimea had been part of Russia for the previous 200 years since the second Russian-Turkish war (see 1787–1791), which had resulted in Turkey officially recognising Crimea as Russian.

In March 2014, Malaysia Airline MH370 disappeared en route from Kuala Lumpur to Beijing. A massive search was undertaken as far south as the southern Indian Ocean but by 2017, with no definite findings, other than some debris belonging to the plane that washed up, the search was called off. To date there is no final result as to the cause of the disappearance but hypoxia (sudden decompression resulting in unconsciousness of all on board) as well as various hijacking theories were all explored, as well as the possibility that it was shot down to prevent a possible terrorist event. There were 239 people on board.

Later in 2014 a further disaster struck Malaysian Airlines when one of its aircraft, carrying 298 people, was shot down over Ukraine, with no survivors. Most of those on board were Dutch with the flight having originated in Amsterdam on its way to

Kuala Lumpur. In September 2016 a Dutch-led team presented their findings that the plane was shot down by a surface-to-air missile fired from Eastern Ukraine where fighting was occurring between Ukrainian nationals and Russian-backed separatists; presumably the target being a military aircraft not a civilian one.

In 2014 President Barack Obama of America and the Cuban President Raul Castro announced that hostilities between the two countries would be ended after 54 years, and diplomatic ties restored. In 2016 Obama became the first sitting US President to visit Cuba since 1928.

> However later, when Donald Trump came to power, many of these diplomatic missions were shut down and Obama's open policies to Cuba were reversed. A series of unexplained radio-frequency-induced hearing injuries occurred to US and Canadian diplomatic staff in Cuba resulted in most staff being pulled back from the island.

January 2015 saw the Charlie Hebdo shootings in Paris, when 17 people were killed at the offices of the satirical magazine – Charlie Hebdo. Two Algerian brothers, Cherif and Said Kouachi, were the killers and referred to themselves as defenders of the Prophet Muhammad. [182] They said that they were avenging cartoons the magazine had published of the prophet. The publication of icons of, or such images of, the prophet is banned under Islam, as are all religious icons. The magazine had been sued for racism following the publishing of the pictures but had won the lawsuit. The magazine had followed up by issuing a special edition naming the Prophet Muhammed as Editor in Chief, and had then been firebombed in response.

Later in the year, in Paris, a series of terrorist attacks occurred throughout the city killing 130 people. The attacks included three suicide bombs outside the Stade de France during a football match, crowd shootings at a café, and a mass shooting at a music concert. The attacks were the deadliest in Europe since the 2004 Madrid attacks. ISIL (ISIS) claimed responsibility for the attacks.

In November 2015, General Elections were held in Myanmar (formally Burma) and the National League for Democracy (NLD) won outright and Aung San Suu Kyi was elected State Counsellor for Myanmar, a newly created position, allowing her to lead the country. Under the actual laws of the country, she could not be president as her late husband and children were not citizens of Myanmar. In 2010, Aung San Suu Kyi had been released after having served 15 out of 21 years under house arrest.

2015 saw the European Migrant Crisis begin. Over 1 million people, mostly refugees fleeing the war in Syria, the conflicts in Iraq and Afghanistan, as well as those fleeing poverty in Africa, tried to move to Europe, many to claim asylum.

The Brexit vote occurred in 2016 as Britain voted to leave the European Union in a referendum.

It had been a member since 1973 and was part of the EU Single Market, an agreement that stipulated freedom of movement of money goods, services and people within the EU. However, when most countries also adopted the Euro as their currency in 2002, Britain did not, keeping its own currency in place.

The result was unexpected and the Prime Minister, David Cameron, who had called the referendum, resigned, and the deadline for the date on which Britain would officially leave the EU was set for 31 Jan 2020.

After one of the most controversial campaigns in US history, in November 2016 Donald Trump was elected the 45th President of the United States. It was the fifth time in history that the winning candidate did not win the popular vote. In this case Trump was running against Hillary Clinton and in terms of pure people's votes, Clinton won 48.2% of the vote whilst Trump won 46.1%. In US Presidential elections, however, the people are voting for state electors who in turn elect their candidate for President. Therefore, the possibility exists that enough electors vote for one winning candidate from the 50 states, but there are more people resident in the losing states that actually voted for the opposing candidate.

Fidel Castro, Cuba's revolutionary leader from 1959 to 2008 and a strong Marxist Leninist, died in 2016.

In 2017 another Mount Etna eruption injured ten people and was one of the largest since the 1971 major eruption which destroyed the mountain cable car and threatened a number of villages on its slope. Etna is still one of the most active volcanoes in the world with over 15 eruptions over the last 100 years.

In August 2017 members of ISIS drove two vehicles into pedestrians in Barcelona and killed 13 people. Two others were killed by the terrorists in separate attacks. Eight of the organisers were killed by the police and three were convicted and jailed.

Later that year, also in Spain, one of the provinces, Catalonia, declared independence. No other country, nor the Spanish government, recognised the declaration and the Spanish president dismissed the Catalan president and his cabinet.

China, in 2018, adopted a constitutional amendment that reversed term limits for the President and Vice President (which had been put in place in 1982), and solidified one-party rule of the country.

In 2018 the Cambridge Analytica scandal occurred. The firm, working with SCL Group, a British PR firm, had an app built that was used by Facebook users. The small print in the app allowed data from those who downloaded it, as well as their Facebook Friends, to be used and sold on. Cambridge Analytica managed to then get hold of the profiles of over 80,000,000 Facebook users. Cambridge Analytica worked on the Trump campaign and its Vice President, Steve Bannon, became an adviser to Donald Trump.[183]

In 2019 Donald Trump was impeached (charged with mis-conduct) whilst in office for soliciting foreign interference in the 2020 election. The allegations were that he withheld aid to Ukraine on the basis that he first wanted the Ukrainian President Zelenskyy to investigate Trump's opposition candidate, Joe Biden. Trump was charged and acquitted on two separate charges, one of abuse of power and the other was obstruction of Congress.

During 2019 riots broke out across Hong Kong against a proposed bill that would allow extradition to the Chinese mainland. Protestors were angered by the chance that the bill would challenge Hong Kong's judicial independence and allow China to extradite persons it wanted and try them in the mainland instead. The bill was withdrawn after months of protests.

In 2019 the new Ecuadorian government revoked Julian Assange's asylum status (for the earlier history of Assange and how he had been granted Ecuadorian asylum in their embassy in London, see 2010). The British police entered the embassy and arrested Assange and convicted him of breaking bail conditions.

He is now in a British jail where he still faces possible extradition to Sweden and / or to the US, but is appealing on various grounds including mental health after being in either asylum or jail for over 11 years.

In December 2019, the first case of COVID 19 was reported in China in the city of Wuhan.

In January 2020 the seafood market where it was believed Covid 19 first originated was shut down and China reported 40 cases of what they called a novel coronavirus, and the term 2019 Novel Coronavirus was coined. By the end of January, cases were reported in Thailand, followed by Japan and then South Korea. Wuhan was placed under lockdown, and travellers from China began to be screened as they entered the US.[184]

On 31 January 2020, Britain officially exited the EU as the Brexit agreement came into being. Having voted to leave in a 2016 referendum, the European Union (Withdrawal Agreement) Act 2020 was approved in the UK and from 31 January 2020–31 December 2020 the UK entered a transition period, no longer an EU member and after 31 December 2020 the transition period was ended and Britain left the single market and the customs union.

In February 2020 the 2019 Novel Coronavirus was officially named Covid 19 and by March 2020 the World Health Organisation (WHO) declared Covid 19 a pandemic.

In the US a nationwide emergency was declared, and a travel ban was imposed banning non-US citizens from travelling to the country from over 26 countries.

By April 2020 lockdowns and travel restrictions began to occur worldwide as governments decided to try and curb the spread of COVID-19. Mask wearing and social distancing measures become the new norm worldwide.

In March 2023 the leader of the WHO said that with statistics on the virus declining, he expected the WHO to declare an end to the pandemic by the end of 2023.[185]

In 2020 Hong Kong passed the Law of the People's Republic of China on Safeguarding National Security in the Hong Kong Special Administrative Region.

Essentially the law gave China further powers in Hong Kong over terrorism activities and to take action over those who might promote secession of the island away from China.

On 06 January 2021 in Washington DC, America, the Capitol Riots occurred. In protesting the certification of the Biden victory over Donald Trump in the November 2020 elections, protestors converged on the Capitol Building, the seat of the House of Congress, the legislative branch of the US government. In a speech made on the day, Trump urged his supporters to protest, but peacefully, as he claimed the vote had been rigged. In the afternoon protests turned to riots and the building was stormed. Over 100 law enforcement officers were injured, and one protestor died during the riots.

One week later, Donald Trump was impeached for his role in inciting the rioting. He then became the first President in history to be impeached twice. However, as with his first impeachment, he was acquitted.

In February 2021 NASA's Mars 2020 Rover, named Perseverance, landed on Mars looking for signs of ancient life and to collect samples of rock and soil. It had taken the Rover almost seven months to travel there. In May 2021 another rover, called Zhurong, landed on Mars, this one belonging to the Chinese National Space Administration.

In Myanmar in 2021, General Min Aung Hlaing staged a coup taking away power from Aung San Suu Kyi and her NLD party (see 2011) and charged her with corruption. Protests broke out across the country and were quelled by the military. A parallel government called the National Unity Government (NUG) declared war on the military govern-ment resulting in continued clashes between the two parties throughout the country.[186]

In the years leading up to the coup, from 2017, the mili-tary had persecuted and displaced the Muslim Rohingya population of Myanmar leading to over one million fleeing the country, many to Bangladesh where the world's largest refugee camp has since formed.

In 2021 the war in Afghanistan, which had started 20 years earlier (see 2001), ended as US forces were pulled out of the country and the Republican government, which had been formed under Hamad Karzai (see 2004), fled.

In 2014 the NATO-led forces had officially handed security of Afghanistan over to the Afghan Republican government. The Afghan government was unable to defeat the Taliban forces and in 2020 the US and Taliban negotiated a deal that agreed for the withdrawal of US troops from the country on condition that the Taliban would not attack US forces or their allies. However, once the US forces were withdrawn, the Taliban launched attacks against the Afghan government (now led by Ashraf Ghani) throughout 2021, eventually causing the collapse of the government, which fled, and the Taliban was restored to power, with an Emirate replacing the republic.

At the close of 2021, in December, the James Webb Telescope was launched into space. This telescope was the greatest science observatory step since the launch of the Hubble Telescope (see 1990) and was designed to see further into space than any other observational machine ever built. It was launched through a partnership between the US NASA (National Aeronautics and Space Administration), the ESA (European Space Agency) and the CSA (Canadian Space Agency). Light emitted by the first stars and galaxies ever formed has moved over billions of years from ultraviolet light to infrared light. Unlike Hubble, which sees ultraviolet light, the James Webb Telescope sees infrared light, meaning it can see further back in time to almost 100 million years after the Big Bang! The telescope was named after the NASA Administrator (the highest NASA Official) from 1961 to 1968, James Webb.[187]

Turkey changed its name to Türkiye during 2021. This was agreed to by the United Nations after a request by the country itself. The name Türkiye is more closely aligned phonetically to the way people of Türkiye call their country.

In 2022 Russia invaded Ukraine.

Following Ukraine's Maidan revolution (see 2014) the pro-Russian government there was ousted. Prior to this, in 2010, Russia had proposed a European Security Treaty that would have prevented NATO expansion into Europe and brought Russia and Europe closer together. In the 1990s President Gorbachev had promoted the idea of Russia's home being in Europe and after Gorbachev, in 2012, Putin himself had stated that "Russia is an inseparable, organic part of Greater Europe, of the wider European civilisation. Our citizens feel themselves to be Europeans." Russia proposed a European Security Treaty that would have stopped NATO enlargement in Europe and kept Ukraine a neutral country between Russia and the NATO members of Europe.[188]

However, when Ukraine ousted the pro-Russian government and sided with a strongly America-aligned Europe, Russia began backing separatists in the Donbas region of Ukraine (comprised of Donetsk and Luhansk).

In 2021 the US-Ukraine Strategic Partnership brought closer to reality the prospect of America arming Ukraine and Ukraine threatening to retake the Donbas region. With Putin strongly against this and having lost all faith in the America-aligned Europe building any meaningful relationship with Russia, Putin had decided to align himself with Asia. In February 2022 China and Russia issued a joint statement opposing NATO expansion with Putin claiming NATO was undermining Russia. Putin then tried unsuccessfully to negotiate a treaty that would ensure Ukraine remained independent but, with these negotiations unsuccessful, Putin launched the invasion.

In mid-2022, the US Supreme Court overturned a 50-year-old law that gave every citizen in the US access to abortion as a legal right. This overturn meant that each individual state could make their own abortion laws including banning abortion if that state so chose.

In July 2022, whilst speaking at a political rally, Shinzo Abe, the former Prime Minister of Japan, was assassinated, shot from behind.

> The assassin's mother had become bankrupt some years earlier in relation to her involvement with the Unification Church to which Abe had political ties. Further investigations revealed the Church pressurised its members to make large donations to it and the political scandal which ensued resulted in the Japanese government passing bills restricting the activities of such church groups.

In September 2022, Queen Elizabeth II, of the United Kingdom, died aged 96.

> Having come to the throne aged 27 on the death of her father King George VI, she became Britain's longest serving monarch and reigned for 70 years. When she was born, she was not first in line to take the throne, only becoming so when her uncle, Edward VIII, who was King at the time, abdicated in order to marry Mrs Wallis Simpson a twice-divorced American. The abdication brought her father to the throne. Elizabeth married Philip, Prince of Greece, in 1947 who died in 2021 aged 99.

> On her death her son, Prince Charles, became King Charles III.

In 2023, two huge earthquakes struck southern Türkiye near the Syrian border. The first was magnitude 7.9 and the second 7.5.

Over 50,000 deaths occurred as a result of the earthquake across the two countries, with over 8 million people living in the affected areas, and over 200,000 buildings destroyed or damaged.

In February 2023 information from the James Webb Telescope revealed that six galaxies were over 100 times larger than they were expected to be just after the Big Bang, meaning that our initial hypothesis as to how the universe was formed, and the Big Bang itself, may not be as accurate as previously thought!

To be continued...

Epilogue

No doubt there are inaccuracies and omittances in this book, as well as areas which are highly subjective.

As much as possible I have tried to keep this to a timeline – simple dates of events and people – without going into detail on subjective matters as to who was right and who was wrong. Nevertheless, from all the wars that are mentioned you cannot help but get a feel as to how destructive we are as a species.

However, if you then take a look at the Alvarez event (end of Chapter 1 and beginning of Chapter 2) you see that after the most destructive event that EVER happened to our planet... it RECOVERED!

It took 4 million years to recover but, in the greater scheme of things (14 billion years), that is not a long time. The planet will recover from what we do to it, but we do need to evolve further first.

Linked to the above, whilst writing this book I read biologist Jeremy Griffith's brilliant summary of his book *Freedom: The End Of The Human Condition*, called *Transform Your Life and Save The World*. [189] You should read it, but, with apologies to Jeremy, my summary of it is as follows.

Jeremy describes the human condition of us having an internal psychological struggle since we came into existence, of our Instinctive Self versus our Conscious Self. Our Instinctive

Self wants us to live in a union of cooperation with each other (because that is how we used to live as very early primates) whilst our Conscious Self wants to explore all our capabilities including selfish tendencies. Thus, we have a good wolf–bad wolf battle raging inside every one of us, leading to guilt over our selfish actions, yet we continue with these selfish actions as we try to justify them through trying to find, and increase, our self-worth.

The problem is that we only know how to gauge our self-worth by competing with our fellow man and judging ourselves on materialistic one-upmanship, and we can only gather these materialistic things by selfishly pushing ourselves ahead of those around us, which we then feel guilty about!

The more we get, the more we need, as we remain trapped inside a cycle of continually needing to justify our actions to ourselves in order to provide ourselves with the recognition and self-esteem we so sorely need. This includes declaring war on each other and all the other terribly destructive actions we take as the human race. However, deep down, we continue to know and believe that we are not evil beings, but good beings, because that is what we are at the core (our Instinctive Self).

So, the take-away from this book is that we just need the timeline to run on a few more centuries or millennia and for the world to evolve further!

We have tried monarchical societies, which didn't work. We have tried, and continue to try, forms of capitalism and communism and to a certain extent have discounted communism as not viable, leaving capitalism to run rampant.

We are now seeing the destructiveness and selfishness of capitalism as we allow our Conscious Self to explore itself unfettered (how much wealth and power do people and leaders need?), but I don't see it working over the long term. Inevitably, as Marx said, the poorer will rebel against the inequality.

Personally, I think we will have to evolve into a version of all three of these societal structures.

A ruling elite who are highly educated and knowledgeable and receive their justification and recognition for what they do through ruling well and making decisions for the betterment of all, i.e. rulers who need the recognition from society (for their own self-worth) that they are good rulers just as much as they need to be well paid for doing so, and they recognise this fact.

Then, people need to be given freedom to make themselves as successful as they want to be, in whatever field they endeavour.

Thirdly, society needs to evolve to a level where we judge each other on non-materialistic things. It needs to become normal to treat each other with respect and kindness, and for those who don't to be frowned upon. So, teachers are judged as well as successful businesspeople, and people who do excel in business or politics or any other field will not want to act in an unscrupulous manner as they will recognise that this effects their own self-esteem and leads to more destructive behaviour. So, whilst people are provided the freedom to make themselves as successful as they can be, they will recognise the pitfalls of doing so and act more responsibly and accordingly.

In other words, we need to evolve psychologically quite far from where we are now. Currently we are allowing ourselves to be led into more destructive behaviour (by those who cannot yet control their Conscious Selves) and it is likely we will allow ourselves to be led like this for quite some time to come before we eventually recognise what is happening to ourselves and rebel.

I think Singapore is the closest to what we should aspire to. Leaders there are highly educated and highly paid, but it is expected of them to perform their duties well, and to a certain extent the shame of not doing so can outweigh any material gain from not doing so.

What about technology? Well, the problem with Marx's view that in an overly capitalist society the poor will rise up is that if the power remains concentrated in the hands of the few, even in a socialist or communist state, the society still doesn't work. This is evidenced from Pol Pot's Cambodia to Stalin or Mao's communism. Marx believed the problem lay in ownership of private property, but history shows that the real problem is in too much concentrated power. Humans, as they have evolved so far, simply can't handle too much power.

Perhaps then, technology will help distribute power better and blockchain technology is doing this, wrestling power away from central banks and governments into collective ownership and responsibility, and non-fungible tokens (NFTs) will allow anyone to control their own intellectual property. Artificial intelligence will result in universal incomes being brought in as fewer people are employed, and huge corporations have less labour costs but are taxed heavily in response. This means that people at home will have more time to take up cottage industries and become creative and have more control over their time and thoughts.

So, where will religion, another major theme in this book, fit into this utopian future? Well, again, as with societies, religion will have to evolve into a combined version of them all. Part of this will be a need to return to faith, but an inclusive faith, more akin to Buddhist beliefs as a way of life, rather than binary faiths that exclude other beliefs. I will explore this more in another book which I am working on, but there is no doubt in my mind that the core to all religion is faith. A belief in something. If you don't have this, you have nothing and whatever you do believe in you can become. Once we truly understand this, we will choose to believe in good things; why would any intelligent being choose anything else if they know it will come true?

Good luck to us all! ☺

Bruce

P.S. If you enjoyed this book and are interested in further books I have written, and am writing, or if you want an updated version of Bruce's Timeline of Our World, please go to www.brucetapping.com for more information.

References

1. Pappas, Stephanie. "What Was the First Life on Earth?" LiveScience. Published March 1, 2017. Starts With a Big Bang. Retrieved October 2021. https://bigthink.com/starts-with-a-bang/.

2. Scott, Andrew C. "When Did Humans Discover Fire? The Answer Depend on What You Mean by 'Discover.'" *Time*. June 1, 2018. https://time.com/5295907/discover-fire/.

3. *Encyclopedia.com*. s.v. "Alvarez Event." Accessed June 8, 2023. https://www.encyclopedia.com/science/dictionaries-thesauruses-pictures-and-press-releases/alvarez-event.

4. O'Neil, Dennis. "The First Primates." Palomar.edu. Accessed June 20, 2023. https://www.palomar.edu/anthro/earlyprimates/early_2.htm.

5. Hill, Jenny. "Paleolithic Egypt." Ancient Egypt Online. Accessed June 20, 2023. https://ancientegyptonline.co.uk/paleolithic/.

6. Bowdler, Sandra. "The Pleistocene Pacific (N.D.)." The University of Western Australia, www.archaeology.arts.uwa.edu.au/about/research/bowdler__research_interests/the_pleistocene_pacific. Accessed 8 Jun. 2023.

7. DK Publishing. *Eyewitness Ancient Egypt*. DK Eyewitness. New York: Penguin Random House. https://www.penguinrandomhouse.com/books/671325/eyewitness-ancient-egypt-by-dk/.

8. Wikipedia. S.v. "Phoenicia." Updated June 9, 2023. https://en.wikipedia.org/wiki/Phoenicia.

9. Softschools.com. "Roman Empire Timeline." Softschools (website). Accessed June 20, 2023. https://www.softschools.com/viewTimeline.action?id=9.

10. Lloyd, James. "Homer." *World History Encyclopedia*. June 19, 2021. https://www.worldhistory.org/homer/.

11. Cartwright, Mark. "The 12 Olympian Gods." *World History Encyclopedia*. September 10, 2019. https://www.worldhistory.org/collection/58/the-12-olympian-gods/.

12. Lahanas, Michael. "Mythical Chronology of Greece." Hellenica World (website). Accessed June 20, 2023. www.hellenicaworld.com/Greece/Mythology/en/MythicalChronology.html.

13 A&E Television Networks. "Hannibal." History.com. Updated May 9, 2023. https://www.history.com/topics/ancient-rome/hannibal.

14 A&E Television Networks. "Persian Empire." History.com. Updated May 30, 2023. https://www.history.com/topics/ancient-middle-east/persian-empire.

15 *Encyclopedia Britannica*. s.v. "Confucius." Accessed June 20, 2023. https://www.britannica.com/biography/Confucius/additional-info#history.

16 Nix, Elizabeth. "Why Is a Marathon 26.2 Miles?" *History* (website). Updated June 8, 2023. https://www.history.com/news/why-is-a-marathon-26-2-miles.

17 "History of China." Travel China Guide (website). Updated January 25, 2023. https://www.travelchinaguide.com/intro/history/.

18 A&E Television Network. "Great Wall of China." History.com. Updated May 31, 2023. https://www.history.com/topics/ancient-china/great-wall-of-china.

19 Song, Candice. "The Terracotta Army: A Complete Guide With Pictures & Infographics." China Highlights (website). Updated December 28, 2021. https://www.chinahighlights.com/xian/terracotta-army/.

20 A&E Television Network. "Did Nero Really Fiddle While Rome Burned?" History.com. Updated August 18, 2020. https://www.history.com/news/did-nero-really-fiddle-while-rome-burned.

21 Bagley, Mary. "Mount Vesuvius & Pompeii: Facts & History." *Live Science*. December 19, 2017. https://www.livescience.com/27871-mount-vesuvius-pompeii.html.

22 O'Brien, Barbara. "History of Buddhism in China: The First Thousand Years." *Learn Religions*. Updated June 25, 2019. https://www.learnreligions.com/buddhism-in-china-the-first-thousand-years-450147.

23 English Heritage. "Hadrian's Wall: History and Stories." History and Stories. Accessed June 21, 2023. https://www.english-heritage.org.uk/visit/places/hadrians-wall/hadrians-wall-history-and-stories/.

24 Wasson, Donald L. "Pax Romana." *World History Encyclopedia*. December 8, 2015. https://www.worldhistory.org/Pax_Romana/.

[25] Johnson, Ben. "Timeline of Roman Britain." Historic UK (website). January 22, 2015. https://www.historic-uk.com/HistoryUK/HistoryofBritain/Timeline-of-Roman-Britain/.

[26] Pruitt, Sarah. "Who Were the Goths and Vandals?" *History* (website). Updated May 31, 2023. https://www.history.com/news/who-were-the-goths-and-vandals.

[27] "Anglo-Saxons: A Brief History." Historical Association (website). Accessed June 21, 2023. https://www.history.org.uk/primary/resource/3865/anglo-saxons-a-brief-history.

[28] Mark, Joshua J. "The Origin & History of the BCE/CE Dating System." *World History Encyclopedia*. March 27, 2017. https://www.worldhistory.org/article/1041/the-origin--history-of-the-bcece-dating-system/.

[29] Abdullah, Aslam. "Hagia Sofia: Church, Mosque or Museum?" IslamiCity (website). July 14, 2020. https://www.islamicity.org/53958/hagia-sofia-church-mosque-or-museum/.

[30] Timmons, Greg. "Muhammad." *Biography* (website). Updated April 6, 2020. https://www.biography.com/religious-figures/muhammad.

[31] BBC. "Muslim Spain." Religions. Updated September 4, 2009. https://www.bbc.co.uk/religion/religions/islam/history/spain_1.shtml#:~:text=In%20711%20Muslim%20forces%20invaded,1492%20when%20Granada%20was%20conquered.

[32] A&E Television Network. "Charlemagne." History.com. Updated July 22, 2022. https://www.history.com/topics/middle-ages/charlemagne.

[33] Nikel, David. "The Viking Timeline: What Happened & When?" *Life in Norway*. September 3, 2019. https://www.lifeinnorway.net/viking-timeline/.

[34] Sikora, Maeve. "The City of Dublin." *Vikingeskibs Museet* (website). Accessed June 21, 2023. https://www.vikingeskibsmuseet.dk/en/professions/education/the-viking-age-geography/the-vikings-in-the-west/ireland/the-city-of-dublin.

[35] Brown.edu. "Gunpowder: Origins in the East (N.D.)." Brown.Edu, www.brown.edu/Departments/Joukowsky_Institute/courses/13things/7687.html. Accessed 9 Jun. 2023.

[36] A&E Television Network. "Tang Dynasty." History.com. Updated April 28, 2020. https://www.history.com/topics/ancient-china/tang-dynasty.

37 Whitelock, Dorothy. "Alfred." In *Encyclopedia Britannica,* online e
    d. Updated June 29, 2023. https://www.britannica.com/biography/
    Alfred-king-of-Wessex.

38 Hudson, Alison. "How Was the Kingdom of England
    Formed?" British Library Board (website). Accessed June
    21, 2023. https://www.bl.uk/anglo-saxons/articles/
    how-was-the-kingdom-of-england-formed.

39 Nikel, David. "The Viking Timeline: What Happened & When?"
    Life in Norway. September 3, 2019. https://www.lifeinnorway.net/
    viking-timeline/.

40 Gliński, Mikołaj. "Historical Facts About the Baptism of Poland."
    Culture PL. March 15, 2016. https://culture.pl/en/article/
    historical-facts-about-the-baptism-of-poland.

41 Klein, Christopher. "The Viking Explorer Who Beat Columbus to
    America." *History* (website). Updated May 25, 2023. https://www.his-
    tory.com/news/the-viking-explorer-who-beat-columbus-to-america.

42 *Encyclopedia Britannica.* s.v. "Macbeth." Updated February 12, 2023.
    https://www.britannica.com/biography/Macbeth-king-of-Scots.

43 Johnson, Ben. "The Domesday Book." Historic UK (website).
    March 25, 2015. https://www.historic-uk.com/HistoryUK/
    HistoryofEngland/Domesday-Book/.

44 A&E Television Network. "Crusades." History.com. Updated March
    28, 2023. https://www.history.com/topics/middle-ages/crusades.

45 A&E Television Network. "Knights Templar." History.com. Updated
    March 28, 2023. https://www.history.com/topics/middle-ages/
    the-knights-templar.

46 Kessler Associates. "European Kingdoms." The History Files
    (website). Accessed June 21, 2023. https://www.historyfiles.co.uk/
    KingListsEurope/IberiaPortugal.htm.

47 *Encyclopedia Britannica.* s.v. "Notre-Dame de Paris." Updated May 30,
    2023. https://www.britannica.com/topic/Notre-Dame-de-Paris.

48 De Beer, Lloyd, and Naomi Speakman. "Thomas Becket: The
    Murder That Shook the Middle Ages." The British Museum (blog).
    December 28, 2019. https://www.britishmuseum.org/blog/
    thomas-becket-murder-shook-middle-ages.

49 University of Oxford. "History" (web page). Accessed June 21, 2023. https://www.ox.ac.uk/about/organisation/history.

50 Benham, Jenny. "Peace of Venice (1177)." In *The Encyclopedia of Diplomacy*, edited by Gordon Martel. Wiley Blackwell, 2018. https://doi.org/10.1002/9781118885154.dipl0470.

51 A&E Television Network. "Crusades." History.com. Updated March 28, 2023. https://www.history.com/topics/middle-ages/crusades.

52 *Encyclopedia Britannica.* s.v. "St. Francis of Assisi." Updated April 24, 2023. https://www.britannica.com/biography/Saint-Francis-of-Assisi.

53 Chaplow, Chris, and Fiona Flores Watson. "The Battle of Las Navas de Tolosa." Andalucia.com (website). Accessed June 21, 2023. https://www.andalucia.com/spainsmoorishhistory/las-navas-de-tolosa.htm.

54 A&E Television Network. "Magna Carta." History.com. Updated October 21, 2021. www.history.com/topics/european-history/magna-carta.

55 Boundless World History. "Great Zimbabwe." Class module. Chapter 11: World Civilization, Lumen Candela. Accessed June 21, 2023. https://courses.lumenlearning.com/suny-hccc-worldcivilization/chapter/great-zimbabwe/.

56 Szczepanski, Kallie. "What Was the Golden Horde?" *ThoughtCo.* Updated October 16, 2021. https://www.thoughtco.com/what-was-the-golden-horde-195330.

57 A&E Television Network. "China: Timeline." History.com. March 22, 2019. https://www.history.com/topics/asian-history/china-timeline.

58 Beattie, Andrew. "The History of Money." Investopedia (website). Updated September 17, 2022. https://www.investopedia.com/articles/07/roots_of_money.asp.

59 Brown, Cynthia Stokes. "Italian Trader at the Court of Kublai Khan." *Khan Academy.* Accessed June 21, 2023. https://www.khanacademy.org/humanities/big-history-project/expansion-interconnection/exploration-interconnection/a/marco-polo.

60 Petrov, Igor. "How Did Switzerland Become Switzerland? The Most Important Chapters in Swiss History Up To 1848." SWI (website). June 30, 2020. https://www.swissinfo.ch/eng/shaping-of-the-federation_how-did-switzerland-become-switzerland--a-summary-of-the-most-important-chapters-in-swiss-history-until-1848-/45810292.

[61] Solly, Meilan. "A Not-So-Brief History of Scottish Independence." *Smithsonian Magazine.* January 30, 2020. https://www.smithsonian-mag.com/history/brief-history-scottish-independence-180973928/.

[62] "The Knights Templar: Trial." Simmons College Library and Information Sciences (website). Updated May 14, 2018. https://simmonslis.libguides.com/c.php?g=832281&p=5941984.

[63] *Encyclopedia Britannica.* s.v. "Hundred Years' War." Updated March 28, 2023. https://www.britannica.com/event/Hundred-Years-War.

[64] *Oxford Reference.* s.v. "Great Schism." Accessed June 21, 2023. https://www.oxfordreference.com/display/10.1093/oi/authority.20111019153937351;jsessionid=FBDCA1BB9B01000CBC-0F418ACC471C85.

[65] *Oxford Reference.* s.v. "Great Schism." Accessed June 21, 2023. https://www.oxfordreference.com/display/10.1093/oi/authority.20111019153937351;jsessionid=FBDCA1BB9B01000CBC-0F418ACC471C85.

[66] Hearst Magazine Media, Inc. "Donatello." *Biography.* Updated May 26, 2021. https://www.biography.com/artists/donatello.

[67] A&E Television Network. "Leonardo da Vinci." History.com. Updated July 13, 2022. https://www.history.com/topics/renaissance/leonardo-da-vinci.

[68] A&E Television Network. "Michelangelo." History.com. Updated September 6, 2019. https://www.history.com/topics/renaissance/michelangelo.

[69] "History of Poland." Intopoland (website). Accessed June 21, 2023. https://www.intopoland.com/poland-info/history-of-poland.html.

[70] "History of Poland." Intopoland (website). Accessed June 21, 2023. https://www.intopoland.com/poland-info/history-of-poland.html.

[71] A&E Television Network. "Ottoman Empire." History.com. Updated February 28, 2020. https://www.history.com/topics/middle-east/ottoman-empire.

[72] Hickman, Kennedy. "Wars of the Roses: An Overview." *ThoughtCo.* Updated December 12, 2019. https://www.thoughtco.com/wars-of-the-roses-an-overview-2360762.

73 *New World Encyclopedia.* s.v. "Bartolomeu Dias." Accessed June 21, 2023. https://www.newworldencyclopedia.org/entry/Bartolomeu_Dias.

74 A&E Television Network. "Christopher Columbus." History.com. Updated April 20, 2023. https://www.history.com/topics/exploration/christopher-columbus.

75 McKelvie, Callum, and Jessie Szalay. "Amerigo Vespucci: Italian Explorer Who Named America." *Live Science.* February 8, 2022. https://www.livescience.com/42510-amerigo-vespucci.html.

76 Hearst Magazine Media, Inc. "John Cabot." *Biography.* Updated August 20, 2020. https://www.biography.com/history-culture/john-cabot.

77 *Encyclopedia Britannica.* s.v. "Vasco da Gama." Updated May 16, 2023. https://www.britannica.com/biography/Vasco-da-Gama.

78 Godoy, Sofia. "A Brief Yet Captivating History of Latin America." Spanish Academy (website). June 25, 2021. https://www.spanish.academy/blog/a-brief-history-of-latin-america/.

79 A&E Television Network. "Michelangelo." History.com. Updated September 6, 2019. https://www.history.com/topics/renaissance/michelangelo.

80 A&E Television Network. "Leonardo da Vinci." History.com. Updated July 13, 2022. https://www.history.com/topics/renaissance/leonardo-da-vinci.

81 A&E Television Network. "Machiavelli." History.com. Updated January 9, 2020. https://www.history.com/topics/renaissance/machiavelli.

82 *Encyclopedia Britannica.* s.v. "History of Goa." Accessed June 21, 2023. https://www.britannica.com/place/Goa/History.

83 Perrigo, Billy. "Martin Luther's 95 Theses Are 500 Years Old. Here's Why They're Still Causing Controversy." *Time.* October 31, 2017. https://time.com/4997128/martin-luther-95-theses-controversy/.

84 Donica, Adrienne. "William Shakespeare." *Biography* (website). Updated April 20, 2023. https://www.biography.com/authors-writers/william-shakespeare.

85 Cavendish, Richard. "The Fall of Calais." *History Today* (website). January 1, 2008. https://www.historytoday.com/archive/fall-calais.

86 Hocken, Vigdis. "The Gregorian Calendar." Timeanddate (website). Accessed June 22, 2023. https://www.timeanddate.com/calendar/gregorian-calendar.html.

87 A&E Television Network. "Spanish Armada." History.com. Updated September 6, 2019. https://www.history.com/topics/european-history/spanish-armada.

88 Salomans, Bobby. "The Dutch East India Company Was Richer Than Apple, Google, and Facebook Combined." *DutchReview*. March 30, 2023. https://dutchreview.com/culture/history/how-rich-was-the-dutch-east-india-company/.

89 Hayes, Adam. "Tulipmania: About the Dutch Tulip Bulb Market Bubble." *Investopedia* (website). Updated November 22, 2022. https://www.investopedia.com/terms/d/dutch_tulip_bulb_market_bubble.asp.

90 "Galileo Galilei." *History* (website). Updated June 6, 2023. https://www.history.com/topics/inventions/galileo-galilei.

91 Hearst Magazine Media, Inc. "René Descartes." *Biography*. Updated May 27, 2021. https://www.biography.com/scholars-educators/rene-descartes.

92 Gefter, Amanda. "Newton's Apple: The Real Story." *NewScientist*. January 18, 2010. https://www.newscientist.com/article/2170052-newtons-apple-the-real-story/.

93 "History of New York." Civitatis (website). Accessed June 23, 2023. https://www.introducingnewyork.com/history.

94 *Encyclopedia Britannica*. s.v. "Richard Nicolls." Updated May 24, 2023. https://www.britannica.com/biography/Richard-Nicolls.

95 Kucha, Glenn, and Jennifer Llewellyn. "The Manchu and the Qing Dynasty." Alpha History (website). Updated December 26, 2022. https://alphahistory.com/chineserevolution/manchu-qing-dynasty/.

96 Mack, Lauren. "A Brief History of Taiwan." *ThoughtCo*. Updated June 3, 2022. https://www.thoughtco.com/brief-history-of-taiwan-688021.

97 Hickman, Kennedy. "English Civil War: An Overview." *ThoughtCo*. Updated January 14, 2020. https://www.thoughtco.com/english-civil-war-an-overview-2360806.

98 *Encyclopedia Britannica*. s.v. "Akbar the Great and the Consolidation of the Empire." Accessed June 22, 2023.

https://www.britannica.com/topic/Mughal-dynasty/
Akbar-the-Great-and-the-consolidation-of-the-empire.

99 National Geographic Society. "Cell Theory." *National Geographic*. Updated May 20, 2022. https://education.nationalgeographic.org/resource/cell-theory/.

100 "The Story of the Piano's Invention." Yamaha (website). Accessed June 22, 2023. https://www.yamaha.com/en/musical_instrument_guide/piano/structure/.

101 "The War of the Spanish Succession." The Royal Hampshire Regiment (website). Accessed June 22, 2023. https://www.royalhampshireregiment.org/about-the-museum/timeline/war-spanish-succession/.

102 Gupton, Nancy. "Benjamin Franklin and the Kite Experiment." The Franklin Institute (website). June 12, 2017. https://www.fi.edu/en/benjamin-franklin/kite-key-experiment.

103 *Encyclopedia Britannica*. s.v. "Seven Years' War." Updated June 19, 2023. https://www.britannica.com/event/Seven-Years-War.

104 Nix, Elizabeth. "What was the 'Shot Heard Round the World'?" History.com. Updated August 30, 2018. https://www.history.com/news/what-was-the-shot-heard-round-the-world.

105 Longitude Found: The Story of Harrison's Clocks." Royal Museum Greenwich. Accessed June 22, 2023. https://www.rmg.co.uk/stories/topics/harrisons-clocks-longitude-problem.

106 *Encyclopedia Britannica*. s.v. "Industrial Revolution Key Facts." Accessed June 22, 2023. https://www.britannica.com/summary/Industrial-Revolution-Key-Facts.

107 *Encyclopedia Britannica*. s.v. "Opium Trade." Updated September 27, 2021. https://www.britannica.com/topic/opium-trade.

108 "The French Revolution (1789–1799)." Sparknotes (website). Accessed June 22, 2023. https://www.sparknotes.com/history/european/frenchrev/summary/.

109 A&E Television Network. "United States Nicknamed Uncle Sam." History.com. Updated September 2, 2021. https://www.history.com/this-day-in-history/united-states-nicknamed-uncle-sam.

110 "10 Facts: What Everyone Should Know About the Civil War." American Battlefield Trust (website). Updated

April 22, 2021. https://www.battlefields.org/learn/
articles/10-facts-what-everyone-should-know-about-civil-war.

[111] "10 Facts: What Everyone Should Know About the Civil
War." American Battlefield Trust (website). Updated
April 22, 2021. https://www.battlefields.org/learn/
articles/10-facts-what-everyone-should-know-about-civil-war.

[112] A&E Television Network. "George Armstrong Custer." History.com.
Updated August 21, 2018. https://www.history.com/topics/early-us/
george-armstrong-custer.

[113] South Africa History Online. "Zimbabwe." South African History
Online (website). Accessed June 23, 2023. https://www.sahistory.org.
za/place/zimbabwe.

[114] Saudi Royal Family History. Retrieved May 2022. https://houseof-
saud.com/saudi-royal-family-history/

[115] *New World Encyclopedia*. s.v. "Internal Combustion Engine."
Accessed June 23, 2023. https://www.newworldencyclopedia.org/
entry/Internal_combustion_engine.

[116] Mister Sparky Franchising. "A Brief History of Electricity." Mister
Sparky (website). Accessed June 23, 2023. https://www.mistersparky.
com/expert-tips/circuits-and-wiring/a-brief-history-of-electricity/

[117] Peterson, Elizabeth, and Callum McKelvie. "Who Invented the
Lightbulb." *LiveScience*. November 2, 2022. https://www.livescience.
com/43424-who-invented-the-light-bulb.html.

[118] *Encyclopedia Britannica*. s.v. "Opium Trade." Updated September 27,
2021. https://www.britannica.com/topic/opium-trade.

[119] Mack, Lauren. "A Brief History of Taiwan." *ThoughtCo*. Updated June
3, 2022. https://www.thoughtco.com/brief-history-of-taiwan-688021.

[120] Petrov, Igor. "How Did Switzerland Become Switzerland? The Most
Important Chapters in Swiss History Up To 1848." SWI (website).
June 30, 2020. https://www.swissinfo.ch/eng/shaping-of-the-feder-
ation_how-did-switzerland-become-switzerland--a-summary-of-the-
most-important-chapters-in-swiss-history-until-1848-/45810292.

[121] BBC. "Otto van Bismarck (1815–1898)." History (web page). Accessed
June 23, 2023. https://www.bbc.co.uk/history/historic_figures/bis-
marck_otto_von.shtml.

[122] The Telegraph Corporate. "A Rich and Unique History." *The Telegraph*. Accessed June 23, 2023. https://corporate.telegraph.co.uk/about-us/.

[123] *Encyclopedia Britannica*. s.v. "British Raj." Updated March 31, 2023. https://www.britannica.com/event/British-raj.

[124] "Charles Darwin." Sparknotes (website). Accessed June 23, 2023. https://www.sparknotes.com/biography/darwin/summary/.

[125] Michael Lynch. "The Emancipation Of The Russian Serfs, 1861" December 2003. https://www.historytoday.com/archive/emancipation-russian-serfs-1861

[126] "Home." The Quagga Project. Accessed June 23, 2023. https://www.quaggaproject.org/.

[127] City of London. "The History of Tower Bridge." Tower Bridge (website). Accessed June 23, 2023. https://www.towerbridge.org.uk/discover/history.

[128] Penn Museum. "The Games." The Real Story of the Ancient Olympic Games. Accessed June 26, 2023. https://www.penn.museum/sites/olympics/olympicorigins.shtml.

[129] *Encyclopedia Britannica*. s.v. "British Raj." Updated March 31, 2023. https://www.britannica.com/event/British-raj.

[130] A&E Television Networks. "Boxer Rebellion." History.com. Updated June 26, 2023. https://www.history.com/topics/asian-history/boxer-rebellion.

[131] Lambert, Tim. "A Brief History of Kenya." Local Histories (website). March 14, 2021. https://localhistories.org/a-brief-history-of-kenya/.

[132] *Encyclopedia.com*. s.v. "Germany's African Colonies." Accessed June 23, 2023. https://www.encyclopedia.com/history/encyclopedias-almanacs-transcripts-and-maps/germanys-african-colonies.

[133] McFadden, Christopher. "The Panama Canal: A Story of Blood, Sweat and Rebellion." *Interesting Engineering*. Updated September 20, 2021. https://interestingengineering.com/innovation/the-panama-canal-a-story-of-blood-sweat-and-rebellion.

[134] The Nobel Foundation. "Albert Einstein Biographical." NobelPrize.org. Accessed June 26, 2023. https://www.nobelprize.org/prizes/physics/1921/einstein/biographical/.

135 Piccotti, Tyler. "Albert Einstein." *Biography*. Updated April 12, 2023. https://www.biography.com/scientists/albert-einstein.

136 Falk, Dan. "What is Relativity? Einstein's Mind-Bending Theory Explained." MACH (website). Updated April 13, 2018. https://www.nbcnews.com/mach/science/what-relativity-einstein-s-mind-bending-theory-explained-ncna865496.

137 Ward, Paul. "The Race to the Pole: 1911–1912 Roald Amundsen and Robert Scott." Cool Antarctica (website). Accessed June 26, 2023. https://www.coolantarctica.com/Antarctica%20fact%20file/History/race-to-the-pole-amundsen-scott.php.

138 A&E Television Networks. "Serbia and Greece Declare War on Ottoman Empire in First Balkan War." History.com. Updated October 15, 2020. https://www.history.com/this-day-in-history/serbia-and-greece-declare-war-on-ottoman-empire-in-first-balkan-war.

139 *Encyclopedia Britannica*. s.v. "Franz Ferdinand, archduke of Austria-Este." Updated June 24, 2023. https://www.britannica.com/biography/Franz-Ferdinand-Archduke-of-Austria-Este.

140 A&E Television Networks. "Dardanelles Campaign." History.com. Updated March 28, 2023. https://www.history.com/topics/world-war-i/dardanelles-campaign.

141 A&E Television Networks. "Russian Revolution." History.com. Updated April 20, 2023. https://www.history.com/topics/european-history/russian-revolution.

142 Harris, Carolyn. "The Murder of Rasputin, 100 Years Later." *Smithsonian Magazine*. December 27, 2016. https://www.smithsonianmag.com/history/murder-rasputin-100-years-later-180961572/.

143 A&E Television Networks. "Joseph Stalin." History.com. Updated April 25, 2023. https://www.history.com/topics/european-history/joseph-stalin.

144 O'Neill, Aaron. *Signatories of the Treaty of Versailles, by Country*. January 2020. Distributed by Statista (website). https://www.statista.com/statistics/1086275/signatories-treaty-versailles/.

145 United Nations. "The League of Nations." The United Nations Office at Geneva. Accessed June 26, 2023. https://www.ungeneva.org/en/about/league-of-nations/overview.

[146] Dorney, John. "The Irish Civil War – A Brief Overview." *The Irish Story* (blog). July 2, 2012. https://www.theirishstory.com/2012/07/02/the-irish-civil-war-a-brief-overview/.

[147] A&E Television Networks. "Great Depression History." History.com. Updated Mary 24, 2023. https://www.history.com/topics/great-depression/great-depression-history.

[148] A&E Television Networks. "Treaty of Versailles." History.com. Updated April 24, 2023. https://www.history.com/topics/world-war-i/treaty-of-versailles-1.

[149] Wikipedia. s.v. "Hyperinflation in the Weimar Republic." June 26, 2023. https://en.wikipedia.org/wiki/Hyperinflation_in_the_Weimar_Republic.

[150] A&E Television Networks. "Weimar Republic." History.com. Updated September 21, 2022. https://www.history.com/topics/european-history/weimar-republic.

[151] A&E Television Networks. "World War II." History.com. Updated May 10, 2023. https://www.history.com/topics/world-war-ii/world-war-ii-history.

[152] Beyer, Greg. "7 Talented Generals Who Shaped World War II." *The Collector*. July 6, 2022. https://www.thecollector.com/most-talented-generals-of-word-war-ii/.

[153] The National WWII Museum. "Research Starters: Worldwide Deaths in World War II." WWII History. Accessed June 26, 2023. https://www.nationalww2museum.org/students-teachers/student-resources/research-starters/research-starters-worldwide-deaths-world-war.

[154] Chen, James. "Bretton Woods Agreement and the Institutions It Created Explained." Investopedia (website). Updated March 21, 2022. https://www.investopedia.com/terms/b/brettonwoodsagreement.asp

[155] Maverick, J. B. "International Monetary Fund (IMF) vs. the World Bank: What's the Difference?" Investopedia (website). Updated December 13 ,2021. https://www.investopedia.com/ask/answers/043015/what-difference-between-international-monetary-fund-and-world-bank.asp.

[156] A&E Television Networks. "Cold War History." History.com. Updated 26, 2023. https://www.history.com/topics/cold-war/cold-war-history.

157 *Encyclopedia Britannica*. s.v. "British Raj." Updated March 31, 2023. https://www.britannica.com/event/British-raj.

158 North Atlantic Treaty Organization. "NATO Member Countries." Updated June 8, 2023. https://www.nato.int/cps/en/natohq/topics_52044.htm.

159 Lee, Ji-Young. "4 Things to Know About North and South Korea." *The Conversation*. Updated August 10, 2017. https://theconversation.com/4-things-to-know-about-north-and-south-korea-80583/.

160 *Encyclopedia Britannica*. s.v. "Federation of Rhodesia and Nyasaland." Updated January 6, 2011. https://www.britannica.com/place/Federation-of-Rhodesia-and-Nyasaland.

161 North Atlantic Treaty Organization. "Cold War: Defence and Deterrence." Accessed June 30, 2023. https://www.nato.int/cps/us/natohq/declassified_138294.htm.

162 CVCE.eu. "Independence for Morocco and Tunisia." Decolonisation in Africa (web page). Updated February 5, 2017. https://www.cvce.eu/en/education/unit-content/-/unit/dd10d6bf-e14d-40b5-9ee6-37f978c87a01/2796f581-3e5a-4dff-9fbe-fd3d48966b38.

163 "History of the European Union 1945-59." European Union (website). Accessed June 30, 2023. https://european-union.europa.eu/principles-countries-history/history-eu/1945-59_en.

164 van Sickle, Keith. "Short History of the Five Republics of France." *The Good Life France* (blog). Accessed June 30, 2023. https://thegoodlife-france.com/short-history-of-the-five-republics-of-france/.

165 "Great Leap Forward: What It Was, Goals, and Impact." Investopedia (website). Updated September 16, 2022. https://www.investopedia.com/terms/g/great-leap-forward.asp.

166 "Singapore Separates from Malaysia and Becomes Independent." HistorySG (website). Accessed July 3, 2023. https://eresources.nlb.gov.sg/history/events/dc1efe7a-8159-40b2-9244-cdb078755013.

167 Haacke, Taylor. "A History of the Woodstock Music and Art Festival, 1969." Culture Trip (website). November 29, 2016. https://theculturetrip.com/north-america/usa/new-york/articles/the-woodstock-music-and-art-festival-1969/.

168 Schneider, Gregory L. "The 1973 Oil Crisis and Its Economic Consequences." *Bill of Rights Institute* (website). Accessed

July 3, 2023. https://billofrightsinstitute.org/essays/
the-1973-oil-crisis-and-its-economic-consequences.

[169] "History of HIV/AIDS." Canadian Foundation for AIDS Research
(website). Accessed July 3, 2023. https://canfar.com/awareness/
about-hiv-aids/history-of-hiv-aids/.

[170] Blakemore, Erin. "The Chernobyl Disaster: What Happened, and the
Long-Term Impacts." *National Geographic.* May 17, 2019. https://
www.nationalgeographic.com/culture/article/chernobyl-disaster.

[171] A&E Television Networks. "Nelson Mandela Released From Prison."
History.com. Updated March 29, 2023. https://www.history.com/
this-day-in-history/nelson-mandela-released-from-prison.

[172] *Encyclopedia.com.* s.v. "Gulf Wars." Accessed July
3, 2023. https://www.encyclopedia.com/history/
encyclopedias-almanacs-transcripts-and-maps/gulf-wars.

[173] University of Minnesota. "Rwanda." Holocaust and Genocide
Education. Accessed July 3, 2023. https://cla.umn.edu/chgs/
holocaust-genocide-education/resource-guides/rwanda.

[174] Gillard, Bridget. "Mother Teresa FSJM: From Wild Adolescent to
Unconventional Sister." *Church Times.* September 30, 2022. https://
www.churchtimes.co.uk/articles/2022/30-september/features/
features/mother-teresa-from-wild-adolescent-to-unconventional-sister.

[175] Council on Foreign Relations. "1999–2021: The U.S. War in
Afghanistan." Council on Foreign Relations. Accessed July 3, 2023.
https://www.cfr.org/timeline/us-war-afghanistan.

[176] Council of Women World Leaders. "Angela Merkel." Accessed July
3, 2023. https://www.councilwomenworldleaders.org/angela-merkel.
html.

[177] Wikipedia. s.v. "2007-2008 Financial Crisis."
Updated July 1, 2023. https://en.wikipedia.org/
wiki/2007%E2%80%932008_financial_crisis.

[178] von Hein, Matthias. "WikiLeaks 'Cablegate' 10 Years On." *DW.*
November 28, 2020. https://www.dw.com/en/wikileaks-cablegate-10-
years-on-an-unvarnished-look-at-us-foreign-policy/a-55755239.

[179] Janjevic, Darko. "The Never-Ending Story of Julian
Assange." *DW.* April 13, 2019. https://www.dw.com/en/
wikileaks-and-julian-assange-the-never-ending-story/a-48316477.

[180] "What Is the Arab Spring, and How Did it Start?" *Al Jazeera*. December 17, 2020. https://www.aljazeera.com/news/2020/12/17/what-is-the-arab-spring-and-how-did-it-start.

[181] Sobolieva, Alisa. "EuroMaidan Revolution." *The Kyiv Independent*. August 24, 2022. https://kyivindependent.com/euro-maidan-revolution/.

[182] *Encyclopedia Britannica*. s.v. "Charlie Hebdo Shooting." Updated April 28, 2023. https://www.britannica.com/event/Charlie-Hebdo-shooting.

[183] Chang, Alvin. "The Facebook and Cambridge Analytica Scandal, Explained with a Simple Diagram." *Vox*. Updated May 2, 2018. https://www.vox.com/policy-and-politics/2018/3/23/17151916/facebook-cambridge-analytica-trump-diagram.

[184] Centers for Disease Control and Prevention. "CDC Museum COVID-19 Timeline." Reviewed March 15, 2023. https://www.cdc.gov/museum/timeline/covid19.html.

[185] Ellis, Ralph. "WHO Leader Expects End of COVID Pandemic in 2023." WebMD (website). March 18, 2023. https://www.webmd.com/covid/news/20230318/who-leader-expects-end-of-covid-pandemic-in-2023.

[186] Maizland, Lindsay. "Myanmar's Troubled History: Coups, Military Rules, and Ethnic Conflict." Council on Foreign Relations. Updated January 31, 2022. https://www.cfr.org/backgrounder/myanmar-history-coup-military-rule-ethnic-conflict-rohingya.

[187] NASA. "The End of the Dark Ages: First Light and Reionization." James Webb Space Telescope Science (web page). Accessed July 5, 2023. https://jwst.nasa.gov/content/science/firstLight.html.

[188] Lieven, Anatol. "For Years, Putin Didn't Invade Ukraine. What Made Him Finally Snap in 2022?" *The Guardian*. February 24, 2023. https://amp.theguardian.com/commentisfree/2023/feb/24/vladimir-putin-invade-ukraine-2022-russia.

[189] Griffith, Jeremy. *TRANSFORM YOUR LIFE AND SAVE THE WORLD Through The Dreamed Of Arrival Of The Rehabilitating Biological Explanation Of The Human Condition*. Sydney, Australia: WTM Publishing and Communications, 2019 https://www.wtmpublishing.com

Index

C

F

H

S

X

Y

Z

Acknowledgements

I'd like to acknowledge and thank the following.

My wife Polina and daughters Ana and Petra – for their patience during the endless evenings of : "OK, Papa needs to work on his book now".

Gareth Howard at Authoright for taking on the project and all the advice given along the way.

Allison Herrera from Down Your Alley Editing for all the help with the references.

About the Author

After schooling in Zimbabwe and the UK, Bruce Tapping dropped out of the University of Cape Town, later completing a BSc through The Open University (UK).

Having left the University of Cape Town he founded Cape Review magazine which went on to become endorsed as The Official Guide to Cape Town by Cape Town Tourism. He sold the publication and moved to London where he was Commercial Director for the Periodical Publishers Association and one of the founders of WeZimbabwe, a charity that ran Zimfest; before he then moved to Shanghai where he was resident for eight years as manager of an Independent Financial Advisory.

He returned to his homeland Zimbabwe where he was founder of travel start up Africabookings.com, which is now part of Hotelonline.co, before taking up his present role managing Malawi, Zambia and Zimbabwe as a consultant for Green Farms Nut Company, one of the largest marketers and processors of Macadamias worldwide.

Bruce has an interest in world history, astronomy and people's belief systems, and this book is the culmination of a 20-year ambition, and five years of actual writing

For more information go to www.brucetapping.com.

www.ingramcontent.com/pod-product-compliance
Lightning Source LLC
Chambersburg PA
CBHW021134090426
42740CB00008B/785